Anne Neville

This was the creature that I woo'd and wonn
Over her bleeding husband stab'd by me:
Such different persons never saw the sunne
He, for perfection, I, deformitie,
She wep't and smil'd, hated and lov'd in one
Such was her virtue, my hypocrisie;
Thus, women's griefes, nor loves, are dyed in graine
For either's colour, time or men can staine.

From 'The Ghost of Richard III', anonymous poem, 1614

Forgive me, Heaven, that I forgave this Man.
O may my story told in after Ages,
Give warning to our easie Sexes ears:
May it Unveil the hearts of Men, and strike
Them deaf to their dissimulated Love.

Queen Ann(e), in 'Richard III', Colley Cibber, 1699

Anne Neville

Richard III's Tragic Queen

AMY LICENCE

AMBERLEY

for Rufus and Robin

First published 2013

Amberley Publishing
The Hill, Stroud
Gloucestershire, GL5 4EP

www.amberley-books.com

British Library Cataloguing in Publication Data.
A catalogue record for this book is available from the British Library.

ISBN 978 1 4456 1153 2
Ebook ISBN 1 4456 1177 8

Typesetting and Origination by Amberley Publishing.
Printed in the UK.

Contents

1. Anne and Richard's shared ancestry.

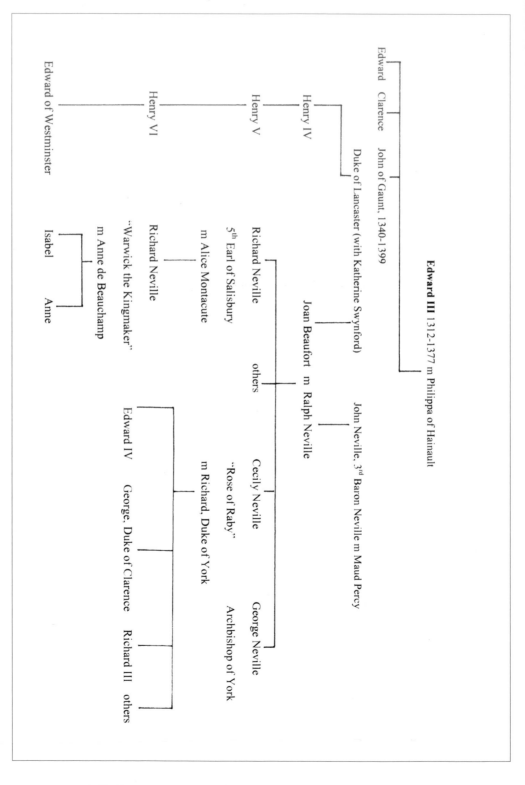

2. Edward III's Yorkist and Lancastrian descendants.

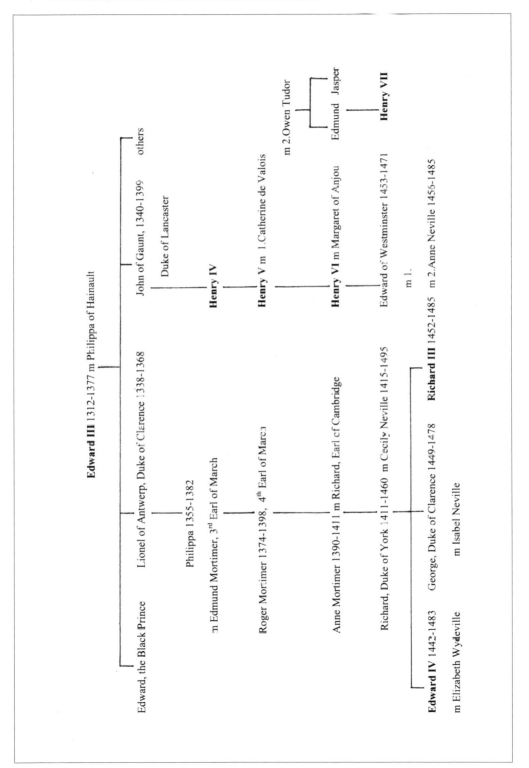

Introduction

Act One, Scene Two. The air is hazy. The room seems to be part medical, part industrial, yet there is a sense of neglect and disrepair. Tiles line the walls and a man in a long white coat stands with his back to the camera, busy over his work. A couple of brown glass bottles and a wooden crutch are visible in the foreground on the right. Rays of opaque light stream through the windows, creating a sort of misty underworld. Discordant jazz plays, low and melancholy.

The double doors in the middle of the scene open and she appears. Only a dark silhouette at first, she steps into the room; a slim, young woman dressed in a black coat with a large fur collar, glamorous with her lipstick, pearls, heels and dark glasses. Yet it is clear from her demeanour that she is in mourning. Reaching behind her, she pulls the door firmly shut before the camera draws close, foregrounding her face as she removes her glasses. Her expression is an uneasy mixture of subdued horror and resignation.

The scene before her is a mortuary. Three bodies lie on marble plinths in a low-ceilinged room where the windows have been shortened with plaster board, making it feel subterranean. She approaches the dead, with her form bathed in shadow, and stops before the corpse of a young man. He lies white and maimed, visibly wounded on the forehead and chest. She leans on the plinth as if the sight of the corpse weakens her, before taking it in her arms and delivering her speech.

*

This is Anne Neville. Or at least it is the actress Kristin Scott Thomas, playing the role of Anne, in Ian McKellen's 1995 film version of Shakespeare's *Richard III*. But it is not Shakespeare as the playwright would have recognised it. The settings and costumes date the action to the first half of the twentieth century; it is martial, modernist, Art Deco. This Anne is more stilettos and sunglasses than kirtle and chemise. The mortuary scene was shot in a lower storage room of the empty Pearl Assurance Building, a vast, greying edifice constructed between 1912 and 1919 in Holborn, London. It was not a ploy to keep down production costs: the grimy, dimly lit basement was perfect for the film's new setting. Written by McKellen and Richard Loncraine, the screenplay updated the story to a fictionalised England of the 1930s, 'a decade of tyranny throughout Europe ... when a dictatorship like Richard III's might have overtaken the UK'.[1] It was a fantasy, a parallel world exploring one of history's 'what-if' scenarios; a vision of the Home Counties being administered by the Nazis or Mosley's Union of Fascists. Thus, a late medieval king was juxtaposed with the rise of the Third Reich in London, echoed in the uniforms, music and set design. Richard III's story was co-opted as part of a wider history, beyond anything the king himself could have imagined. Recalling the process of writing, McKellen explained, 'we talked about it in the near-present tense and imagined it taking place yesterday rather than yesteryear. This, I suppose, was what Shakespeare intended.'[2] McKellen was right. As the Bard was writing, in 1591, the events he described were part of recent history, but as an entertainment, legend and a degree of dramatic licence were central to his work's success. In 1955, Laurence Olivier and Claire Bloom's memorable version of the scene followed more traditional lines and forty years later, McKellen reinvented its setting to draw modern parallels. In this way, Shakespeare's play is subject to constant revision; each generation adds a new chapter to the afterlife of the text, for better or worse. Similarly, these changes continue the on-going narrative of Anne Neville, daughter of the Earl of Warwick, the legendary Kingmaker. Her life has undergone several phases of reinvention by later generations for the purposes of entertainment and propaganda, which is the very reason her brief existence is remembered. For the historian, Anne herself is not too dissimilar from a 'text', a set of clues to be decoded according to the standards of her day, which may have been mishandled and misrepresented through time. The process began early. Just as Olivier and McKellen adapted Shakespeare, so the Bard distorted actual events of the fifteenth century to better serve his dramatic intentions.

The real Anne was not the sophisticated beauty Kristin Scott Thomas suggests; by modern standards she was a child when the key events outlined in this scene actually took place. In the year that she was widowed, 1471, Anne was only fourteen years old. That year she also lost her father and father-in-law, in violent circumstances, while she was alone among her former enemies. She would have had reason enough to grieve. McKellen altered Shakespeare again to portray her cradling the dead body of her husband, rather than that of the murdered Henry VI, and Scott Thomas leaves the audience in no doubt about the extent of her emotions. Yet the grief that the role demands is misleading: Anne had been married for about five months, but the union had been arranged for political reasons and was possibly consummated only briefly. After a long association with the Yorkists, Warwick had performed a dramatic U-turn and allied his younger child with their Lancastrian foes. Anne barely knew her boy-husband and no evidence survives to suggest she held him in any affection. The loss of her father was far more significant. It meant that Anne was left alone in the paradoxical position of the teenage widow, midway through the civil wars that were commensurate with her lifespan.

Clearly Shakespeare's 'history' was a fiction, re-animating well-known figures from the past and putting words into their mouths, within an abridged time-scale. Previous chroniclers, storytellers and historians like Rous, More, Holinshed, Hall and Vergil had done no less. However, Shakespeare's dramatisation of the incident has become so famous that it has almost entirely eclipsed historical fact in the popular imagination: the powerful scene develops along familiar lines as Anne's grief is interrupted by Richard, Duke of Gloucester, the alleged killer of her relatives. According to the play of 1591, Anne recoils in horror from the blood-stained apparition, which displays the often-repeated physical deformities that were correlative in the Tudor mind with immorality and evil intentions. McKellen follows this interpretation. Playing the part of the king himself, his hunch-backed figure, dressed in military uniform, appears from behind the widow as Anne bends over her husband's corpse. Sensing his approach, she turns in revulsion to see the 'fiend' and curses him, yet Richard is able to manipulate her emotions to the extent that she agrees to become his wife before the exchange ends. Even as the villain, the character's Machiavellian powers of persuasion cannot fail to impress.

In reality though, Richard was an old friend, perhaps more. His father, the Duke of York, had married Anne's great-aunt and the young Gloucester had spent several years living as Warwick's protégé at the family home of Middleham Castle. The earl may even have been the boy's godfather. The children would have been brought together regularly, in ceremonial and informal situations, so it is not impossible that an early friendship had blossomed between them, surviving Anne's arranged marriage with the enemy. After all, her family's sympathies lay first with the Yorkists, then with her Lancastrian husband: next she would marry the boy she had known, whose family had made her a widow. Shakespeare truncates this: Richard forces Anne to accept his ring alongside her husband's corpse, despite her curses. The actual ceremony took place over a year later in July

1472 and the pair lived together, apparently in harmony, for over a decade. It may even have been a love match. The eighteenth-century Ricardian Horace Walpole mentioned that Catherine, Countess of Desmond described him as 'the handsomest man in the room'. There is no denying though, that the alliance was financially expedient to both, so much so, that they were prepared to enter a marriage that was possibly invalid in the eyes of the medieval Church. Together, they were crowned in 1483: Anne was Richard's companion, his wife, the mother of his child and his queen. Did he then go on to murder her, as Shakespeare suggests?

McKellen shows a rapidly deteriorating Anne. The haggard appearance of the wife contrasts sharply with the earlier elegance of the widow. In the back of a limousine she hitches up her skirt and, according to McKellen's screenplay, 'finds the appropriate spot in her much-punctured thigh'. Her unnamed drug of choice is described in the screen play as 'calming' and she closes her eyes and 'waits for it to work', while the orchestra plays triumphantly. Later she appears 'doleful' and sad, later still, in a drugged stupor, in a world of her own and finally, catatonic.[3] The last the audience see of her is a motionless form, lying in bed with wide, staring eyes. A spider descends and lands on her face, scurrying away as she remains unblinking. McKellen's Anne Neville is dead. Obviously, the fifteenth-century queen's death was not attributable to recreational drugs but the rumours of her demise were just as sinister. Popular culture has upheld Anne as another of Richard's victims, with Shakespeare placing her among the accusatory ghosts that disturb his sleep before battle. This is unsurprising as the circumstances of her death are shrouded in mystery and, for once, the corrective facts are harder to establish. In early 1485, the corridors of Westminster Palace whispered of jealousy, flirtations, affairs and illness, as some contemporaries suggested Richard might have been planning his second marriage while Anne was still alive, perhaps to a foreign princess, perhaps to his own niece. Aged only twenty-eight, the queen passed away amid an eclipse of the sun and the chroniclers were swift to draw their conclusions. Did Richard really play a part in her death? Did he 'eschew her bed' as she was fatally ill, possibly contagious? Was she poisoned to make way for a younger, more fecund model? Perhaps she was lovingly tended, yet unwittingly administered with medicines that could themselves prove fatal. The truth of Anne's demise remained unresolved at the time and the dramatic regime change that followed compromised the objectivity of many witnesses and chroniclers. It is time to tease out the facts from the fiction.

Anne
and
Warwick

1

Battles and Births
1453–1456

His lords are lost, his merchandise is lost, his commons destroyed,
the sea is lost, France is lost
Complaints of Jack Cade's rebels, 1450[1]

It was summer 1453, the thirty-first year in the reign of the Lancastrian Henry VI. The nights were long and warm and the royal household had left its overcrowded lodgings in the Palace of Westminster in favour of some sport and relaxation in the country. By August, the court had settled into Clarendon Palace, near Salisbury, to enjoy riding, archery and pursuing the hart in the surrounding royal parkland. A former hunting lodge, the location had been a favourite one with English kings since before the Norman Conquest, where spacious rooms of 40 feet in length stretched over two floors with vaulted ceilings, tiled floors and fireplaces flanked by marble pillars. As the heat of the day mounted, the glazed windows with their stained glass images were thrown open and the scents of summer flowers and herbs drifted up from the formal gardens outside. It was an idyllic retreat for a monarch who increasingly eschewed worldly cares and allowed his wife and her favourites to take over the reins of government. Early in the morning, as the Palace was stirring, Henry could be found on his knees in the chapel, offering up his devotions to its marble altar and crucifix flanked by the figures of Mary and John. The king was known for his piety, asceticism and dislike of suffering but he was still a young man and relatively healthy according to the standards of the day. It was completely unexpected, therefore, when he suddenly suffered a seizure and took to his bed, lifeless as if paralysed, unable to speak or understand what was being said to him.

Suddenly, panic took hold. Nobody knew what to do or how to react when the king suffered his collapse. At first, his puzzled courtiers merely helped him into bed, hoping that a good night's rest would prove restorative: in hushed tones, they summoned his most intimate assistants, advisers, his confessor and sent word to his wife, the queen. Footsteps echoed along the tiled floors and up stone staircases; horse hooves clattered into the courtyard outside and urgent whispers filled the royal bedchamber. The king was urged to eat, to drink and finally, when these proved fruitless, to sleep; perhaps he had simply overtired himself and all would be well the next morning? But when Henry's servants went to rouse him in the early light, they found him unchanged. Weeks passed and the king did not improve. In fact, his condition appeared to be worsening, verging on the catatonic: he had descended into a deep state of shock, similar to receiving bad news or a sudden fright, as Norfolk landowner John Paston suggested in a letter home. Other contemporaries described Henry losing control of his body and wits, as if the man himself had withdrawn, leaving just the physical shell. Keen to conceal the extent of his incapacity, his servants waited for two months before packing up the household at Clarendon and removing to Windsor, where he was put to bed in more familiar surroundings. It was given out that he was resting; the country must not yet know that its king was as virtually useless as he had been when he inherited the throne as a baby. Still nothing could rouse him from his stupor and members of his court tiptoed about his room, where the wan figure lay among the velvets and silks of the impressive bed of state. Old favourites leaned over him and spoke in soft tones, yet the king could not distinguish them from the servants bringing in his food or building up the fire. Nor could he recognise his heavily pregnant wife, Queen Margaret, her dress unlaced across her expanding belly, soon to deliver the much longed-for Lancastrian heir.

Yet there was no obvious cause for such a dramatic collapse. The doctors summoned to Windsor could offer little real help, as their understanding of mental illness was as imperfect as their knowledge of the workings of the human body. They would have made their observations of his appearance, consulted the king's astrological chart and examined his urine, before reaching a diagnosis based on the four Galenic humours, which categorised patients according to differing degrees of heat and moisture. Three physicians and two surgeons administered him with powerful drugs to no avail and soon he was in the sole care of Gilbert Keymer, Dean of Salisbury, 'an expert, notable, and proved man in the craft of medicine'.[2] The royal diet was adjusted to allow for the humours to be balanced according to the properties present in his food, so an over-heated, dry patient would be given meals of cold, wet ingredients like lettuce while the fiery seeds of mustard were to be avoided at all cost. The king's condition would have necessitated force-feeding by a trusted and intimate servant, reducing him to the status of a baby; passive, dependent and helpless. The initial response to Henry's collapse was probably the universal remedy of bleeding, applied to almost every ailment, to draw dangerous matter out of the body, which in this case, was deemed to be an excess of black bile. He would also have been given various medicines, ointments and powders mixed from natural ingredients chosen for their medicinal and superstitious qualities. But ultimately, the doctors were baffled and, as usual in the medieval period, when events defied logical explanation, superstitious and religious answers were sought. Madness was interpreted as a function of individual morality, as a punishment for sin or a test of character, although Henry's pious lifestyle placed him above the usual reproaches. Perhaps some witnesses considered it the trial of a man unsuited to kingship, a response not too dissimilar from modern interpretations, though their explanations would encompass divine and supernatural causes rather than schizophrenia or depression.

The autumn days passed but the king did not improve. His absence was beginning to be noticed and those citizens and courtiers who believed in the real power of witchcraft feared he was the victim of some form of enchantment. Henry's condition was dangerously suggestive of daemonic possession or the influence of *maleficium*, the Latin term for 'mischief,' or magic of evil intent. These were very real and active threats in the fifteenth century; it was believed that spells, chants and magic rituals could injure and even kill, as could the presence of evil spirits. In 1484, the Pope would issue a 'witch-bull' outlining the activities of witches and a manual of witch-hunting, *Malleus Maleficarum, the Hammer of Witches*, appeared in print. It was a subject that was given considerable credence and importance in late medieval logic. Only twelve years had passed since Eleanor, Duchess of Gloucester, wife of the heir to the throne, had been convicted of treasonable necromancy and paraded through the streets of London. She had finally died, in the summer of 1452, after spending the remainder of her life in captivity, the news no doubt stirring memories of her activities for the inhabitants of the capital. Priests may have been summoned to Westminster to pray for the king to overcome any evil spirits holding his soul and sanity in their grip. Making their devotions in the Abbey, they may well have brought holy relics, the consecrated host and phials of blessed water, across the short distance to the king's bedchamber, or even conducted their ceremonies there.

Once the spiritual remedies had failed, the physical alternatives encompassed a range of painful possibilities. It was not unknown for patients to undergo the highly dangerous process of trepanning, when a hole was drilled into the skull to release humours or demons, as described in some contemporary medical tracts and images.[3] Doctors might also use cautery; the application of heat in the same way that wounds were cauterized, in order to divert inflammation away from another part of the body, such as the brain. They also recognised the likelihood that his condition was genetic. Henry's madness of 1453 may well have been inherited from his maternal grandfather, the French King Charles VI, who suffered from intermittent periods of mental illness, claiming different identities, being unresponsive and believing himself to be made of glass. As a result, France had become embroiled in political turmoil and power struggles; now the same fate threatened to befall England. In a deeply superstitious age, where the king's health was held to be a mirror of the health of the nation, strong leadership was required to maintain peace and this illness was a potential disaster. It was imperative that his madness should be cured.

Writing in the sixteenth century, physician Andrew Boorde's advice on the treatment of 'them the whiche be madde and out of theyr wytte' clarifies the dangerous overlap of medical understanding with superstition. He identified three different kinds of madness – lunatics, frantics and possessed 'daemonics' – but the regime to which they were all subjected sounds sufficient, to the modern mind, to ensure the total loss of any remaining sanity. Primarily, such individuals were considered a danger to others and should be kept in 'savegarde ... in some close howse or chamber where there is lyttell light'. The room must not have painted walls or hangings, nor pictures 'for such thynges maketh them full of fantasyes'. Citing the case of a murderous maniac named Mychell, who killed his wife in a fit, Boorde advocates that the lunatic must be 'allowed no knife or shears or girdle' and be guarded over by a keeper 'whom he fears'. No words must be spoken to him, except for 'reprehension or gentyll reformacyon'. He must be shaved once a month, drink no strong liquor and eat a little warm meat and 'moderate suppings' three times a day.[4] These instructions had unique implications when the sufferer was of royal blood. As an anointed king, Henry VI's status as the ruler and protector of his people was undermined, for his lunacy transformed him into a potentially malignant force, with the resulting ramifications for his country.

Frailty of any kind could potentially prove the downfall of a ruler; as Shakespeare's Claudius states about his step-son Hamlet, 'madness in great ones must not unwatched go'. If Henry had previously been considered a weak, easily led king, he never fully recovered from this redefinition, even after his madness abated.

Henry VI had inherited the throne in 1422, when he was only nine months old. His warmongering father was a hard act to follow, even if his son had been a grown man on accession. Revered as a hero in his own lifetime for his victory at Agincourt and the conquering of vast swathes of French territories, Henry V had contracted dysentery and died suddenly at the age of thirty-five, fulfilling his own brother's prophecy that he was 'too famous to live long'. The baby's inheritance was a dubious one. Having been engaged in expensive wars for over the eponymous Hundred Years, the country had amassed a wealth of foreign properties which the boy felt obliged, by the memory of his father, to maintain. The young Henry VI was crowned in England 1429 and then, as King of France, at Notre Dame in 1431, following the burning of Joan of Arc. His two uncles, John, Duke of Lancaster, and Humphrey, Duke of Gloucester, whom Henry V had appointed Regent and Lord Protector and who oversaw his upbringing, had died in 1435 and 1447 respectively. After that, keeping a foothold in the many English territories abroad was to prove difficult. And it was a difficulty the young man did not seek. By nature he was gentle and unworldly, unable or unwilling to make decisions and easily manipulated; he had no inclination for the martial arts or desire to prolong a state of war. One condition of his marriage to Margaret of Anjou in April 1445 had been his agreement to relinquish the provinces of Maine and Anjou to France, a clause that was initially kept secret and was as controversial as expected when it became public knowledge in 1446. By 1451, the English-held territories in Normandy, Bordeaux and Gascony had been lost through the incompetence of Edmund Beaufort, the Duke of Somerset, as Commander of the French Campaign. In 1453, the final blow came when English forces were routed at Castillon, marking the traditional end of the Hundred Years' War. It may be that this loss precipitated Henry's collapse. The royal finances were also in disarray with huge debts being owed to the Court's suppliers. On one infamous occasion, the royal family sat down to dine, only to be told there was nothing to eat! The royal routine continued, 'but payment there was none', causing additional, unpopular taxes to be levied.[5] An anonymous chronicler of the 1460s described the king as 'simple and led by covetous council and owed more than he was worth'. Many attributed this mismanagement, as well as much of the bad decision-making of the 1450s, to the king's unpopular favourites. Now that John, Duke of Lancaster, and Humphrey, Duke of Gloucester, were out of the way, a number of ambitious English noblemen saw their opportunity to pull the strings of government. Many of them clustered around the real power behind the throne, Henry's young wife, Margaret of Anjou.

The young queen found herself in an awkward position at the onset of Henry's illness in 1453. As a couple, they were temperamentally very different. According to their contemporary, Henry's adviser and Carthusian monk John Blakman, the king was pure, truthful and devout; he rejected the immodest fashions of the day and frivolous pastimes in favour of reading the scriptures and worship. Famously, he was scandalised at the sight of naked bathers and desired them to be clothed, disliking the fashion that allowed the female neck to be exposed. His views on sex were equally prudish and his confessor continually advised him not to have 'his sport' with the queen. Margaret, however, was young, intelligent, energetic and beautiful; at the time of her marriage, when she was fifteen, she was 'already a woman, passionate and proud and strong-willed'.[6] She conceived after almost eight years of marriage and the inevitable rumours implicated the unpopular Duke of Somerset as the potential father. As Henry lay incapacitated, he may have heard the screams of his wife, coming from her apartments in the Palace, when she went into labour that October. The child proved to be a boy. After his birth, Edward of Westminster was shown to the king for his blessing on New Year's Day 1454, but Henry said nothing. He merely looked at him and cast his eyes down again, supposedly refusing to acknowledge the child, although this may have been more to do with his inability to communicate. When he did finally recover, the following Christmas, he expressed surprise at the existence of the infant, whom he said must have been conceived by the Holy Ghost. Others at court favoured a different explanation.

Somerset had already replaced Margaret's previous ally, William de la Pole, Earl of Suffolk, who had met an untimely death on board a ship on his way to exile in 1450. These favourites were felt to have an undue influence over a young man who was unsuited for kingship and was content to let others fill his regal shoes. Now that Henry VI had fallen ill, Margaret and her faction were in a position to assume almost complete power over the invalid and, by extension, her son. It appeared that the same conditions that had caused chaos in France were about to disrupt England's already fragile monarchy. Factional rule, bankruptcy and national humiliation over French losses led to public calls for reform and retaliation against those considered culpable. Civil conflict was looming; in 1450, Jack Cade had headed a rebellion against the 'false council' of Henry's advisers but his death had not silenced the widespread complaints of the day. Chaos seemed to lurk just over the horizon. Boorde's suggestion that a madman required a 'feared keeper' was a difficult one, too: who would be prepared to rule the king in his incapacity and what would happen to them in the event of Henry's return to health? Several prominent candidates emerged at the Westminster Court, including the Duke of Somerset, whose own claim to the throne was not inconsiderable. However, there was another duke, whose inheritance placed him even closer in blood to the king, who was not prepared to stand by and watch his rivals dominate. The challenge that he mounted to them in the 1450s stemmed partly from bitter personal rivalry but was also for the wider 'common weal', which he saw as being adversely affected by the current status quo.

Ambitious and driven, Richard, Duke of York, was head of the Plantagenet family. The rivalries of the fifteenth century stemmed, in part, from Edward III fathering so many children and now the order in which three of those sons had been born was of crucial importance. First had been Edward, the Black Prince, whose early death meant his son Richard II had become king in 1377, next in line was Lionel of Antwerp, Duke of Clarence, and finally, John of Gaunt, Duke of Lancaster. In 1399, Richard II had been deposed and murdered by the Lancastrian line of descent through Gaunt, which had placed his son, Henry Bolingbroke, on the throne as Henry IV. In turn, he was succeeded by his son Henry V and grandson Henry VI. However, as the great-great-grandson of the second Plantagenet sibling, Lionel of Antwerp, Richard of York should have taken precedence over the claim of this younger branch of the family. It also placed him before Somerset, another cousin as a result of the descent from John of Gaunt he shared with the king. York considered he had been passed over unfairly because his claim was carried through the female line, rather than the all-male exclusivity of the Lancastrians, which was thought superior. Additionally, his family had suffered disgrace when he was a child. His father's title and lands had been attainted after his involvement in a plot against Henry V but when the boy's uncle died at Agincourt, the four-year-old was allowed to inherit the Dukedom of York. Before Queen Margaret gave birth in October 1453, York was the heir to the throne and had previously attempted to assert his rights for the 'common weal': he was rumoured to have been responsible for Suffolk's death in 1450 and later marched on London, intent on dislodging the other unpopular favourites. The rivalry between York and Somerset had become increasingly personal when Beaufort had replaced his cousin as Lieutenant of France in 1448, after which the majority of the remaining English possessions there had been lost. York blamed Somerset for this and attempted to oust him from power but his rival had tricked him into being captured, forcing him to promise not to take up arms again. York's subsequent appointment as Lieutenant of Ireland had briefly removed him from the scene but now he was the leading duke of the land and the man to fill Henry VI's shoes.

Despite their common ancestry, the contrasts between the duke and the king could not have been more profound. York was ambitious, organised and soldierly yet he was more than his royal cousin's equal in terms of wealth, being the second-greatest landowner in England after him. His annual income was almost £6,000, twenty times that of Somerset, although by 1450, the crown owed him something in the region of £40,000. Queen Margaret loathed him and deliberately excluded him from consultations over Henry's future but when the extent of the king's illness became apparent, Parliament recognised York's claim and he was appointed Lord Protector. One of his first acts was to impeach Somerset and have him imprisoned in the Tower, in spite of the queen's protests. Finally, with his enemy out of the way, the capable York had the reins of government in his hands and national disaster could be averted. He was also in a position to reward his supporters, none of whom had been more loyal than his nephew-in-law, Richard Neville, who came to be known as Warwick the Kingmaker. Neville's father, Salisbury, was the brother of York's wife Cecily. It was through this connection that the Neville family, including their two daughters, Isabel and Anne, would play a central role in English politics in the coming decades.

It was Cecily Neville who provided the initial connection between Richard of York and Richard Neville, Earl of Warwick. A granddaughter of John of Gaunt, she was known as the beautiful 'rose of Raby', after the castle where she was born, and 'proud Cis'. At fourteen, she had married the duke and went on to bear him thirteen children, of whom six survived to adulthood. Cecily and her brother Salisbury had themselves come from a large family. One of the youngest of an impressive twenty-three children, she was only thirteen years older than her nephew, the Earl of Warwick. He, in turn, was betrothed to the wealthy heiress Anne de Beauchamp in 1434, when they were children of six and nine, and married two years later at Abergavenny, perhaps in the castle chapel or else in the church of Benedictine Priory. Such early marriages were not uncommon among the biggest landowning families of the day, although the pair were young by even that standard and would not be expected to live together as man and wife for many years to come. At first, there was no question of rebellion or of siding with York against the king. The young man's career advanced quickly at his cousin Henry VI's Lancastrian court; in 1445, he was knighted at the Coronation of Margaret of Anjou and later is likely to have seen military service with his father, the Earl of Salisbury, in the Scottish wars of 1448–49. On the death of the previous heir, he was permitted to inherit the Warwick title through his wife, although the claim was subject to dispute over the coming years. One of those questioning his right was the unpopular Duke of Somerset, who had married Anne de Beauchamp's elder half-sister and laid claim to the lands Warwick inherited in the 1440s. Thus York and Warwick already had a common enemy in Edmund Beaufort.

On a personal level, Warwick appeared charming, charismatic and capable. The Tudor chronicler Edward Hall sang the praises of 'a man of marvellous qualities ... witty and gentle demeanour ... among all sorts of people he obtained great love, much favour and more credence, which he increased by his abundant liberality and generous housekeeping', bringing him 'favour among the common people'.[7] By the time of the king's illness, Richard and Anne were already the parents of a daughter, Isabel, born on 5 September 1451. Considering that their marriage was probably consummated in the mid-1440s, when Richard reached his mid-teens, the birth of one female child could scarcely be considered prolific and the family legacy was entailed in such a way that only a male child could claim it in its entirety; otherwise the various lands, wealth and titles would be split. As yet, the much-desired son had not materialised to inherit the entire package but the couple were still hopeful. In the summer of 1453, when Margaret's favourite, Somerset, looked poised to take charge, Warwick joined forces with Richard of York and supported his appointment as Lord Protector. From this point onwards, the lives of these two men and their offspring would be closely linked. York's success brought Warwick increased power, yet it also made him more enemies.

Even though the birth of Queen Margaret's son in October 1453 was a cause for national celebration, York was not content. Edward of Westminster had supplanted him as heir to the throne and he had been relieved of his regency in February 1455, after Henry's recovery appeared to be lasting. It was not easy being relegated from his position of power, when he considered he had done a better job than Henry or Somerset. During his tenure, he had also won many nobles over to his side as a preferable ruler to the king or the queen's favourites and introduced the strong leadership and relative stability that impressed the citizens of London. The contemporary 'Davies' chronicler claimed the common people loathed Somerset 'and loved the Duke of York because he loved the Commons'.[8] The unpopular minister had been imprisoned in the Tower but was now released and it appeared that things would return to the way they were before, if not worse, while others asserted that baby Edward of Westminster was actually Somerset's son. Henry was finally able to acknowledge the boy but the possibility of a Beaufort-dominated minority in the event of his relapse or death could push York out completely. While the duke was keen to regain some of his former influence, the queen was equally desperate to oust him and when Margaret and Somerset called a meeting of the Great Council at Leicester, to deal with the king's enemies, York and Warwick found themselves excluded. One informal explanation was given – that the queen feared the duke and earl would arrive bearing arms – but the clear implication was that they were the problem and the meeting had been called to discuss how best they could be disabled. This proved sufficient to provoke York to action. Gathering his allies, he raised an army of almost 2,000 and marched towards London, intent on destroying the hold of the court party on the king. A manifesto of their intentions was sent to Henry, who was still in the capital, but it was intercepted and destroyed by Somerset who raised troops of his own and began to march north.

The armies met in the compact little town of St Albans on 22 May 1455. Before any arrows were fired, York attempted to negotiate with Henry, who had arrived with Somerset's army, asking him to hand over his unpopular counsellors. Somerset had, he claimed, been 'disloyal to his country', lost French territories and 'reduced the entire realm of England to a state of misery'.[9] The hard-line reply which the messengers brought back only inflamed the situation. Prompted by his favourites, Henry wrote that anyone arming against the king was guilty of treason and would suffer the usual penalty of hanging, drawing and quartering. He then dressed in full armour, sat astride his horse and raised his standard in the marketplace, but it was a military gesture he was unable to sustain and he would remain there throughout the conflict, finally retiring when wounded in the neck by an arrow. As historian Robin Storey has stated, 'if Henry's insanity was a tragedy, his recovery was a national disaster'. The king's reinstatement and reliance upon the faction headed by his wife and Somerset had made conflict inevitable between the dukes. When he read the official response to his attempts to negotiate, York knew he must defend himself and his claim to the throne, or risk losing his position and now, his life. Fighting swiftly broke out. The town was ill equipped to contain what may well have been close to 7,000 men, locked in hand-to-hand combat through the narrow streets and back lanes, into the inhabitants' gardens and homes, with witnesses describing the piles of dead bodies, running with blood. The townsfolk must have thought that hell had descended.

For the families living around the market square and those engaged in trade and business, the impact of this carnage has often been overlooked in historical accounts. Many locals must have been drawn in, attempting to defend their property or repel intruders intent on claiming their living spaces as an arena for slaughter. With fighting taking place literally on their doorsteps, the wise may have fled out into the fields surrounding the town or into sanctuary at the abbey and waited until the chaos was over. Surviving objects from the fifteenth century on display in the Museum of St Albans, such as thimbles, needles, pegs and shoes, serve as powerful reminders that the fighting ranged over a primarily domestic landscape. The scene when the families returned must have been nightmarish; property damaged, gardens trampled, blood pooling in the gutter and the familiar transformed into the horrific. In the market square, the heart of the town, where the fighting was at its thickest, it is not difficult to imagine the faces of terrified residents behind the windows, watching events unfold. Safe in the abbey, Abbot John Whethamstede described the troops breaking down houses and through back gardens between two inns, blowing trumpets, shouting 'á Warwick' and 'slaying all those that withstood them'. The horror of the experience is brought vividly to life in his descriptions that followed: 'I saw a man fall with his brains beaten out, another … with his throat cut and [another] with a stab wound in his chest, while the whole street was strewn with corpses.'[10]

The period of fighting, though, was blessedly short. Having once been told of a prophecy that he would die 'under a castle', Somerset was indeed killed with a poleaxe outside the marketplace's Castle Inn, although some sources have described it more as a formal execution. York and Warwick may have deliberately targeted him, using a manoeuvre that took them through private gardens into the main square. His death effectively ended the fighting. All was over in less than an hour. Revolted by the sight of blood, much of the royal army now deserted, leaving Henry bleeding from a wound to the neck inflicted by a stray arrow. He took refuge in the nearby home of a tanner, cursing those who would 'smite a king anointed so'. About seventy lords were killed beside Beaufort; others hid in the abbey, hiding their armour and disguising themselves as monks. While the day was a decisive victory for the Yorkist faction, the locals' ordeal would continue as the jubilant troops rampaged through the streets, looting and destroying homes, although they stopped short of pillaging the abbey, where Henry had retired for the night. It was not until the following day that York, his father Salisbury and Warwick escorted the king back to London, where York assumed Somerset's title of Constable of England.

By that autumn York was effectively King of England in all but name, as he had been as Protector and Defender of the realm. The death of Somerset created a temporary vacuum at the heart of the queen's party and Margaret was increasingly occupied with her husband's health, although the dead duke's heir looked to pose a considerable threat once he had recovered from his battle wounds. One of York's first steps was taken to ensure his own safety. His first Parliament passed an Act defending the role he had played at St Albans as an attack upon the 'great tyranny and injustice' of Somerset's government. None of York's allies were to be 'empeched, sued, vexed, hurt or molested in thaire bodies, goodes or lands' as a result of the events of 22 May.[11] The pardon was secured and a peace of sorts had been reached but there was still an undercurrent of suspicion. York and Warwick clashed with Parliament over the sensitive issue of who should accept responsibility for the battle, prompting their followers to stuff 'their Lordes barges full of wepon dayly unto Westminster' in case of attack before the passing of the Bill exonerating York and his followers from any blame, which was 'groged [begrudged] full sore' by many.[12] A letter in the archives of Milan, written to the Archbishop of Ravenna, stated that King Henry had forbidden anyone to speak of the recent battle 'upon pain of death' and that York now 'had the government' and 'peace reigned' at which the people 'were very pleased'.[13] Yet the anonymous correspondent did not realise that the Lancastrian king was virtually under house arrest.

Parliament might have cleared York and his associates of accusations of treason but it did not clear the air. His most powerful enemy, Queen Margaret, was temporarily occupied at Greenwich, as Henry VI's mental state began to deteriorate again. In spite of the best medical care the era could offer, his previous symptoms reappeared, casting doubt on his ability to resume control, if he had ever managed it in the first place. However, the situation was not the same as it had been in August 1453, as Henry now had a living male heir. If York temporarily held the reins of power, it was only ever to be until young Edward reached his majority and was able to reward or punish his Protector as he saw fit. And, as the son of the 'warlike and hostile' Margaret of Anjou, the latter was more likely. The queen was keen to assert her son's rights and keep York at a distance, to which purpose she had had the boy invested as Prince of Wales at Windsor the previous year but, as an only child, he was still vulnerable. While his extreme youth rendered him incapable of rule, York must have been mindful of the circumstances in which Henry VI had acceded, back in 1421, and been anxious to avoid a similar situation. As York and Warwick were now in control, exploiting the loss of their mutual enemy, the royal family retreated. The tradition of royal nurseries at Greenwich may well have been established at this time: the little boy was probably there with his parents, while Margaret desperately tried to regather her supporters and rouse her husband again. Among other things, York was responsible for the settlement of 10,000 marks a year on the two-year-old prince: in a decade or so, the boy would be considered able to exercise his own will and York had no doubt that the queen's influence meant he was potentially nurturing his future worst enemy.

Born in 1453, Edward of Westminster was one of four children whose lives would shape the coming decades and the course of English history. At the time of his birth, he had the full expectation of becoming king after Henry VI, just as his father and grandfather had succeeded; he was invested as Prince of Wales at the age of two and raised for this role. His mother, Queen Margaret, was still young at twenty-three when she gave birth, but she would not conceive another child, perhaps due to the sexual incompatibility between her and Henry VI. This could have been the result of his disinclination, fuelled by long-term mental illness or other medical issues. Young Edward's conception and birth had been controversial but this was not insurmountable. Although popular rumours regarding his paternity might have exploited the unlikelihood of the king fathering a child, in order to spread the damaging theory that he had been supplanted in his wife's bed by any one of her favourites, there was no proof. In fact, it was not uncommon for couples to experience difficulties in trying to start, or build, a family: some branches of other noble medieval families became extinct as a result.

While opposing the queen's faction at court, Warwick and his countess were confronted by questions as to their own fertility and parenthood. With only one surviving daughter, it is possible that other children had been conceived and lost during the 1440s and 50s. One note in the family accounts lists that eggs were provided for the countess during Lent 1453, due to her weakness resulting from sickness and pregnancy, which may not necessarily have been related to her earlier live birth. It is quite likely that she was pregnant at the time, two years after Isabel's birth, but later lost the baby. Both her own siblings had recently died young: her brother Henry had only produced one daughter, who had not survived infancy, while her half-sister had produced four children. On the earl's side, there were no obvious problems with fertility, as he was one of the ten of his parents' offspring to reach adulthood, and although one of his sisters, Cecily, bore only a single surviving girl, another, Alice, bore eleven children. The Warwicks must have wondered whether they would ever become parents again. However, in the autumn of 1455, soon after the Battle of St Albans, Anne conceived. It was good timing, coinciding with the Yorkists' success and Warwick's new position at the duke's side. For standing by his ally in the Parliament of February 1456, when Henry VI resumed personal control, Warwick was rewarded with the lucrative position of Captain of Calais. By this time, the countess's pregnancy would have been confirmed and, although the couple would not have wished to tempt fate, the first cautious provisions for the child's arrival would have been put in place.

In late May or early June 1456, Countess Anne took to her chamber at Warwick Castle and awaited the start of her labour. Situated on high ground in a bend of the River Avon, the earliest parts of the building were datable as far back as the Norman Conquest, but later additions had so significantly improved its defences and levels of comfort that, by mid-fifteenth-century standards, the castle had become known as the Windsor of the North. Anne would have had every material comfort to assist her lying-in: her chambers hung with tapestries and closed off to exclude draughts and daylight, provisioned with candles, linen, religious relics and texts. Women of the household would have brought regular supplies of food and drink and whatever was required on a daily basis, while friends, relations and a local midwife kept her company. Anne knew she would be lucky to survive the ordeal. As she lay secluded in her darkened rooms, she recalled from experience that the coming hours would test her to the limit; she would have known of women who had lost their lives or those of their babies in labour.

The pregnancies of Anne's aunt-in-law, Cecily Neville, illustrate just how precarious young lives could be in the mid-fifteenth century. Her experiences as a mother began just three years after Anne's betrothal to the Duke of York, with the birth of her short-lived first daughter, Joan. All through the countess's youth and early married life, Cecily continued to deliver children, at a rate of approximately one a year until the occasion of Anne's second confinement, in 1456, a year after

Cecily delivered her thirteenth and final child. That baby, a girl named Ursula, did not live long, leaving the four-year-old Richard of York as Cecily's youngest child. Of her complete family, only seven babies reached adulthood, giving her an infant survival rate of just over 50 per cent, which was not uncommon. The Duchess of York was fortunate to have survived such a number of births, so closely spaced, across a span of seventeen years. In cases of straightforward deliveries, the rate of maternal mortality has been estimated at between 1 and 2 per cent[14] but as soon as complications arose, the chances for both mother and child lessened significantly. For those in attendance, there was no formal training or regulation and certainly no understanding of the nature of germs or the need for basic cleanliness, in fact, religion and superstition superseded hygiene. The countess would have prayed to the saints for intercession in their labours or may have held religious or superstitious artefacts; the consecrated host or holy water may have been brought into her chamber from the castle chapel or a cross may have been laid on her swollen belly. While pain relief was forbidden on religious grounds, the oils of lilies and roses were thought to lessen the pains of contractions, while some followed more bizarre rituals, including chants, charms and talismen. The event was so significant that Warwick absented himself from Parliament in order to be present. He must have been waiting anxiously in one of the many impressive chambers of Warwick Castle, hearing the screams of his wife as the hours wore on. Finally, on 11 June, the child arrived. It was another girl. They named her Anne.

This is the story of four children born in the 1450s. Richard of York (1452), Edward of Westminster, Prince of Wales (1453), and Anne Neville (1456) were the first three. The fourth, who had been conceived shortly before Anne's birth and would arrive the following year, would outlive them all. In November 1455, a marriage had taken place between the niece of the recently deceased Earl of Somerset, Margaret Beaufort, and the king's half-brother, Edmund Tudor. Henry VI himself is said to have chosen twelve-year-old Margaret, who was Edmund's ward, for this match; Edmund, at twenty-four, was twice her age. He was one of at least six children born to Henry V's French widow, Catherine of Valois, and the keeper of her wardrobe, Owen Tudor, in a secret and illicit match. Even by the standards of the time, Margaret was unusually young to enter into marriage in its full sense but, in fact, she had already been 'married' once before, as an infant, before the connection was annulled for political reasons. As an heiress and the sole surviving child of her father, her wardship was a valuable commodity for those who could ally her with their own families, although consummation was usually delayed until girls reached the age of fourteen, considered to be the onset of physical maturity. Within months of the marriage, though, Margaret was pregnant. Soon afterwards, she was also widowed, when the Lancastrian Edmund was captured by Yorkist William Herbert and imprisoned in Carmarthen Castle, where he died of the plague. The girl awaited the birth of her child at Pembroke Castle, Wales, under the care of her brother-in-law Jasper. As might have been predicted, even then, the process of labour was long and difficult for a thirteen-year-old, bringing her close to death and possibly resulting in lasting physical damage. Yet she survived, as did her son, Henry Tudor, born on 28 January 1457, who would, ironically, become Herbert's ward and later use his dead father's family connections to ascend the throne as Henry VII.

Richard, Edward, Anne and Henry. As children of the mid-fifteenth century, they were lucky to survive birth, infection, illness, accident and murder. Their average age at death would be thirty-three, although one of them would attain just half these years and only one other would live longer. This was pretty much the average life expectancy for aristocracy males, when a healthy baby might be expected to die before his thirty-fifth birthday, factoring in childhood disease and death in battle. For baby girls, who might expect to be engaged in frequent childbirth, expectations varied, although every pregnancy and birth made her more vulnerable. Born within five years of each other, these four children were the inheritors of a civil turmoil that had been the making of their parents' generation, through which they had to forge their own path. All three boys had claims to the English throne and two of them would be crowned king. Two of them would also become Anne's husbands, and she herself would experience a splendid Coronation of her own. They grew to maturity amid conflict caused by inheritance, royalty, insanity and marriage, in which their own struggles to assert their claims against those of their rivals would prove deadly. As they lay in their cradles, took their first steps and began to form their first words, these paths were still waiting to evolve. It is hindsight which now dictates this juxtaposing of their arrivals, although the imminent future may not have proved such a surprise as, even in the mid-1450s, many of these impending changes were already unfolding. Henry VI's incapacity, in comparison with the Duke of York's ability, indicated where power was about to shift. For the infant Anne Neville, though, the political intrigues of the next few years would be distant in more ways than one. She was about to leave the English shores over which the three boys would later fight to the death.

2

Castle Life
1456–1458

I am ful yong
I was born yisterday
Death is ful hasty
on me to ben werke.'[1]

The infant Anne arrived safely inside the impressive grey stone bastion of Warwick Castle. In her first moments, she was carefully checked by the midwives and her umbilical cord was cut, anointed with balm and tied. She would have been rubbed in scented oil and had her mouth washed in wine or sugar water, in front of the fire, before being tightly bound and lain in her cradle. Like her mother, she was fortunate in having survived the birth process but the next few months could potentially prove fatal. The women of the household would keep a special eye on the new child and make sure her linen and bedclothes were scrupulously clean, as well as washing down the floors and walls of the chamber where she slept. Animals, undesirables and those suffering from any sort of illness would be kept out. As the countess recovered from the rigours of labour, finally allowed to rest, she would have looked across to the tiny form sleeping soundly, with only its little pink face visible through the layers of fabric, and felt relieved that the child was alive and had no visible defects. This may have been the point when her husband Richard tiptoed in to congratulate his wife and take a peek at the newborn. Did his smile conceal his disappointment that the child was not a boy?

Born into one of the leading aristocratic families of the day, Anne's chances were probably better than many of her contemporaries but her wealth could not insulate her from the many childhood infections, illnesses and accidents that were a frequent part of medieval life.

Parish records in rural Essex villages indicate that mortality rates in the under-fives were between 30 and 50 per cent[2] but in such communities, survival could be determined by unpredictable and uncontrollable factors such as the weather, which affected the yield of harvests and the survival of animals. At Warwick, Anne would have benefited from the closed community of castle life, with tradesmen, craftsmen, cooks, storerooms and clean water being accessible within the walls. Built to withstand attacks and sieges, the little enclosed community could survive on its own for months and would have had doctors, nurses and clergymen on the staff. The countess also would have been in charge of a still-room, where the essences of flowers and plants were 'distilled' to make medicines, perfumes and treats; there would be potions and lotions, balms and charms available if either mother or child fell ill. The prevalence of certain diseases such as the plague, pox and forms of the dreaded sweat during the fifteenth century made it a particularly dangerous time for fragile members of society, especially the very old and very young. Even royal families were not immune to the sudden deaths of their juvenile heirs: Joan of Navarre, the second wife of Henry IV, had lost her first two babies while, closer to home, Anne's own cousin had died at the age of five, passing the Warwick title into the Neville family.

At birth, Anne Neville had every conceivable material advantage. By being born wealthy and one of only two infants in the household, she improved her chances a little more, although she may have adversely affected those of Isabel, then turning six. The terrible catalogue of juvenile fatalities listed in contemporary court records show that older siblings were more at risk when a new baby entered the family, perhaps because maternal attention was divided. Yet this was of particular concern in urban environments, where many more immediate dangers lurked on the doorstep and there were fewer attendants for the average middle-class child. Isabel was fortunate that her parents' wealth meant she was well cared for while their focus shifted to the new arrival. On average, though, girls stood less chance of survival than boys. London statistics of the 1440s reveal that female children were 22 per cent more likely to die young than their brothers, although this may highlight the relative value and greater care placed on male heirs by a late medieval society.[3] It has been estimated that a quarter of all medieval children died before their first birthday, an eighth were lost between the ages of one and four, while a further 6 per cent did not reach their tenth birthday.[4] To ensure her salvation, even if the worst occurred, Anne was baptised soon after her birth, at the nearby collegiate church, St Mary's, in Warwick, the resting place of many of her de Beauchamp ancestors.

Anne would scarcely have remembered her early days, yet they would have been typical of fifteenth-century views of childrearing among the aristocracy, consisting of little more than feeding and sleeping. In common with most ladies of rank, Anne's mother would not have breastfed her child, as it was considered to interfere with her role and duties. To be tied to a routine of constant lactation would have prevented a noblewoman from managing her household and honouring social and administrative commitments, perhaps even appearing at court. If her husband's role necessitated his absence, she would be required to take over the running of their estates, as is illustrated from the letters of Margaret Paston at this time, who had to repel continual attacks upon the family's property while her lawyer husband John was in London. She may also need to be available to listen to and resolve the complaints of locals, in an extension of her husband's good lordship. It also meant her fertility returned more quickly and she was able to conceive another child sooner. The conception patterns of some, taken from Essex parish records, indicate that this did actually happen within a few months, although, for the countess, there were to be no more children.

The Earl of Warwick, though, was a different matter. It is rumoured that he had an illegitimate daughter, born in the North of England, who was named Margaret. She was married in June 1464, placing her birth date around 1450 or slightly earlier, possibly indicating that her conception took place when her father was campaigning in Scotland in 1448–9. On her marriage to Richard Huddleston of Coverdale, Warwick made her an annual settlement of 6 pounds and settled on her the estates of Upmanby and Blennerhassett, in Cumbria, after which she went on to bear three children of her own in the 1470s and 80s. Her husband and a John Huddleston were trusted enough to be called upon by Edward IV to muster troops in Cumbria in 1480, in the event of a Scottish invasion. In July 1483, Richard was granted the 'lordships, manors and lands' of Thomas Grey, Marquis of Dorset, who had fled to Brittany after his involvement in a failed rebellion. That December, the office of Master Forester and Keeper of the Forest in Snowdon, North Wales, was added to Huddleston's titles, for which he received 'the accustomed fee' and the castle of Beaumaris.[5] Margaret was to serve at her half-sister Anne's court and outlive her, remarrying when widowed and dying well into the reign of Henry VII. The Thomas Huddleston who entered the Middleham household as a young man in the 1460s may have been a relation of her husband, perhaps a cousin or sibling; one younger brother, William, was to marry Warwick's niece Isabel. The earl was not alone in producing illegitimate children and it would not have been considered to be a reflection of the success of his marriage. Such liaisons were common. Edward IV and Richard III were both to father extramarital offspring and there was little choice for their wives but to endure the situation.

The baby Anne had her own mini-establishment separate from those of her parents. In all probability, this was an extension of that already created for Isabel, with a few special extra appointees to meet the needs of an infant. Her days were overseen by a mistress, or lady governess, which was a position of privilege and responsibility held by a trusted associate or member of the extended family unit, even, possibly, a figure from the countess's own childhood. The mistress would be assisted by a dry nurse and other servants to supply the basics of food, clean linen and basic hygiene. The wet nurse to whom Anne would have been handed for feeding may have been a new arrival, unless there was another suitable, recently pregnant woman within the castle walls. Whoever had suckled Isabel Neville following her birth in 1451 may well have been no longer lactating, as parish records and diaries of the period suggest that the term of breastfeeding lasted on average between nine months and a year. However, women did become professional wet nurses, suckling a string of babies and prolonging lactation. It is possible that the Neville's first wet nurse had sustained her milk supply by working for other families but equally likely that a new woman was appointed. Possibly she came with a recommendation from another family of rank, but at this time, women of lower social ranks were considered most suitable to the task. The criteria for her appointment would have been physical and moral. She must be of good character and not drink too much nor eat garlic and spicy foods but, typically, appearances were taken as a mirror of health. The wet nurse should have clear eyes and skin, good teeth and no visible signs of illness or weakness, as these were thought to be transferable through her milk, as was her character. Anne's mother and the mistress of the girls' household probably examined several possible girls from the surrounding town before selecting the most suitable. Where wet nurses were not available, children were fed with animal milk sucked from rags or horns and bread soaked in milk.

Anne's first year would have been an inactive one, as babies were swaddled tightly in their cots for the majority of the time to prevent inadvertent and self-inflicted injury. The air was also considered damaging to their skin and babies were regularly rubbed with butter or oil to close up their pores. A series of Italian images by Lumberto da Montevarchi depicting the 1479 miracle of Monna Tancia show the sort of tight swaddling Anne would have experienced, with a child wrapped in bands from the shoulder down to the ankles. Other contemporary church frescoes also portray this method, such as the *Santa Liberato* in St Peter's chapel, Vercelli, where two infants are reduced to white cocoons with only their heads protruding. One modern reproduction of a cot dating from around 1465 has been made at the archaeological site of an abandoned medieval fishing village at Walraversijde in Belgium. Woven from straw or reeds, like a basket, it is a deep, kidney-bean shape set on rockers. Some fourteenth- and fifteenth-century manuscripts depict cots as more shallow, rather like large temporary trays, such as in Bologna's image of the birth of John the Baptist, which sits flat on the floor with low sides. At Pembroke Castle in Wales, a reconstruction of the room where Henry Tudor was born in 1457 includes a solid rectangular wooden crib with minimal detail on its rails and knobs. Hanging and swinging cradles survive from the time, as do those with impressive geometric, natural and animal carvings: impressive eagles would have sat guard over the occupant of one surviving crib, dating from around 1500. As the daughter of one of the richest landowners in the country, Anne's cot would have been more substantial and highly decorated, probably made from oak. She would have spent a lot of time in it.

At court, the royal baby, Edward of Westminster, had been amply provided for. The arrangements would have been overseen by Margaret of Anjou, probably with minimal involvement from the king. Besides the lady governor, the boy's first household included a nursery nurse, four rockers for his cradle, yeomen, grooms and officers 'for the mouth' whose job it was to 'see the nurses meate and drinke be assayed [tested]' so long as she was employed, while later a physician was to keep watch over whatever she fed her young charge. Boys were more likely to be suckled for longer, up to the age of two or three, whereas girls tended to be weaned soon after the age of one.[6] Edward's state cradle, hung with buckles of silver and pommels, lined with ermine, velvet and cloth of gold, was equipped with a mattress, two pillows and numerous coverings of similar rich materials. Anne may have slept in something more like the smaller, practical crib described in 1486 by Margaret Beaufort, mother of Henry Tudor. Made 'of tree', it was painted 'with fine gold and devices', a yard and a quarter in length. Five silver buckles were set on each side to hold the swaddling bands, and therefore the child, in place. The accompanying bed linen was scarlet, grey, blue and gold.[7]

As the spring of 1457 approached, Anne was released from her swaddling bands and encouraged to take her first steps in the safety of her chambers. An illustration from a 1440 book of hours completed for Catherine of Cleves, showing the Holy family at work, places a toddling Jesus in an early walking frame. Made from twelve pieces of wood, in the form of an open box or cube, it is narrower at the top than the bottom where four large wheels help the child move, while giving some protection in an environment where carpentry and weaving is being done. Anne may have learned to walk inside a similar frame or else been guided by her nurse. Her world would have encompassed little more than the great chamber, the solar and the family's private living quarters, usually on the first floor above the Great Hall where servants and other castle employees were fed and slept. The medieval manor house of Stokesay Castle in Shropshire has a well-preserved solar of this type, reached by an interior wooden staircase. Warwick Castle had been extended during the late fourteenth century and the domestic buildings date from then, hung with tapestries and warmed by large fireplaces. A bed, recorded among the castle descriptions of 1400, was made of red damask embroidered with ostrich feathers, with a coverlet and dressings, three curtains of red tartarine, eighteen matching tapestries and six red damask cushions. When improvements were made in the 1420s to these rooms, plaster of Paris was used to enhance the whiteness of newly built walls. As the daughters of an earl, who had access to the rich diversity of London's international trade, the girls would have been surrounded by the best-quality furnishings and fashions of the day.

Anne wouldn't have remembered her early months at Warwick. In any case, the family were about to relocate and the world she knew would be left behind. Before her first birthday, her father was appointed to the prestigious position of Captain of Calais, an important strategic territory which had been in English possession since shortly after Edward III's victory against the French at the Battle of Crécy in 1346. The eleven-month siege, described by the chronicler Froissart, had resulted in the famous capitulation of the burghers of Calais and the town's transference into English hands. Froissart records that one of the first 'conquerors' of the town was the then Earl of Warwick, so Anne's father's position had historical precedence, although he would not have been wise to emulate the previous earl's record. In 1347, the first English rulers of Calais were commanded to expel the town's men: 'Take here the kayes [keys] of the towne and castell of Calys … putte in prison all the knyhts that be there and all other soudyours [soldiers] that came there symply to wynne their lyveng, cause them to avoyde the towne and all other men, women and children, for I [Edward III] would re-people agayne the towne with pure Englysshemen.'[8] Such national cleansing was common in conquered territory but hardly made for an auspicious start, helping to exacerbate the conflicts which followed. Calais was still a much-desired territory, coveted by the French and Burgundians on either side, creating an uneasy tension for the English inhabitants, which Anne and her family now became. Packing up the household, they waited for weather conditions to be favourable before embarking on one of Warwick's own ships across the Channel. Perhaps the six-year-old Isabel was old enough to be excited at her first glimpse of her new home, the walled medieval city with its imposing churches, towers and castle.

This 'brightest jewel in England's crown' covered an area of about 20 square miles, including the fortified town and surrounding marshland, with the defensive castles of Guines and Hammes. Although Calais lies only 20 miles from England as the crow flies, the Channel crossing could represent considerable difficulties for a fleet of wooden vessels in bad weather. This meant that, although it was technically English territory, the geographical distance represented a real political limbo and sanctuary for its inhabitants, which Warwick would exploit. By 1400, as many as 12,000 people lived within the city walls, while one map of 1477 shows the 'pale' extending north to include Ghent and Bruges and south beyond Arras and encompassing those residents too. Placed between the warring King of France Louis XI and Phillip III, Duke of Burgundy, it allowed England to maintain a European gateway for the staple trades of wool, tin, lead and cloth as well as relationships with both countries, neither of whom wished to see the area fall into enemy hands.

Calais itself was an impressive city. The manuscript illustrations from Jean de Waurin's *Chroniques d'Angleterre* make a feature of the town's high, smooth defensive walls and pointed turrets which the Warwicks would have glimpsed as their ship approached. A later map, drawn in the reign of Henry VIII, shows the walled town in some detail with its castle, church and marketplace, while the Cowdray engravings of 1545 give a vivid flavour of the port, forts and buildings. The crenelated town walls with their many towers are passable through an impressive gateway, giving out into the closely packed streets where a significant number of smooth and crow-stepped gable roofs are visible. In the picture, the thirteenth-century Calais Castle is also drawn, outside the walls, a solid, square structure clearly built for defence with a tower in each corner. Its windows are tiny and high, along with a number of the traditional arrow slits. Although the castle no longer stands, replaced by the sixteenth-century citadel, the comparable Castle Olhain north of Arras may give an impression of its appearance, with squat, round towers and drawbridge. Fort Risban, standing at the entrance to the harbour, was a reminder of the Crécy siege that could scarcely have been forgotten; then the fort had been a wooden structure; by Anne's day it was walled and mounted with cannon. Much of medieval Calais was destroyed in the conflicts of the twentieth century, but a description of the visiting Paul Hentzner in 1598 lists the still extant St Mary's church, or Église Notre-Dame, with its early fifteenth-century tower. The twelfth-century Watch Tower is another rare survivor, despite being split into two by an earth tremor in 1580!

Warwick and his countess were resident in the castle soon after his appointment in May 1457. Isabel and Anne were almost certainly with them, although there were other precedents for the care of aristocratic children in their parents' absence. In 1419, Margaret, Duchess of Clarence, took her sons with her when she went to join her husband in Normandy but left her daughters behind under the care of the prioress at Dartford. The girls, Joan and Margaret, were then thirteen and ten respectively. Others were sent out to board with respectable families, as were Anne and Elizabeth Bassett, aged twelve and eleven, step-daughters of Lord Lisle, who was appointed to the Calais captaincy in 1533.[9] Anne's extreme youth may have been both an argument for her residence with her parents and a reason for her to stay in England. On balance, it seems most likely that she and Isabel did go, crossing the Channel sometime in mid-1457 with her retinue of nurses and rockers. As the family would have been lodged within Calais Castle and Anne's household and routine were resumed, the difference between her old life and the new may not have been that great; she was simply exchanging one medieval fortified castle for another.

Just as at Warwick, Anne would have found life in a medieval castle divided into two realms; the separate households of her father and mother. The nursery was probably a subsection of those chambers presided over by the countess; an exclusively female zone, where a secluded life was encouraged and the girls were chaperoned when they interacted with the men in her father's employ. From the beginning, Anne and Isabel would have been brought up in the expectation of their future roles as wives and mothers. Their presence in Calais would have brought them into contact with French and Flemish, as well as their own native tongue, but speaking other languages was more common than an ability to write them among noblewomen of the day. The education they received is not to be compared with modern standards or concepts of the term; it was to fit medieval girls for the running of their own households, teaching them courtesy and deportment, how to handle servants and etiquette as well as such useful skills as the use of medicinal herbs, spinning, sewing and the production of domestic textiles. The main educators of girls of all classes were their mothers; unlike their brothers, the majority stayed at home in their early years, as observers and participants in the daily lives of their elders. Thus, female education was part of an oral tradition, dependent upon the skills and abilities of the mother and the social sphere she occupied.

There was time for play while the girls were still young. Toys dating from around 1300, recently discovered on the banks of the Thames, suggest that some figurines, such as knights, were mass produced in moulds and that girls may have played with smaller versions of the family's crockery and tableware.[10] Anne and Isabel would also have had their own 'poppets', wooden or cloth dolls, probably made by their mother, or women of the household. They would have sung songs, recited tales and learned simple prayers in their early years, as they learned the more formal process of reading essential for their future duties to check domestic documents and accounts. If Anne's contemporary Margery Paston could read and write fluently, as her letters demonstrate, there is no doubt that the Earl of Warwick's daughters could. The remnant of Richard III's library held in the modern British Library contains books bearing the signatures 'Anne Warrewyk' and 'R Gloucester'. It is probable that prayer books commissioned for the girls, which would be read to them until such a point as they could read for themselves. *The Babees' Book* of 1475 was 'turned out of Latin into my common language'[11] to help infants learn the alphabet by negative example; 'be not too Amorous, too Adventurous nor Argue too much'. The book advocated moderation in all activity and emotion. Babbling or the synonymous 'jangling', tale-bearing and meddling were also undesirable qualities, as were excesses of excellence, gladness, kindness and lovingness. Anne may have learned through games such as 'Crambo', a variant of the 1430 'ABC of Aristotle' or similar poems that explore rhyme.

Other children's entertainments of the time included Barley-Break, Cat after Mouse and other chasing games, variants of hopscotch and skipping, nine pins and shuttlecock, whip-tops and marbles, although the earl's daughters may not have got to play the rowdier Hot Cockles or Blind Man's Buff. There is the possibility that there may have been other children in the castle, perhaps those of the family's employees, who were considered of sufficient, albeit lower, status to play with the girls. Many of their class would have had pets of some kind, especially dogs or birds, separate to those used for hunting and hawking. Within the walls of Calais Castle, they may have had a small garden to attend and flowers to pick and store or dry for medicinal and household use.

Indoor pursuits included cards, dice, chess, tric-trac or backgammon, juggling and games like the popular Penny Prick, which involved throwing stones at pennies balanced on pins, and the well-known game referred to by Chaucer called Drawing Dun out of the Mire. Some versions of well-known board games like chequers were considered unsuitable, such as Queke-Board and Hand-yn-Hand-out, which were banned under a statute passed by Edward IV in around 1478.[12] The girls would also have spent hours at embroidery and learning to play instruments. Undoubtedly, as daughters of an earl, Anne and Isabel would have had some opportunities for play, although this would be more than balanced with training for their intended future roles. They would not be children for long.

Many of the instructional manuals of the day were aimed at boys, but one notable exception sheds a little light on the qualities considered desirable in the rearing of girls. In the 1430 poem 'How the Good Wife Taught her Daughter', the ultimate goal for both subjects is the girl's marriage: the mother instructs her child 'full many a time and oft' 'a full good woman to be … if thou wilt be a wife'. The qualities most valued are piety, good husbandry, modesty, thrift and honesty. Before marriage, the daughter must

> Look wisely that thou work
> Look lovely and in good life
> Love God and Holy Kirk
> Go to Church whene'er thou may
> Look thou spare for no rain.

Of particular relevance for wealthy children, like the Nevilles, was the message of charity and generosity:

> Gladly give thy tithes and thy offerings both
> To the poor and the bed-rid – look thou not be loth
> Give of thine own goods and be not too hard
> For seldom is the house poor where God is steward.[13]

Other texts like Symon's 'Lesson of Wisdom', from around 1500, *The Little Children's Book* and John Russell's 1460 *Boke of Nurture* urge children to be obedient, God-fearing, humble, clean, kind to animals and respectful towards their parents. In one, they are instructed to rise at six, perform their devotions, wash face and hands, cast up their bed, dress in clean clothes according to rank and be off about their business. The slightly later *Young Scholar's Paradise* urged them to shake off their 'sluggishness' after a 'moderate sleep' of seven hours and think 'of things that for thy soul's health sweet melody brings'. They should follow four key principles: to have a virtuous and godly mind, aim at the liberal arts, act moderately and grow up to be civil. However, while Anne and Isabel were being instructed in the arts of becoming young ladies, the world around them was becoming increasingly less civil, to the point of national conflict. Playing with their poppets and singing rhymes within the tapestry-hung walls of Calais Castle, they would have been aware of their father's absences but with no real understanding of how significant his role was to prove in the coming struggle.

3

Warring Cousins
1458–1460

But loe I found another thing,
I was disdained of the king,
And rated as a varlet base,
that so betraid the good dukes grace[1]

Calais had become a problematic inheritance for many reasons, both for England and for Warwick. Although it provided an important gateway for trade, it was also a significant drain on the English coffers; Parliament had refused to pay the garrison's wages in 1454, totalling a huge £40,000. Given that the town housed the largest standing army of professional soldiers of different nationalities, the blocking of proper funding for weapons and manpower left the area weakened when an attack was mounted by the resentful French in May 1455. Queen Margaret, fearing Warwick's intentions regarding such a large sum, withheld it, so he began to regain the trust of the soldiers by paying their arrears and wages out of his own pocket, before leading them in an expulsion of the invaders. Soon, though, the problem grew beyond Calais' walls. As an island, dependent on sea-based trade, England had always been vulnerable. Foreign attacks had been feared back in 1452, when Henry VI had summoned all South and East Coast ship owners to assemble at Sandwich in case of Channel raids. The Confederation of Cinque Ports had been designed to protect local ships from becoming prey to foreign pirates, although its members often indulged in acts of piracy themselves. It was not until August 1457, however, that a French general, a previous friend of Margaret, mounted a devastating attack on the English seaport of Sandwich, setting off renewed fears of a full-scale invasion. Now the queen had little choice but to trust the earl. As a result, Warwick was given the commission of Lord High Admiral to keep the seas clear for three years and granted £1,000 expenses. It is difficult to overestimate how powerful this position was, considering that Warwick was already head of England's largest standing army, at Calais, and was now able to control sea traffic. It also gave him license to indulge in his own acts of piracy.

There was a long history of piracy between England and France, dating back to before the outbreak of the Hundred Years' War. One of the most famous, whose legend lingered into Anne's lifetime, was John Hawley, politician, merchant, privateer and pirate, whose adventures were already legendary at the time of his death in 1408. His fleet seemed to be ubiquitous, appearing wherever he was feared and avoided: 'Blow the wind high, blow the wind low, it bloweth good to Hawley's Hoe.'[2] It has been suggested that Chaucer, visiting Dartmouth in the 1370s, used Hawley as his model for the character of the Shipman in *The Canterbury Tales*,[3] who had no conscience when drawing draughts of Bordeaux wine as the trader, or owner, slept and never lost a fight:

> Ful many a draughte of wyn had he ydrawe
> Fro Burdeux-ward, whil that the chapman sleep.
> Of nyce conscience took he no keep.
> If that he faught, and hadde the hyer hond,
> By water he sente hem hoom to every lond.[4]

The role of a pirate often overlapped that of a privateer, a private sailor authorised to defend their country. Chaucer was, in fact, sent by Richard II to arrange for the release of a Genoese merchant ship that Hawley had captured, but by 1403, the privateer's reputation had improved and he was honoured for repelling a Breton raid. However, Hawley then got in trouble when he preyed upon the ships of Breton merchants which were under the protection of Sir John de Roche, resulting in a court case that lasted eight years. His fortunes plummeted again when he was imprisoned in the Tower until he promised to return his plundered goods. In 1449, another Dartmouth man, Captain Robert Wenyngton, captured a number of trading vessels from Brittany, the Low Countries and Prussia, which he held on the Isle of Wight, so that Henry VI was forced to compensate them for their losses. In 1450, piracy was so proliferate in the Channel that over fifty Hanseatic ships were seized that year alone, with their cargoes of salt being sold in London. In 1458, two cases appear in the Close Rolls which highlight the nature of the piracy taking place on England's south-west coast under Warwick's rule. One Portuguese ship, the *Saint Mary de Nazareth*, under the command of Lewis Vaskes, had put into the port of Dartmouth the previous December and had not yet been allowed to leave.[5] Another fleet of Calais ships and soldiers, 'furnished and arrayed for war', took, by force, three Dutch vessels at Tilbury Docks in Essex. In these, they found letters of patents from Henry VI to a Venetian merchant, allowing them to intercept cargoes of wool from London ships, which they disposed of 'at their pleasure'. For this crime, they were fined £3,200 and the aggrieved wool owners were granted passage to trade with Italy until they had recuperated their losses.[6] They had got off lightly, as one William Maurice had been hanged, drawn and quartered for his activities back in 1421. In the spring of 1458, Warwick was heading back to England but in the light of his recent activities and the queen's distrust of him as an ally of the Duke of York, he would have to tread carefully. His piracy could give Margaret the ammunition she needed. On the surface, though, all appeared amicable.

On Lady Day, 25 March 1458, the rival factions behind the throne were drawn together in a last-ditch attempt at solidarity. Crowds were converging outside St Paul's Cathedral and the atmosphere in the capital was tense. Londoners were unsettled by the presence of armed troops, who had been arriving for weeks and kicking their heels while waiting for their opponents to put in a presence. York, Warwick and his father, the Earl of Salisbury, had been invited to attend a special reconciliation with the king, organised by Thomas Bourchier, Archbishop of Canterbury. This meeting was to be followed by a mass of thanksgiving, when enemies would walk hand in hand, known to history as the Loveday. However, it was all a sham; there was little love felt between the queen and the Yorkists, whom she held responsible for the massacres and looting after the Battle of St Albans. Heading a large number of troops, Warwick had already evaded one attempt to capture him on his way to Westminster and knew that, in spite of appearances, the queen was his sworn enemy. The crowds watched uneasily as the combatants emerged from the cathedral. Warwick was arm in arm with Henry Holland, Duke of Exeter, York's son-in-law, who was reputedly furious at having been replaced as Lord High Admiral, and the young Henry Beaufort, Duke of Somerset, burning with hatred at the man whom he held responsible for his father's death at St Albans. A contemporary ballad recorded the public truce:

> In Yorke, in Somersett, as y undyrstonde
> In Warwikke also ys love and charite

In Salisbury eke [also] and yn Northumberlond
That every man may reiouce the concord and unite.[7]

A series of magnificent jousts followed at the Tower, held in Margaret's honour, although perhaps only Henry VI was deceived by his enemies' 'lovely countenance[s]' and 'token that love was in the heart and thought'.[8] The optimism of popular ballads, calling on the citizens to rejoice in the new peace, overlooked the tension created by the thousands of armed guards that thronged the streets. A marriage was also arranged between the queen's seventeen-year-old ward, Isabella Ingaldscthorpe, and Warwick's younger brother, John. However, within months, hostilities had broken out again. The owners of German merchant ships, upon which Warwick had been preying in the Channel, appealed to Henry and Margaret for support, providing the queen with the opportunity she needed. In the autumn of 1458, she attempted to have the earl indicted for piracy and rumours followed that Somerset's men were about to break into his London property with murderous intent. Warwick appeared at court in order to answer the summons, guarded by 600 men. Margaret insisted he should stand trial and he retaliated by accusing her of insincerity on the Loveday. The next day, Warwick's supporters rioted in London and later, as he visited Westminster, the earl narrowly avoided being killed by an 'accident' in the palace kitchens. Some accounts have suggested that Warwick embroidered this event, which was little more than an accident, but it indicates the depths that mutual hostilities had reached and is not at all impossible. That November, at a council meeting, his men clashed again with those of the queen, after which there was little the earl could do but flee; he fought his way to his barge, waiting on the Thames, and fled back to Calais.

After this, the descent to civil war was rapid. Margaret attempted to establish an alternative power base in the North, where she raised an army and ordered 3,000 bows to be made. A Royal Council was summoned to Coventry in 1459 to deal with the thorny problem of Henry VI's enemies, but York, Warwick and Salisbury were excluded, leaving little doubt who those 'enemies' were and that significant steps were to be taken against them. In response, the Earl of Salisbury held a family meeting at Middleham Castle to declare allegiance for the Duke of York and when, that autumn, Warwick brought an army across the Channel from Calais, a pitched battle could hardly be avoided. Warwick and Salisbury both set off to march to York's stronghold at Ludlow Castle on the Welsh border. The intention was to join forces and head south to London but the

queen's men intercepted Salisbury midway between their strongholds
of Ludlow and Middleham.

It was a Sunday morning, 23 September 1459, St Tecla's day, when
the armies met at Blore Heath, part fields and part woodland. The
weather was wet and the muddy ground churned over by the feet
of horses and men. The king's forces, which have been estimated
as numbering between 6,000 and 12,000, were ranged behind a
huge hedge across a brook from Salisbury's much smaller army of
3,000–6,000. However, Warwick's father, then aged about sixty, was
a seasoned commander of the Scottish Wars and the long-running
Percy–Neville family feud. He might have been outnumbered but
his superior military tactics allowed him to win the day. In order to
protect his men, Salisbury ordered huge defensive ditches lined with
sharpened sticks to be dug, encircled them with carts and wagons
and waited to be attacked. Seeing the odds stacked against them,
though, his army initially feared the worst and supposedly fell to their
knees and kissed the earth, which they believed would be their final
resting place. They underestimated their commander, though, who, by
drawing the royal army out towards them, was able to feign a retreat
before turning on the enemy and slaughtering the leaders. Salisbury's
men shot the horses out from under the opponents, which led to
the defection of around 500 terrified men to their side. After about
an hour of hand-to-hand fighting, many Lancastrians deserted and
Margaret's army collapsed, yet the engagement continued well into the
early hours. Salisbury ordered cannon to be fired into the darkness to
give the appearance that the fighting was lasting longer than it had and
deter further attacks. According to Gregory's Chronicle, 'the batayle
… lastyd alle the aftyr none, fro one of the clocke tylle v aftyr non, and
the chasse lastyd unto vii at the belle in the mornynge'.[9] About 3,000
men lay dead, the majority of whom were Lancastrians.

The queen herself is rumoured to have watched the battle from the
church spire at Mucklestone and, witnessing the defeat, instructed her
blacksmith to reverse her horseshoes, to deceive her enemies about her
flight. She is then supposed to have executed the smith, one William
Skelhorn, in order to preserve his silence, to which 'Skelhorn's anvil'
stands testament in Mucklestone churchyard today. Legend has it that
little Prince Edward, then aged six, may have been with her; it appears
she had him order and witness the executions of his enemies in the
coming years. This story has all the trappings of a highly unlikely
romantic legend but it is consistent with contemporary portrayals of
the martial and cunning nature of Henry VI's wife and the impression
perpetrated of her as a mother. Margaret may have watched from nearby

but it is unlikely to have been at Mucklestone, as the village was located behind Yorkist lines at that point. Another account has both king and queen arriving together at the battlefield the following morning, only to find it deserted in the wake of the Yorkist victory. From there, Salisbury had headed off to join Warwick and York at Ludlow, where, it was planned, their combined forces should be able to defeat the Lancastrians decisively. Blore Heath was to guarantee nothing, though. It was after this victory that their fortunes began to turn.

That October, the triumphant Yorkists occupied Worcester and headed for the cathedral. Overlooking the River Severn, there had been a place of worship on the site since the seventh century and, by the accession of Henry VI, it had been developed and extended as a home to a community of Benedictine monks. Warwick would recognise the green limestone and yellow sandstone details still standing today, the crypt and circular chapter house as well as the newer additions of the central spire and cloisters. In 1459, it was to play host to a symbolic display of loyalty. Kneeling before the altar, the Duke of York and Earls of Warwick and Salisbury swore an oath of loyalty to the king. It was a move designed to repudiate the charges levelled against them and reinforce the stance they had taken over St Albans. Once again, they stated their dispute was not with the person of the king himself but the influence of his 'evil councillors'. Their words were written down and handed to the king in person by the Bishop of Worcester: Henry VI, however, or rather Queen Margaret, was not impressed. She was still convinced that York intended to supplant her son Edward, then days short of his sixth birthday, correctly as it turned out. As the royal armies approached Worcester, the trio headed back towards Ludlow but were pursued. Again, they attempted to offer their loyalties in a letter addressed to Henry lamenting the complaints of his true subjects; this was intercepted by Margaret's men, who forged a reply, inviting them to meet the king on the battlefield. This was the challenge they had anticipated, so the Yorkists decided to take a stand at nearby Ludford Bridge. On 12 October, they set up their guns and awaited reinforcements.

Those reinforcements did not come. Unexpectedly, the Yorkists were seriously outnumbered, almost two to one, and morale plummeted. At Blore Heath they had fought against the troops of 'unpopular favourites' while Henry was elsewhere. It did not help now that the royal standard was visible in the Lancastrian camp, indicating the presence of the king himself, which meant that to engage with his armies was a different act entirely. Much has been made by modern historians of Henry's absence during key battles or the stories of him wandering about dazed, to be discovered sitting under trees, but the view of Henry VI as completely ineffectual has not gone unchallenged. No doubt his presence in full armour was a significant factor here, regardless of the role he played in the fighting; it may well have contributed to the overnight defection of 600 men Warwick had brought from Calais. York tried to counter their fears by putting out a rumour that the king had died but as Henry himself remained visible, this only cost him further support. As news of further desertions arrived, the Yorkist leaders envisioned a crushing defeat and recognised this was the moment to withdraw rather than engage. At midnight, they feigned a visit to Ludlow for supplies, leaving their armies in the field and did not return. It was a low point in their command. York and his second son, Edmund, Earl of Rutland, fled to Wales then on to Ireland. Warwick, Salisbury and York's eldest son, Edward, Earl of March, headed to the West Country where a supporter, Sir John Dynham, provided them with a boat for Calais. The armies they left behind were pardoned but Cecily, Duchess of York, and her two youngest sons, George and Richard, were left at Ludlow to become Lancastrian prisoners under the care of their aunt, Anne, Duchess of Buckingham. This was the seven-year-old Richard's first experience of the changing fortunes that battle could bring.

The king's troops then went on to plunder Ludlow, described by the chronicler Gregory as a terrible act of misrule; they were 'wetshod in wine', as the town was looted and women 'defouled'.[10] York Castle was robbed and the properties and estates of Yorkist lords were desecrated. According to the Davies chronicle, the king's advisers then began to gather 'riches innumerable' from the poor and 'rightful heirs'; for which 'the hearts of the people were turned away from them that had the governance of the land, and their blessings were turned to cursings'.[11] Not only was England no longer safe for the Yorkists, it was becoming a dangerous, lawless place for many of the king's subjects. The failure to curb these destructive activities would seriously damage the Lancastrian cause in the next few years.

The whereabouts of Warwick's family is unclear during this period. It is possible that he left them in the safety of Calais Castle during the upheavals of 1458–9, but there is also the chance that, at some point, they crossed the Channel with him and were for a short time resident again in Warwick Castle. If this was the case, the eight-year-old Isabel would certainly have been aware that her father was in danger, even if her younger sister was not; perhaps the family prayed together in the chapel for his safe return. At this point, the Warwicks were still hoping to conceive a male heir, so it is likely that husband and wife took every opportunity to be together. The dynastic imperative among the aristocracy was strong: it was engrained in them from their early years, so Richard and Anne may not have wished to have wasted valuable months or years, as both were now in their thirties and considered comparatively middle-aged by the standards of the day. Records of births indicate that many noblewomen of the era experienced their menopause in their mid to late thirties, so time was running out if the countess was to produce a son. Cecily of York frequently travelled with her husband through England and France, as the birthplaces of her children in Rouen, Dublin and Fotheringhay indicate. Wherever the family had been during this episode, they were reunited in Calais that autumn, along with Anne's paternal grandparents, Earl Richard and Alice, Countess of Salisbury, Warwick's uncle, Lord Fauconberg, and the seventeen-year-old Earl of March, York's son, Edward. He was a tall, handsome young man of athletic build, already skilled on the battlefield and a lover of good company, women and entertainment. In the years ahead, the Neville girls would come to know him better, as their king and as brother-in-law to them both.

That November, a royal council was summoned to Coventry, which came to be known as the Parliament of Devils. Led by the Lancastrian Dr John Morton, later Archbishop of Canterbury under Henry VII, it passed Acts of Attainder against York and his sons, Warwick and Salisbury. York's wife Cecily and young sons were brought into the chamber to witness his disgrace in his absence and hear the lords swear a new oath of allegiance to Margaret and Edward. Such Acts represented serious capital crimes, the penalties of which extended to the families and heirs of those on whom they were passed: their lands, income and titles were confiscated, making their heirs legally 'dead'. A large proportion of the confiscated estates were given to Owen Tudor, father-in-law to Margaret Beaufort. This attainder was the final straw which put aside all pretence of reconciliation and incited open attack. And none were more willing to attack than the young Duke of Somerset, Henry Beaufort, whose personal vendetta against Warwick now led him to plan an invasion of Calais. Following Warwick's disgrace, Beaufort had been appointed to the position of Captain of Calais, but holding the theoretical title and taking possession of the town were two different things entirely. Hearing of this, Warwick made a pre-emptive strike on Sandwich, where Somerset had been gathering his forces; a number of distinguished prisoners were taken and the entire enemy fleet was captured. Having also been deprived of his position as Admiral, to which Exeter had been reappointed, Warwick's best means of attack was surprise. Six months later, he was planning an invasion.

In July 1460, Francesco Coppini, the papal legate to England, wrote to King Henry VI explaining his recent actions. Coppini had been appointed by Pope Pius II to try to end the civil conflicts and involve the Lancastrians in a crusade against the Turks; he was successful in neither but his record of the mounting insurgence in Calais remains. First, Warwick had attempted to find a peaceful solution – 'The lords of Calais had called me, requesting me to mediate for the conclusion of peace and extinction of civil discord in your realm' – after which Coppini 'besought [Henry] piously to ponder these matters'. His efforts were rejected by Margaret of Anjou, after which the legate 'found everything in confusion, in consequence of a new state of things and fresh accidents, and that the lords were on the point of crossing over to England, saying they could wait no longer by reason of emergencies'. To Henry, he wrote that Warwick and his men were still 'disposed to be devoted and obedient to your Majesty, and desirous to maintain and augment the commonweal of the kingdom' but wished to be 'restored to favour', which the 'envy of their rivals' had cost them. Warwick implored Coppini to mediate for him with the king in order to avoid bloodshed and offered to 'accept whatever was fair and just', making their pledges in writing.[12] Soon after this, the earl launched his invasion with about 2,000 men, using the already reconnoitred Sandwich as his foothold. From there, he marched to Canterbury and on to London. By the time he reached the capital in early July, he had amassed between 20,000 and 30,000 men. With Margaret attempting to establish a royal power-base further north, the city willingly opened the gates and not only welcomed the Yorkists but advanced them a loan of £1,000. Warwick headed to St Paul's to give thanks. Coppini had travelled to England in support of the 'lords of Calais' and witnessed the next three battles of the wars, leaving his own record in letters. It would cost him his job: two years later, he would be dismissed in disgrace for taking sides.

Two battles, fought over the next six months, were to prove decisive in the struggle between the cousins and turn the wheel of fortune decisively against Anne's family again. The first came in July 1460, when Warwick's army met that of the king at Northampton, resulting in a significant victory for the Yorkists. Much had changed since the royal standard had waved proudly at Ludford Bridge; the plunder following the battle had shifted the mood of the people against the king and many were now willing to take up arms against him as he sheltered from the rain in his tent. Later, the behaviour of the Lancastrians and their armies at Ludlow would be described in Parliament as tyrannical and remorseless. They were accused of 'destroying and despoiling the realm on their way, not sparing God's church or refraining from its violation, and that of his ministers; ravishing and seducing nuns, maidens, widows and men's wives; shedding innocent blood like tyrants', which was enough to strike fear into the heart of the realm and allow Yorkist support to spread out of the capital and further north.[13] In contrast, Warwick had learned from the mistakes made at St Albans in 1455 and gave orders that his men should not show violence towards ordinary soldiers once the day was won.

Mirroring the dismal national mood, the armies faced each other amid terrible weather. The heavy downpour turned the field into a marsh and rendered the carefully prepared Lancastrian cannon useless. Now Warwick, Salisbury and Edward, Earl of March, easily had the upper hand. Part of the king's forces defected, allowing Warwick to march into the enemy camp and take Henry into his custody; after only about half an hour, all was over. Around 300 Lancastrians lay dead in the field and the queen fled west to the Welsh stronghold of Harlech Castle with Prince Edward. Warwick returned to London, making public displays of loyalty to the king, in whose name a new Parliament was summoned that October. Henry VI was present when Warwick's brother, George Neville, Bishop of Exeter, preached a humiliating sermon on the failings of his reign. However, none of the assembled lords had any idea just how dramatic the occasion would become.

More than one influential player was absent. Margaret and Prince Edward remained in Wales, attempting to raise troops to liberate Henry, but also, Richard, Duke of York, had been in exile in Ireland during the battle. Now he was on his way back to Westminster and was planning an extraordinary entrance. His arrival in the city must have been impressive, heralded by trumpeters, followed by an army dressed in his livery of blue and white, with his great sword carried before his horse, in the custom of kings. Over his head flew the royal standard, a reminder of his superior descent from Edward III. Abbot Whethamstede recorded the well-known story of the duke marching into the palace with more trumpeters and armed men, crossing the great hall and entering the chamber 'where the king usually holds his Parliament with the commons', where he put his hand on the king's throne, 'like a man taking possession'.[14] However, the necessary audience was missing. An anonymous correspondent, describing the scene to John Tiptoft in a letter, confirms that when York arrived at 10 a.m., the lords were in the Parliament chamber 'except the kyng' and the commons were in session in their 'place acustumed', which at this period was the monks' refectory. In a highly symbolic gesture, York went to stand under the cloth of estate to assert his hereditary claim to the throne over that of Henry VI, announcing that 'he purposed nat to ley daune his swerde but to challenge his right'.[15] Word quickly spread along the corridors of Westminster and people hurried to witness his declaration. However, York had misjudged the mood. Shuffling in embarrassment, they did not react as the duke had hoped, prompting his son Edward to act as messenger between those assembled that day. First, Warwick warned him that the people would turn against him if he tried to strip Henry of his crown and then, even Henry himself reminded them they had all sworn loyalty to him. Technically, although York's right was strong, the declaration was made in a time of peace, when Henry VI was under Yorkist control and very much alive.

Parliament hastily withdrew to Blackfriars to discuss how to deal with this insistent and overmighty subject. The more the lords explained to York the awkwardness of the situation, the more the duke insisted on his right and began to make plans for his Coronation, which Waurin claims he had planned as early as 13 October, although others cite 1 November. Ever keen to interpret the symbolic or superstitious, one record related how the Commons' discussions were interrupted when the crown, which hung in the middle of the house, suddenly fell down, 'which was take for a prodige or token that the reign of King Henry was ended'.[16] According to Vergil, the falling crown incident had happened earlier, when it rolled off Henry's head as he took his seat in Parliament: either way, it was taken as a 'signe prodigious'. Finally, a compromise was reached in the Act of Accord. Henry was to continue to reign, with York resuming his role as Lord Protector and being named his formal heir. It gave the duke a degree of protection: 'If any person or persons scheme or plot the death of the said duke, and are provenly convicted of overt action taken against him by their peers, that it be deemed and adjudged high treason.' At a stroke, Henry VI's own son, Edward of Westminster, was removed from the line of succession: 'The heirs of the body of the same King Henry IV, did or do possess a hereditary right to the said crowns and realms, or to the heritage or inheritance of the same, shall be annulled, repealed, revoked, negated, cancelled, void and of no force or effect.'[17] Perhaps Henry had little choice but to agree; perhaps he had listened to the rumours about the boy's paternity: in any case, the Act was passed. It was to be expected, though, that the boy's mother would not accept this: if nothing else, Margaret was tireless in her fight to protect her son's rights and immediately sent a letter to London written in her son's name, asserting his right to the throne. It was clear to the queen that there would no longer be a peaceful solution; her enemy, York, had to be permanently removed.

Prince Edward's disinheritance swung a little public sympathy back in his family's favour but Margaret needed to act decisively. In Wales and Yorkshire she was able to recruit large numbers of troops under Henry VI's half-uncle, Jasper Tudor, while she sailed north to attempt to draw the Scots into her cause. York and Salisbury knew they had to strike back before they were outnumbered, so leaving Warwick in charge of Henry VI in London, they marched north to meet her challenge.

It has been suggested that the children's nursery rhyme 'The Grand Old Duke of York', marching his 10,000 men up and down the hill, might date from the encounter that followed, or even the colourful mnemonic 'Richard of York gave battle in vain'. The rout that led to the Battle of Wakefield certainly entered the history of the conflict as memorable and decisive. York, along with his second son, Edmund, and Salisbury, kept the Christmas of 1460 at Sandal Castle. An impregnable stronghold close to the city of Wakefield, it was an old Norman motte-and-bailey settlement, built on a natural ridge. The keep was circular, with towers rising four stories high, surrounded by a 6-foot wall and deep moat. Here, York and his family and their troops, numbering between 3,000 and 8,000 men, were surrounded by a Lancastrian army from Pontefract. The anticipated support from Warwick or Edward, Earl of March, who was then in Wales, had not yet arrived but York decided not to wait. If his men had remained within the castle walls, they would have been safe, but for some reason, they ventured outside to confront their enemies: Hall and Waurin suggest half the enemy force was concealed in the woods, or that they displayed false colours or lured the inhabitants out under promise of a ceasefire. At a loss to explain the lapse in York's usual military abilities, historians have suggested that Salisbury's nephew, John Neville, may have betrayed them or else they were caught out when foraging for food after a long siege. Hall described York's position as 'like a fish in a net or a deer in a buckstall', although when cornered, he fought 'manfully'. Perhaps it was trickery, perhaps bravery. The result was the same. York was killed in battle, as was his brother Thomas; his sixteen-year-old son Edmund, Earl of Rutland, was cut down as he fled and Anne's grandfather, Salisbury, was taken prisoner to Pontefract Castle where he was beheaded. The heads were displayed on the Micklebar Gate, the traditional entry point for monarchs into York, as a 'terror to the rest of thadversaryes',[18] with the duke's dressed in a paper crown.

For Margaret, it was a decisive victory. Now she needed to bring her troops south and convert it into the readeption of her husband

and reinstatement of her seven-year-old son. However, one man in particular stood in her way: Anne's father. With so many of his Yorkist allies wiped out in one stroke, Warwick became, in the words of Vergil, 'thonely man upon whom all the weight of the war depended'. This was not strictly true, as the eighteen-year-old Edward, Earl of March, now took on his father's role as head of the family and his claim to the throne. Between them, the future king and his kingmaker would continue to fight York's battle; their fortunes had plummeted but there were more battles to come, which were still to bring them their greatest victory. Writing in January 1461, Coppini advised a fellow Italian, staying with Queen Margaret and Henry Beaufort, to warn his hosts not to 'be arrogant because of the trifling victory they won, owing to the rash advance of their opponents', otherwise they would bring 'desolation upon the whole realm' because the 'feelings of the people are incredibly incensed against them'. Coppini's advice would prove correct, as the Lancastrian triumph at Wakefield proved to be short-lived: soon they would be ejected from the English throne entirely. York's death had made way for a new commander in the field, a soldier of experience and daring, who, for a while, appeared undefeatable. He was also a family man, a husband and father to two small girls. Warwick's success would bring Anne back home.

4

Boy and Girl
1461–1465

Three glorious suns, each one a perfect sun;
Not separated with the racking clouds,
But sever'd in a pale clear-shining sky.
See, see! they join, embrace, and seem to kiss,
As if they vow'd some league inviolable:
Now are they but one lamp, one light, one sun.
In this the heaven figures some event.[1]

Anne's world, and that of her contemporaries, was changing. The fortunes of those four babies born in the 1450s had fluctuated as the rivalry between Lancaster and York deepened. Now aged four and a half, Anne was suddenly the daughter of the most powerful man in England, on whose shoulders rested the responsibility of defending the City of London and guarding King Henry VI, while the queen's pillaging troops marched south. At a remove from the action in Calais, Anne would have been unaware just how critical the situation in London had become, although her mother's sympathies must have been roused by the plight of York's widow and children; perhaps their prayers were also extended to them in the castle chapel. In England, though, grieving for her husband and second son, with her eldest boy Edward, Earl of March, leading an army of his own, Cecily of York took steps to protect her babies. Following the defeat at Wakefield, she had been in the 'custody' of her sister Anne, Duchess of Buckingham, but now she sent her two youngest sons, Richard and George, to Utrecht under the protection of Philip the Good, whose son their sister Margaret would eventually marry. Aged eight and eleven, they arrived at the Burgundian household without any indication of the length of their stay, or whether they would even see their home again.

On the other side, the fortunes of Edward of Westminster had improved with the death of York. As the newly reinstated heir to the throne, his early years had been spent in flight from the scene of battlefields and he was used to scenes of conflict and bloodshed. Legend has it that the boy himself pronounced the death sentence on those knights who had failed to prevent his father's capture. Queen Margaret had used him as a rallying point in the North, relying on his presence to draw men to his cause and rewarding them with badges of loyalty. Early in 1461 it appeared that he was about to be fully restored to his former life, with only the Earl of Warwick remaining of the old enemy. However, his mother and Henry Beaufort had mismanaged their armies, unable to control the continual looting as they progressed south. This meant that Westminster, after which the seven-year-old was named, was now terrified of the boy's approach.

Three more battles early in 1461 sealed the Lancastrian party's fate. On 2 February Edward, Earl of March, won a decisive victory at Mortimer's Cross in Herefordshire against Henry VI's father-in-law, Owen Tudor. Following the death of Henry V, his widow, Catherine of Valois had contracted a secret match with her groom, Tudor, and borne him at least two sons, the now deceased Edmund, father of Henry VII, and Jasper, who fought at his father's side. Now a widower aged about sixty, Owen Tudor appeared at the head of a Lancastrian army in order to defend his son-in-law's right. The signs were not propitious though, with even the planetary forces seeming to support the Yorkists. Before the fighting began, Edward of March witnessed the phenomenon of a parhelion, or 'sun-dog,' which appeared as three suns in the sky, taken to be a sign of divine favour. Using Welsh recruits, he was able to prevent the different parts of his enemies' forces from meeting up and captured Tudor, who was later beheaded. As the old man laid his head incredulously on the block, he commented that it had been used to 'lie in Queen Catherine's lap'. Jasper Tudor survived the encounter and escaped into exile, although his young ward, Henry Tudor, was left behind. The four-year-old boy was removed from his mother at the Tudor's residence of Pembroke Castle and placed under the guardianship of the loyal Yorkist, William Herbert of Raglan Castle, who had fought for Edward's victory.

Elsewhere in the country, the Earl of Warwick had met with less success. He and Edward of March had intended to join forces to defeat Margaret but Edward had been forced to engage with the Tudors at Mortimer's Cross before they could meet up. This left the earl outnumbered. Only two weeks later, with Henry VI in his custody, Warwick's army met a Lancastian force at St Albans and the unfortunate town was again subjected to intense fighting and destruction. Six years had passed since the destruction of that terrible first battle, time enough for the physical damage to have been cleared away, with properties and gardens repaired and replanted. The memories, however, remained. Aware of Warwick's technique of dividing his army into three and his north-facing positioning, the Lancastrians swung round to take him by surprise. Fighting was again concentrated within the town and in the domestic settings of back yards and houses, lasting several hours until Warwick's troops were finally repelled. Henry VI had supposedly spent the duration of the battle singing and laughing under a tree; now he was reunited with his wife and son, knighting the young Edward, who then went on to knight thirty more Lancastrians himself. Nothing should have prevented their victorious army marching straight into London and reclaiming the throne. Except they didn't. Their hesitation was fatal to their cause, allowing Edward, Earl of March, fresh from his triumph at Mortimer's Cross, to enter the city himself and gain its support. London welcomed the handsome, strong, 6-foot-4 warrior, who went on to declare his hereditary right to the throne.

Both sides thought they had won a decisive victory. March's position in London gave him the advantage but a final encounter was needed to settle who was to emerge as the winners and claim the throne. The opposing armies met at Towton, on Palm Sunday, 29 March. Yorkist leaders Edward, Warwick and the earl's uncle, Lord Fauconberg, faced a Lancastrian army headed by Henry Beaufort, Duke of Somerset, while Henry VI and Queen Margaret waited to hear the outcome at York. The Lancastrians also had Sir Andrew Trollope, who had served under Warwick at Calais before defecting to the other side, Henry Percy, 3rd Earl of Northumberland, with whom the Nevilles had long been in dispute, and Sir Henry Holland, who was married to Anne of York, March's elder sister.

What followed has been called the largest and bloodiest battle on English soil, after which Edward himself estimated that more than 28,000 soldiers lay dead on the snow-driven field. Modern scholars have put the number somewhere between 50,000 and 75,000. Trollope and Percy were killed and Holland fled north to join Henry VI and his family in their Scottish exile. His wife, Anne of York, received his lands and officially separated from him in 1464. At least three-quarters of the noble families of England had members who fought on that day and after the battle, 113 attainders were issued. The fighting had lasted for hours but the Yorkists eventually emerged as the victors; Henry VI and his family fled to Scotland and

Edward of March was crowned, as King Edward IV, at Westminster that June.

It was around this time that Warwick's family packed their bags and returned to England on a more permanent basis. Edward had rewarded his right-hand-man with the position of Admiral of England and King's Lieutenant in the North, which required him to leave Calais behind. The transportation of a great household like the earl's would have entailed much organisation and hard work before the piles of crates and boxes were finally loaded into the ships sitting waiting in Calais harbour. Anne and Isabel would have watched their mother overseeing the servants' activities and perhaps helped to select which items they most wanted to take. Bulkier objects were likely to have been left behind although much of the furniture of the period was designed to be dismantled. Other chattels would follow on later ships; perhaps the family and their belongings required a small fleet, given the requisite numbers of dresses and accoutrements that society required a countess and her daughters to possess.

The surviving household accounts made in the aftermath of the deaths of noble and aristocratic individuals makes clear the extent of their wardrobes. An inventory of Catherine of Aragon's effects, made in 1536, when she was living in disgrace with a pared-down household, lists forty-eight separate hangings for walls and windows, seven sets of embroidered bed linen including counterpanes, testers, curtains and canopies, five cupboard cloths, nine carpets, fourteen cushions, twenty-one pillows, twenty-four sheets and eight blankets. This was before account was made of the finer linen in her 'wardrobe stuff' and that designated for use at her table. The general household and 'kitchen stuff' does not begin to list her own personal effects and items of clothing: comparable lists for the countess and her daughters would have been exhaustive even before the chests of clothes, gowns, kirtles, surcotes and all the layers of under-linen were loaded on board ship.[2] Whenever they travelled and however long it took, Warwick's family were back in residence at Middleham at some point in 1461.

It seems logical to suppose the Nevilles' arrival coincided with Edward IV's Coronation, when other significant exiles returned to the country, including the young York brothers, now second and third in line to the throne. Finally, it was considered safe enough for Edward's brothers, Richard and George, to leave their Burgundian exile, where their mother, Cecily, had sent them after the crushing defeat at Wakefield. They had fled from England as the sons of an attainted traitor and returned as part of the ruling royal family. That June they were made Knights of the Bath and given the titles by which they have come to be known in popular history and drama; the eleven-year-old George became Duke of Clarence while eight-year-old Richard was elevated to the Dukedom of Gloucester.

Anne's base for the next few years was to be Middleham Castle in Wensleydale, Yorkshire, an impressive twelfth-century bastion which had been acquired by the Nevilles through marriage in 1270. In its heyday, it would have had the appearance of a typical defensive stronghold, with its moat and drawbridge, huge walls, towers, gate and the three-story keep with 12-foot-thick walls encompassing the family's living quarters. At 32 by 28 metres square, this keep was one of the largest in England, placed squarely within the castle's solid walls. Early in the fifteenth century, Anne's great-grandfather, the fourth Lord Neville, had undertaken a significant programme of rebuilding, improving the south and west ranges and making more modernisations to accommodate his large family. The new rooms were mostly given over to domestic use, with latrines, fireplaces and views over the countryside; wooden bridges were built on the first floor to connect the new range with the family's original rooms in the keep. The family would thus be elevated above the squalor created by the castle's catering arrangements, such as cooking, slaughter and provisioning, which took place on the ground floor. Most of the community's activity centred around the Great Hall, which would serve as a local court and meeting place as well as for the usual feasting and entertainment that punctuated the daily and annual routine. At the back of the hall stood the chapel, added around 1300, as well as the entrance to the Great and Inner Chambers, which Anne would have known well. Divided by a wooden partition, each had a fireplace, cupboard, small side room or 'closet' and latrine.[3] The fourth Lord Neville also converted a tower into a gatehouse, with stone seating on the inside; perhaps the young Anne sat here and watched the household traffic pass by as millers brought flour to be baked in the new ovens, animals were herded for slaughter, hops delivered to the brewhouse or horses led through to be shod in one of the many workshops that enabled the castle to be self-sufficient.

The thick walls of Middleham Castle would have enclosed a large household, supporting around 200 people in a microcosm of the royal court and of wider medieval society. These would have included a variety of ranks, from those among the immediate family, to the dean of the chapel, almoner, cofferer, marshall, clerks, ushers and those waiting at table, washing laundry or cleaning. Anne's father, Warwick, would have spent a lot of time engaged in acts of 'good lordship', overseeing the smooth running of the local area and investigating disputes: on a national level, he was also away more on diplomatic and government business. During the early 1460s, he fought alongside his brother John, Lord Montagu, to repel the Lancastrian attacks on the Scottish borders, where Queen Margaret was hoping to invade and reclaim the throne for her husband. Anne spent more time, therefore, with her mother, who was described by the family chronicler, John Rous, as a devout lady: decorous, generous and with a strict sense of etiquette; exactly what was expected of a great lady of her day. Rous notes that one of her particularly favoured duties was to attend the deliveries of children in the neighbourhood. Other duties expected of a lady included in the 1412–13 *Household Accounts of Dame Alice de Bryene* are overseeing her many staff and making purchases for the household, especially of luxury items such as spices, salt, wax and candles. The even earlier *Manual for his Wife*, written by the Householder of Paris in 1392, listed among her tasks the skill and cultivation of a garden, particularly grafting and the cultivation of roses in winter; she should also know how to order meals and give instructions to her butcher, poulterer and spicer and that she should be skilled in the preparation of soups, sauces and meat for the infirm and ill. The author also allowed his wife her pleasure in 'rose trees and … violets' and her desire to 'make chaplets and dance and sing'. After all, she was only fifteen. Perhaps the young Anne Neville also took delight in such things.[4]

The *Orders and Rules of the Princess Cecill*,[5] written sometime after 1495, outlines the daily routine of Richard's mother, Cecily Neville, later in life. It gives an impression of the lifestyle of those of similar rank, much of which would be relevant for the household of her future daughter-in-law. The day started when she rose at seven, dressed for the day and heard mass in her chamber before she proceeded into her private chapel for more devotions. After this she ate her first meal at eleven, called 'dinner', during which religious texts were read aloud, usually the lives of female saints such as Maude, Bridget or Katherine. After eating, she gave an hour's audience to any who were waiting to see her, followed by a short nap. Rising after fifteen minutes, she spent the rest of the afternoon in prayer until roused by the 'first peal of evensong'. Then, until the last peal of the bell, she 'drinketh wyne or ale at her pleasure', before attending chapel again. Supper followed at five, which was clearly a more social occasion, during which she recited the lessons heard during dinner to those assembled to eat with her. Finally, the time had come for recreation: now Cecily 'disposeth herself to be famyliare with her gentlewomen' to the season of 'honest mirth', then, an hour before bed, drank wine and retired to her private closet to pray, before laying down to sleep at eight.[6]

However, this routine was not representative of the entire life of 'proud Cis', as the locals nicknamed her; perhaps the later strictures of the widow were partly a penance for the throne room she created at her home of Fotheringhay Castle, where she received visitors with 'the state of a queen' or the thousands of pounds she and her husband spent on clothes and jewels. For aristocrats of their rank, though, second only to the king, this was expected, even desired as a necessary indicator of their status, as outlined by Sir John Fortescue in *De Laudibus Legum Anglae*. Cecily's gold cup cost £54, one shopping trip to London acquired £606 worth of clothes and the duke's 'white rose' collar cost £2,666.[7] It may have been even more important for the Yorks to maintain their regal status in contrast with King Henry's preference for a simple life and dislike of contemporary fashions and worldly goods, which had prompted Fortescue's work. Richard and Cecily's surviving sons, Edward, Edmund, George and Richard, would grow to adulthood with a strong sense of entitlement and the understanding of the need to physically project their majesty.

The *Orders and Rules* for Cecily's household lay out the terms of service for the castle's large staff. Head officers and married ladies were assigned quantities of bread, ale, fire and candles; breakfast was not offered except to the officers resident at the castle, as some were housed in the town. Those who fell ill were permitted 'all such thinges as may be to thaire care' and those who became 'impotent' or unable to carry out their work were to have the same wages as long as Duchess Cecily lived. Three days a week, the family was served with roast beef or mutton; on fast and fish days they had salt fish and two fresh dishes; presumably the estate encompassed some ponds as its position inland would have made regular supplies difficult. The payments for fresh produce were made weekly on a Friday, and on Saturday they had butter and eggs. No mention is made of children, although Cecily and Richard of York had a large family. Compiled after her death, and most of theirs, it probably represents her routine as a widow, although her lifelong practices are likely to have influenced the habits of her sons, as Edward IV's household reforms, the *Liber Niger Domus Regus Angliae*, may suggest. Conscious of her position, the surviving images of Cecily and her daughter Margaret, reared under this regime, speak of elegance and opulence.[8] Life for the Countess of Warwick would have not been too dissimilar and, soon, one of Cecily's sons was to come and live under her regime at Middleham.

Returning from Burgundy in 1461, aged almost nine, Richard of Gloucester initially lived at Sheen and Greenwich with his siblings

Clarence and Margaret, attending Edward IV's Coronation on 27 June. It is likely that Anne and Isabel Neville were also present at this momentous occasion, given their father's role in his accession. Perhaps they stood with their mother in Westminster Abbey, dressed in velvet or damask, or the other impressive fabrics that their rank permitted, while the countess sported one of the new winged or butterfly headdresses, watching the proceedings. Among the feasting and jousting that inevitably followed, Warwick's children and Edward's siblings would have come into contact, either seated at the head table or enjoying the entertainment. Anne and Isabel may well have attended key events at court, staying at their father's town house of the Erber, when not at their northern base of Middleham. So it is likely that Richard was known to them both by the time he joined Warwick's household. It was customary among the nobility and aristocracy to place teenage children among families of equivalent rank in order for them to receive social or military training suitable for their future positions. For girls, their education as ladies would encompass traditional skills such as needlework, dancing and music as well as those required to run households of their own in the future. Adolescent boys, known as 'henxmen', were trained in the art of warfare and chivalry, as well as languages and those skills of diplomacy that would open doors at the highest level. Often, they grouped around a young man of similar age, establishing friendships and loyalties that would last a lifetime.

The date of young Richard's arrival at Middleham is uncertain; it may have been as early as 1461, although other historians have suggested he did not enter Warwick's tutelage until 1464. Certainly in 1461, the nine-year-old boy was mentioned in the king's household accounts, when his goods were conveyed to and from Leicester and the capital, as well as the necessary furnishings for his time at Greenwich. Thomas Bourchier, Archbishop of Canterbury, who was related to the Yorks by marriage, received compensation for supporting the king's brothers 'for a long time and at great charges' so Richard may well have been resident in his household for a period of time.[9] While nine years old was not too early for Richard to begin his chivalric training, it appears that his elder brother George, Duke of Clarence, had begun this process when he was ten. Clarence was now the centre of his own establishment at Greenwich, continuing his chivalric training among his peers. The sons of the aristocracy matured early, when youth and strength were often as crucial as experience when it came to combat. Fourteen was considered to be a significant milestone in the maturation of boys and Edward himself would declare Richard of age when he reached sixteen, after which he would take an important administrative and legal role, before fighting his first full battle at the age of eighteen. Edward IV had become king just before his nineteenth birthday. Now it was the role of the Earl of Warwick to prepare his young charge for this military and chivalric future.

It is possible that Richard was already a frequent visitor to Middleham Castle or Warwick's other properties. Certainly, he would have been familiar to the Neville family. Several historians have suggested that the earl was Richard's godfather and, as such, he would have played a parental role in his education even before the boy became a more permanent resident under his roof. This would have begun as early as 1461, certainly when Warwick was at Westminster or about the king's business. The relationship between the king and the earl had never been stronger than in the year of his accession. After that, things would slowly sour and, by 1464, major disagreements of policy had already arisen between the cousins, although they had not yet reached the proportions of later years that resulted in their complete breach. Edward was clearly making arrangements for his siblings in 1461 as, that November, his Parliament instructed the Sheriff of Gloucester to pay Richard £40 a year for life.[10] Around 1465, an entry in the Roll of the Exchequer recorded money 'paid to Richard, Earl of Warwick, for costs and expenses incurred by him on behalf of the Duke of Gloucester, the king's brother', so he was clearly at Middleham by then. Additionally, to pay for the boy's upkeep, Edward awarded Warwick the wardship of Francis Lovell, heir to Lord Lovell. Two years younger than Richard, Lovell probably arrived in Wensleydale on the death of his father in around 1463, but the pair were to become lifelong friends. Also present were Robert Percy of Scotton and Richard Radcliffe, or Ratcliffe, of Lancashire, who were to fight and die alongside their future king. Ratcliffe's grandfather was comptroller of the household of Edward IV, a position that the young Robert Percy would assume for the duration of Richard's reign. Thomas Huddleston and Thomas Parr, Richard's future esquire, were also probably present as the sons of Warwick's Cumbrian retainers, along with James Tyrell of Ipswich. Warwick's schoolroom may have been even larger; other boys may also have passed under his tutelage during those years in a hothouse for the environment that one historian has referred to as the 'flowering of British chivalry'. There is also another possibility. Young aristocrats were often sent away to be raised in households of their intended future partners. Perhaps, even at this early stage, Warwick was considering the king's brother as a match for one of his daughters.

Actually, Warwick was frequently absent from home during 1464–
65. Always favouring a French alliance over the Burgundian match
Edward IV favoured, he had travelled back across the Channel to
negotiate a marriage for the king, which had been called off, much
to the earl's chagrin. However, he was kept busy in the royal service,
visiting the Cinque Ports on the Kent and Sussex coast in November. At
the end of the month he was at York and, after celebrating Christmas,
was at Coventry on 10 January and six days later, at the opening of
Parliament in Westminster, staying at his London home, the Erber,
where he remained until that March. Between mid-May and mid-
July, he was in Calais, then back in Warwick in August before being
recorded making offerings at the church of St Mary's, Warwick, along
with the countess, their daughters and Richard, Duke of Gloucester
in September 1465.[11] Richard may well have accompanied him on
some of these minor missions or, alternatively, was in residence at
other Warwick properties such as Barnard Castle, Penrith and Sheriff
Hutton.

Given the routine of the Warwick household, Richard and
Anne Neville would have seen each other regularly while he was
at Middleham. Although Anne's existence would have been more
sequestered and her presence in the Great Hall less frequent, the
pair's proximity cannot but have bred a degree of intimacy. Out
of the window, the little girl may have seen the youths tilting in
the yard or riding out with hounds and hawks; indoors, she may
have heard them reciting their Latin, listened to them practise their
instruments in the evening or knelt beside them in prayer in the
chapel. Isabel was closer to Richard in age and it is even possible
that friendship developed between them first. All three are recorded
as attending the enthronement of the girls' uncle, George Neville,
as Archbishop of York in September 1465, at Cawood Castle,
participating in the legendary feast that saw the consumption of
gargantuan quantities of fish, flesh and fowl. According to Leland's
account, Warwick was acting in the honoured role of steward
and among the 'estates sitting in the chief chamber', Richard was
seated alongside 'the earl's daughters', under the watchful eyes
of the Countesses of Suffolk, Westmorland and Northumberland,
clearly considered to be part of the Warwicks' intimate family. The
countess was placed separately in the second chamber; obviously
at the ages of nine and fourteen, Anne and Isabel's table manners
were considered up to scratch, as modelled in Hugh Rhodes' *Boke
of Nurture*:

An ye be desired to serve, or sit, or eat meat at the table,
 Incline to good manners, and to nurture yourself enable...
 Before that you sit, see that your knife be bright
 Your hands clean, your nails pared is a good sight.
 When thou shalt speak, roll not too fast thine eye;
 Gaze not too and fro as one that were void of courtesy.[12]

Rhodes himself was a member of Edward IV's chapel, a man 'of worship, endowed with vertuuse moral and speculatiff ... modestiall in all other manner of behaving'. He would have composed his advice to young people at the same time as Richard and the Neville girls were growing up; perhaps Warwick and his countess used his advice, or else their own version of it. At table, Anne and Isabel would have learned not to fill their spoons too full, not to dip bread in their soup, slurp too loudly or put their meat in the salt cellar, to eat small morsels and not to quaff or scratch, fidget or pick their teeth. Displaying good manners towards their table companions was essential:

An a stranger sit near thee, ever among now and then,
 Reward him with some dainties like a gentleman
 If thy fellow sit from his meat and cannot come thereto,
 Then cut him such as thou hast, that is gently to do.[13]

Seated together, the young trio would have eaten through their share of the dishes prepared by the sixty-two cooks in the kitchens that day. Recorded by Leland, the three courses included such delicacies as frumenty with venison, hart, mutton, cygnets and swans, capons and geese, peacock and rabbits. The small birds eaten numbered woodcocks, plovers, egrets, larks, redshanks, martinets, partridges and quails, while among the sweets were dates, fritters, quinces, wafers as well as the marzipan subtleties in the forms of a dolphin, dragon, St William and St George. This did not even include the fish courses, with salmon, sturgeon, lobster and lampreys, conger eels, trout and turbot among many others. Around 300 tuns of ale were consumed and 100 of wine and under the quantities listed, the amount of 'spices, sugared delicates and wafers' made was recorded as 'plenty'. Around 13,000 puddings were consumed. Following the feast, guests were given damask (rose) water to wash in and hippocras to drink. The three children cannot help but have been impressed, even accustomed as they were to the finest cuisine and the most formal of occasions. Forbidden by etiquette to discuss the food, perhaps their formal manners allowed for little conversation in spite of the friendship that existed between the families. Perhaps even at this stage, the thirteen-year-old boy and the nine-year-old Anne were already fond of each other; was Anne already more than just one of 'the earl's daughters' to Richard, Duke of Gloucester?

5

Romance and Chivalry
1465–1469

In person she was seemly, amenable and beautiful and in
conditions full commendable and right virtuous[1]

What did he look like, this young man who came into Anne's
Middleham world? The question of Richard's appearance has proved
contentious since the late fifteenth century. A flurry of accounts
written in the aftermath of Bosworth quickly established the myths of
deformity that the Tudors required as a correlative to the late king's
perceived moral distortion. Shakespeare's Richard of 1591 manages
to use his powers of persuasion to make Anne submit to a match
with a 'hunch-backed toad' but no taint of abnormality was present
when the two children were growing up in the 1450s. The origins of
this misrepresentation stem from the use of two words in a poem,
'A Dialogue between a Secular and a Friar', recording the family's
history in the Clare Roll. According to the chronicler, Richard was the
eleventh child of twelve, some of whom had already perished. Other
sources list another short-lived or stillborn daughter, Joan, born earlier
in the marriage around 1438.

Sir, aftir the tyme of longe bareynesse,
God first sent Anne, which signifyeth grace,
In token that at her hertis hevynesse
He as for bareynesse would fro hem chace.
Harry, Edward, and Edmonde, eche is his place
Succcedid; and after tweyn doughters cam
Elizabeth and Margarete, and aftir William.
John aftir William nexte borne was,
Whiche bothe he passid to Goddis grace:

George was next, and after Thomas
Borne was, which sone aftir did pace
By the pathe of dethe into the heavenly place.
Richard liveth yet; but the last of alle
Was Ursula, to him God list calle.[2]

The penultimate line, stating that 'Richard liveth yet', has been interpreted as an indicator of his poor health, leading to descriptions of him as a sick and weakly child. There is no other evidence to support this, though, and recent historians have argued that it is more a statement of fact in comparison with his deceased siblings. The author was simply stating that Richard had survived in comparison with Thomas and Ursula, his immediate siblings. At the time of writing, Richard was still a child 'in his pupilage' and therefore still at risk from various infantile illnesses. The statement that he 'liveth yet' could, in fact, be an affirmation rather than indication of any physical problem; rather, it suggests strength and survival.

The Neville family chronicler, John Rous, was initially favourable to Richard, describing him in 1484 as a 'most mighty prince' who ruled 'commendably ... cherishing those who were virtuous' to the 'great laud of all the people'. The line drawing which accompanies his text shows a knight holding a sword, whose limbs appear in perfect proportion, his features regular, almost beneficent. It is not too dissimilar to an illustration featured in the chronicle of French writer, Jean de Waurin, where a figure in a green hat, thought to represent Richard in his early twenties, clearly has well-formed limbs, straight spine and even shoulders. It may be that Waurin and Rous were diplomatically flattering their ruler by glossing over his impediments or perhaps, that these defects were not necessarily visible at the time of writing or were hidden under clothes. After the victory of Henry VII in 1485, Rous produced a second version of his history, although he was unable to access and amend his original, positive account. This later, Tudor-friendly version introduced the idea of Richard's monstrous birth, which depicts him arriving after an impossible two-year gestation period, sporting a full set of teeth. Rous' dramatic U-turn may have been his attempt to curry favour with the new regime, or else he could have been influenced by his belief that Richard was responsible for the death of Anne, whose family were his patrons. Whatever prompted Rous to rewrite history, his second account of 1491 was to trigger the legends of the late king's deformities.

This dramatic horror story influenced another account of Richard's life and reign, written by Thomas More between 1512 and 1519, in which the boy was breech-born, little, 'croke-backed' and 'hard-faced', which served his purpose in presenting the dead Yorkist as a villain. Equally, the author had served as a page in the household of the Lancastrian Archbishop Morton and may have based his version of events on conversations with one of Richard's adversaries. Tudor historian Polydore Vergil built on More's account, which was further developed by Edward Hall in the 1540s, seeking to justify the Tudor invasion of 1485. These three negative portrayals formed the main influence on Shakespeare's interpretation, which developed Richard into the 'poison bunch-backed toad' that was the supposed physical manifestation of his wickedness. By the time the play was composed, in around 1591, the tradition of the king's deformity was well established and, by 1614, it had inspired an anonymous author to produce the poem 'The Ghost of Richard III', drawing together the worst of the legends about his appearance and deeds, which survives in a single manuscript copy in the Bodleian Library:

> My mother Languish't many a tedious houre…
> My legges came foremost, an unequall payre…
> Hollow my cheeks, upon my brest black hayre,
> The characters of spleene and virulent deedes;
> My beetle-brow, and my fyre-cyrcled eye
> Foreshow'd me butcher in my cruelty…
> So, mountaine-like was I contract behind
> That my stretch't arms (plumpe with ambitious veines)
> Might crush all obstacles and throw them downe
> That stood betwixt my shadow and a crowne…
> Th'amazed women started, for each jaw
> Appear'd with teeth, which mark made these ils good
> That I should worry soules, suck humane blood.[3]

However, none of the contemporary chroniclers, Mancini, Commines and Croyland, make any mention of Richard's deformities. The Italian, Mancini, certainly had a motive to do so, writing in 1483 about the 'suspicious' disappearance of the princes, which were even then reputed to have been killed by their uncle. Based in London, Mancini never met Richard but he certainly repeated the rumours of the day. He had no compunction about giving his opinion on the new regime, titling his account *The Occupation of the Throne by Richard III*. When he left the country that summer, he had little need to flatter the new king and could have presented any unpleasant truths without fear of reprisals. The Burgundian Commines had probably never visited England but wrote an account based on meetings with Richard's contemporaries in exile, notably his nemesis Henry Tudor. While he states that King Louis of France thought Richard a 'cruel and evil' murderer, he does not exploit the opportunity to discredit his appearance. The English Croyland Chronicle calls Richard's later activities 'seditious and disgraceful' but makes no mention of his looks.

Accounts written by those who knew Richard give the impression that the thirteen-year-old boy took after his father, the Duke of York, in appearance, being dark-haired and wiry. The Silesian, Nicolas von Popplau, who visited Richard's court in 1484, described him as slim and lightly built with slender arms and thighs, although he admitted the king was actually three fingers taller than himself. The Scottish Ambassador, Archibald Whitelaw, confirmed in the same year that Richard was small, although none seemed to doubt his strength and prowess in battle. Horace Walpole claimed that Catherine, Countess of Desmond, remembered Richard and had called him the 'handsomest man in the room' although her death in 1604, at the reputed age of either 120 or 140, may push credibility to the limit. It hardly seems possible that she lived to such an advanced age and could remember him herself: perhaps she was recalling what her mother or grandmother had passed down, or even her much older husband, as suggested by John Ashdown-Hill. Her marriage in 1529, assuming it was her first and that her death date is correct, might suggest a birth date of between 1500 and 1515.

Handsome or not, Richard was clearly an impressive youth, being made Admiral of England at ten, Commissioner of Array for nine counties at the age of twelve and Constable of England a few years later. While Vergil paints a bleak picture of Richard during the reign of Henry VIII, one description he gives confirms the late king had been 'slight in figure, in face short and compact like his father'. Taken in isolation, this is probably quite close to the truth. The earliest surviving portraits of Richard from 1516 onwards, based on lost originals, have shown signs of tampering and cannot be trusted. The famous 'broken-sword' picture, held at the Society of Antiquities, has been x-rayed to expose the crudely painted hump that was added by a later artist. Although the post-Tudor depictions of Richard have eclipsed those written during his lifetime, their dubious veracity and ulterior motives should not be allowed to distort less well-known portrayals of Richard as a young man. The thirteen-year-old boy whom Anne Neville came to know was probably short, strong and slender with dark hair.

When Richard's body was discovered in a Leicester car park in September 2012, a number of scientific tests run by the University of

Leicester were finally able to establish the truth about his appearance. According to the skeletal analysis, Richard was of 'unusually slender' build and had both arms of similar size, of which he would have had normal use, although they were almost 'feminine' in delicacy, confirming von Popplau's description. He would have been above average height, at around 5 foot 8, except for the presence of spinal curvature, which would have significantly affected how tall he stood. The bones made it clear that Richard suffered from idiopathic adolescent onset scoliosis, a condition that caused his spine to bend into an 'S' shape. He was not born with this and the reason for its development is unclear; it would have begun some time after his tenth birthday and may have caused back pain and breathlessness, as a result of the additional pressure on his heart and lungs. It can result in uneven muscular development on the back and uneven limb length, rib prominence and slow nerve reaction, yet the young man was clearly to become a competent and strong soldier. As Richard was still a child at the onset of his condition and had not yet undergone his adolescent period of growth, he was likely to have experienced greater spinal curvature as he aged, although his life expectancy did not differ from that of his peers. Investigators at the University suggested that his spine would have had a 'stiff' and 'abnormal' curve and resulted in asymmetry to the chest wall. However, with this concealed under his clothing, he may still have looked and walked like anyone else, with perhaps one shoulder slightly higher. An examination of the end of his clavicles, the two bones that form the collar, showed the right-hand side to be larger than the left and may have resulted in one shoulder being held higher than the other. If this was a mild condition, diplomacy would probably have dictated that it went unmentioned during his lifetime. After his ignominious death, however, such apparent signs of divine displeasure would have been exaggerated.

Also, in February 2013 a facial reconstruction was completed, based on Richard's skull. Rebuilt by Professor Caroline Wilkinson at the University of Dundee, a series of pegs were attached to the bones, allowing for the muscles and flesh to be laid over them. Gradually as the layers built up, a recognisable face emerged, not unlike the earliest portraits, dating from the 1520s. The face of Richard III had a strong nose and jaw but the reconstruction captured a pleasantness, a softness about the mouth and eyes, even a half smile. Dressed in dark wig and soft velvet cap with its dangling jewel, after the style of the portraits, it exudes a certain unexpected charisma. It was not difficult to see the man whom Anne Neville may have fallen in love with.

The appearance of the young Anne is even less certain. While Richard's physical shape has occupied historians for centuries, hers has barely merited any attention. One depiction of her in the Beaufort Pageant gives a stylised glimpse of her head and shoulders only. Her long hair hangs down, while her sloping form and sketchy facial features are typical of fifteenth-century ideals of beauty, which give a mere representation and evoke little personality. The Rous Roll shows a young woman with hair down to the waist, while her face has the simplicity of a woodcut, with its wide forehead, high arched brows, straight nose, prim small mouth, strong chin and eyes cast down to the left. John Rous, the Chaplain of Guy's Cliffe near Warwick, was born in 1411 and was therefore likely to have seen Anne in person, although his many images of her ancestors and family are too similar to be very helpful. The representation of queens in all forms was bound by conventions of beauty, loyalty and status. Rous' illustration of a young woman conforms with these, depicting her with long, flowing hair brushed back off her face and the heavy-lidded eyes popularised by the legendary beauty of Elizabeth Wydeville. Other contemporary manuscript images and statuary depict young women with a recognisable set of aesthetic ideals; sloping shoulders and large forehead, the wide hips thrust forward and rounded belly suggestive of fertility. Rous' pen portrait of Anne as 'seemly amiable and beauteous and in conditions full commendable and right virtuous and according to the interpretation of her name, full gracious' is similarly platitudinous.

It was also a consistent act of late medieval flattery to describe aristocratic beauties, especially queens, as golden-haired, with all its correlations to wealth and fecundity, even if this was obviously a departure from the truth. Writing about the cult of the Virgin Mary, Marina Warner identifies the association of fertility, innocence and purity with blonde hair, resonant of haloes.[4] Other royal attributes included fair skin, sparkling eyes, fine features, curved brows, red lips and cheeks, blue or grey eyes and the sinuous, large-bellied body. On attaining regal status, women seem to have miraculously acquired these, with the notable exception of the foreign and therefore 'dark' Margaret of Anjou. As a literary conceit, this form of beauty is found in Chaucer, the Pearl poet, Boccaccio, Matthew of Vendôme, Geoffrey of Vinsauf, Guy of Warwick and others; it is also the traditional depiction of many virginal saints such as those written by Osbern Bokenham in the 1440s. The Croyland Chronicler remarks that Anne was 'alike in complexion' to her niece, the blonde Elizabeth of York, ten years her junior, whose interchanged clothing also suggested Anne was slender as a teenager.

Her elder sister Isabel, now fourteen, was probably of similar appearance. Thirteen months older than Richard, it may have been she who developed a friendship with the young duke first. Anne was only nine years old, which is a significant remove from the sort of companionship two young teenagers would be able to offer each other. Hindsight has led the majority of historians and novelists to speculate whether the Duke and Duchess of Gloucester's marriage was based in juvenile affection which developed during his time at Middleham. The other romantic possibility, though, was that Richard was actually drawn to Isabel, who was subsequently wed to his brother, although this has received little consideration and is pure speculation. Emotion aside, if Richard was considering one of the Neville girls as a suitable future wife, he may not necessarily have had a preference for one over the other. When early marriages were contracted, death sometimes intervened and the intended spouse was replaced by a sibling near in age, in order to preserve the settlement. When negotiations were being drawn up for the marriage of Edward IV's daughter, Elizabeth of York, to Charles, the Dauphin of France, clauses were inserted to allow the young man to marry one of her sisters in the event of her premature death. This safeguard did prove necessary early in the following century, when the death of Prince Arthur led to the remarriage of his teenage widow, Catherine of Aragon, to her brother-in-law Henry VIII. By the time Richard was in a position to take a wife, and hoped to assume Warwick's mantle, Isabel was unavailable.

The three children would have come to know each other well during the 1460s. However, on one occasion, the relationship between the king and Warwick was to foreshadow their later opposition. In 1465, Richard would have attended a significant event at which the girls may not have been present: the Coronation of Edward IV's queen. Through the early 1460s, Warwick had been working towards a French alliance, cemented by a marriage between the king and Bona of Savoy, the teenage sister of Queen Charlotte, wife of Louis XI. At the last minute, just as the arrangements were on the verge of being concluded, Edward made the startling admission that he was already married. His bride of five months was the widowed Lancastrian Elizabeth Grey, *née* Wydeville, a beautiful blonde from a large and aspirational family. The ceremony had been conducted in secret on May Day 1464, at the Wydeville seat of Grafton Regis, where Edward had arrived on the pretext of hunting. The unexpected news came as a personal blow to Warwick, who had previously worked in harmony with Edward, whose secrecy and encouragement of the French marriage made the Kingmaker look a fool. He already had cause to quarrel with the family, as Elizabeth's brother, Anthony, Earl Rivers, had been responsible for amassing a fleet at Sandwich with the intention of invading Calais in 1460. The plot had failed, resulting in the capture of Scales and his parents as they lay in bed in Sandwich town. They were then brought to Calais as Warwick's prisoners, where he had berated them as traitors and the 'sons of knaves' in Edward's presence. Now Scales was made a Knight of the Garter and his sister was England's queen. The family were also pro-Burgundian and resented the influence Warwick had previously exerted over the king. Warwick himself was not present at her splendid Westminster Coronation at Whitsun 1465, having been sent on an embassy to Burgundy, so it is unlikely that the countess and her daughters may have attended. There is the chance that Anne's mother may have had some ceremonial role to fulfil as the wife of the most powerful magnate in the country, but no record remains of her duties. One fact suggesting this is her absence from Middleham for most of that year, when she may have been occupied with the new queen's establishment or else visiting her other properties at Warwick, Hanley Castle in Worcestershire, Tewkesbury or Cardiff.

Elizabeth and Edward had met, according to local legend, in the forest near her family home of Grafton. She was the daughter of the aristocratic Jacquetta of Luxemburg, whose first marriage to John of Lancaster had made her the first lady in the land after Queen Margaret and a staunch Lancastrian. Her second union with Richard Wydeville, Earl Rivers, was a forbidden love match, which produced fourteen children, the eldest of whom was Elizabeth. The blonde beauty, variously described as 'icy' and 'haughty' by her enemies, had been married to Sir John Grey and bore him two sons before his death at the Second Battle of St Albans in 1461. The late medieval and early Tudor chroniclers agree that the amorous Edward was struck by her beauty upon seeing her and determined to have her, as he had many other women on whom his fancy had fallen. Elizabeth held out for more, though. Refusing to become his mistress, she became, instead, his queen. It was an unpopular match among the king's family and Parliament from the start.

Besides Warwick's existing dislike of the Wydevilles and the humiliation over his attempts to conclude a French alliance, the rise of Elizabeth's relatives upset many of the old established figures at court who were bypassed in favour of the parvenus. The Great Chronicle of London commented on the increasing hostility and Warwick's annoyance that Edward 'maketh more honourable account of new upstart gentlemen than the ancient houses of nobility'. Rivers held the position of Lord Treasurer, and, wealthy through a profitable marriage himself, was also Governor of the Isle of Wight and Elizabeth's other siblings were matched above their previous station. Warwick was particularly incensed by the match between Katherine Wydeville and Henry Stafford, Duke of Buckingham, the queen's ten-year-old ward, suggesting that he had intended Buckingham as a husband for one of his daughters. According to Mancini, Edward's second brother, George, Duke of Clarence, did not try to conceal his personal dislike of the new queen, nor did their mother, Duchess Cecily, who attempted unsuccessfully to persuade her eldest son to abandon the marriage. Edward, however, would not be influenced and Richard, at the age of twelve, was more diplomatic. If he was shocked or displeased by the secret marriage, he did not show it. Unsurprisingly, it was from this marriage that the seeds of discord were sown among the brothers and their cousins. Later historians have even gone as far as to trace back the fall of the House of York to this rash, romantic act which propelled the Wydevilles into the centre of national politics. By the middle of 1465, though, it was clear that the queen and her relatives were staying put; that summer, Elizabeth conceived a child and by the autumn, her growing belly advertised her success.

The earl, countess and their daughters were certainly present at the christening of Edward's eldest child, Elizabeth of York, born in February 1466. The visiting Bohemian Gabriel Tetzel recorded that there were eight duchesses and thirty countesses in attendance, standing in silence as the queen was seated on a golden chair.⁵ As the girl's godfather, Warwick fulfilled a ceremonial role and probably remained in London to witness the queen's churching that March. The family would have stayed in their town house of the Erber, where, rumour had it, the household was so large that six oxen were consumed at breakfast each day. From its location on Stowe's map, between Newgate and old St Paul's, the family could access Westminster by road via Charing Cross along the Strand, or else take a boat upstream from Blackfriars or Puddle Wharf. Perhaps Anne and Richard were reunited for the three-hour feast that followed, or else enjoyed the music and festivities that night, where Edward's sister Margaret was recorded as dancing with two dukes, who were quite possibly her brothers George and Richard. They may also have been at court during the process of negotiations that led to the foreign alliance Edward had long sought. While Warwick continued to push for closer Franco–English relations, his rival Anthony Wydeville, Earl Rivers, had led a party that visited Bruges in the spring of 1467, following the signing of a peace and trade treaty with Philip of Burgundy.

That June, Anthony, Comte de la Roche, the 'Grand Bastard of Burgundy', son of Philip and half-brother of Charles the Bold, arrived in England for an extended visit. An impressive figure, with an international reputation for jousting, a crusader against the Moors and holder of the Order of the Golden Fleece, he took part in a magnificent tournament held at Smithfield as the guest of Edward and Earl Rivers. In Rivers' own words, the purpose of the joust was to avoid slothfulness 'and to obeye and please my feire lady'. The event may have been designed to entertain such fair young ladies as Warwick's daughters but it could also be brutal. According to Gregory's Chronicle, de la Roche's horse 'was so brusyd that he dyde a whyle aftyr'. The chronicler recorded how, whether by 'fortune, crafte or cunnynge', the Bastard 'lay out' all men and horses in the field. Seated prominently in the specially erected scaffolding, Anne would no doubt have witnessed, with interest, everything that took place. Smithfield itself was a large grassy space or 'smoothfield', long used for livestock markets, public gatherings, executions and drying laundry. It was situated on the eastern side of the Tower, accessible by the Postern Gate, which for the Warwicks would have required a journey home through the heart of the city itself, along one of its major thoroughfares such as Thames Street, taking them as far west as they needed to go before turning north at Blackfriars.

There was a long precedent of tournaments held at Smithfield, with the impressive spectacle of 1442 still in recent memory, when Henry VI acted as umpire between Sir John Astley and the Chevalier Philip Boyle of Aragon. This encounter was depicted in the Hastings Manuscript, written around 1475, where the complicated dress of the combatants was described, from their woollen hose and thick cordwain shoes to the satin-lined doublet, mail gussets and full metal armour. Another contemporary manuscript, *How a Man Schall be Armyd*, provides the only surviving image of a knight being dressed for combat on foot, as his valet ties on his mail skirt before beginning to assemble the complex jigsaw of body pieces, with the traditional weapon of the poleaxe and more unusual *ahlspiess*, a four-sided spike, depicted at the side.[6] Quadrangular lists were erected, in which the combatants faced each other wearing embroidered armour and wielding axes.[7] The arena was immediately beside the west doors of St Bartholomew's church, where trials by combat had been held since the 1350s. The most defining encounter was that organised by Richard II in 1390, when sixty knights, accompanied by sixty ladies from around Europe, descended on the capital, where preparations had been made by Chaucer in his capacity as the king's clerk and records of the event were made by the French chronicler Froissart. Etiquette for such events was set by Margaret of Anjou's father René, in his 1406 vividly detailed tournament book, which lists that 'noble and rich prizes should be given by ladies and damsel'. It would not have been a passive experience for Anne: the ladies are constantly referred to by René as visiting and observing coats of arms, attending suppers, making complaints, exercising compassion and the most beautiful and noble of them leading processions.[8] Among the ritualised responses, the knights were bound to promise their patronesses:

I humbly thank my ladies and damsels for the honour it has pleased them to do to me: and although they could easily have found others who could do this better, and who merit this honour more than I, nevertheless I obey the ladies freely and will do my loyal duty, asking always that they forgive my mistakes.[9]

Then, when it came to receiving prizes, the King of Arms must say,

Behold here this noble lady, my lady of such a place N., accompanied by the knight or squire of honour and by my lords the judges, who have come to give you the tourney prize, because you have been judged the knight or squire who has fought best today in the melee of the tourney, and my lady prays that you will take it with good will.

As René outlined,

the lady should uncover the prize, and give it to him. Then he should take it and kiss her, and the two damsels if he likes. And then the king of arms, heralds and pursuivants should shout his battle cry around the whole room. And this done, he should lead the lady to the dance, and the judges, the knight of honour, the king of arms and the pursuivants should lead the two damsels back to their places, without sounding the trumpets any more.[10]

As the daughters of the leading magnate of the land, Anne and Isabel may well have played a part in the distribution of prizes, perhaps receiving kisses and even taking part in the dancing. A great hall was set aside for this, with hanging wooden chandeliers, bowls to hold torches, tapestries, minstrels' gallery, a side board of pewter and silver as well a dressing-room for the women to 'refresh themselves or rest'.[11] Along with feasts and court pageantry, such encounters would have been the most exciting form of entertainment for those in Anne's circle;

the pinnacle of what fifteenth-century secular culture had to offer and not to be missed. When Anne's husband, Richard of Gloucester, became Constable of England, part of his job was to update the rules for tournaments; perhaps Anne recalled the Smithfield event and made her own contribution.

The primary motive for the 1467 visit of the Burgundians was to discuss the proposed marital alliance between Charles the Bold and Margaret of York. With relations between the two countries improving along cultural, trading and political lines, Edward was encouraged to host a lavish tournament at Smithfield for his guests. In fact, though, it was the magnificent three-day duel on horse and foot, fought between Earl Rivers and the Bastard of Burgundy, which turned out to be the memorable event, eclipsing the true diplomatic purpose of the visit. Warwick would have wished to keep an eye on the development of the negotiations, still holding out his vain hopes that Edward would ultimately return to the idea of a French alliance. This occasion, with all its protocol and pageantry, marked a final glorious flourish in the tradition of late medieval tournaments; in fact it was also the last recorded use of the Smithfield site. Later incarnations under the Tudors would take different forms and represent a nostalgic return to older traditions.[12] It was certainly the Burgundians who led the way in the elaborate ceremonial and pageantry of these formalised conflicts by the 1460s but what Anne may have witnessed at Smithfield was impressive enough. In fact, the 1467 festivities became a prototype for the perfect tournament, being copied a decade later for the celebrations of the marriage of the four-year-old Richard, Duke of York, to Anne de Mowbray. By this date, her marriage would have made Anne the boy's aunt, so it is likely that she was there to witness the splendid occasion. The party of 1467 was cut short, however, by the death of Philip of Burgundy and accession of his son, Charles the Bold, which sent his courtiers hurrying back home. If anything, this cemented the proposal and Warwick had to accept that the match would go ahead, regardless of his dislike.

In the summer of 1468, Earl Rivers was given the honour of leading the party escorting Margaret to her wedding and the pomp and ceremony was resumed. Warwick had ridden with her when she left Westminster but it was Scales who accompanied her across the sea to Burgundy, marking a reciprocal chivalric gesture but also, perhaps, a significant indicator of Edward's shift in trust. The bride arrived through decorated archways where red and white wine flowed from the bows of archers and hippocras poured from the breast of a pelican sitting in a golden tree. The wedding took place on 3 July, in a temporary wooden hall, 140 feet by 70, with upper galleries, turrets and glass windows with gilded shutters, its thirty-two rooms hung with tapestries. Nine days of festivities encompassed banquets of swans, peacocks and 'unicorns', dances, plays, wild animals, music and 'mechanical surprises'. The *pièce de résistance*, though, was the tournament of the Golden Tree, organised by the Bastard of Burgundy in Margaret's honour. A narrative thread linking all the events presented the 'lady of the Hidden Ile', who required her knights to carry out three great tasks on her behalf, encountering ogres, dwarves and mysterious figures lurking in the woods; the victors hung their coats of arms on the golden tree itself. One participant arrived chained inside a black castle from which only the ladies could free him with a golden key. However extraordinary these fantasies were, the ensuing fighting was real enough, with the host sustaining a broken leg in action.

In the same year as the Burgundian wedding, the teenage Richard of Gloucester was reaching maturity. The days of hunting, hawking and practising in the tilt-yard were soon to be translated into royal service on a national level and combat in the field. A little verse by John Hardyng neatly sums up the transition from late medieval aristocratic boyhood to the manhood of a leading magnate:

> At fourteen they shall to field I sure
> At hunt the deer; and catch a hardiness...
> At sixteen year to war and wage
> To joust and ride, and castles to assail.

When Richard turned sixteen that October, his elder brother, the king, declared him officially of age and bestowed upon him the previously Lancastrian titles of Halton and Clitheroe, in order to provide for his upkeep. He was already a Knight of the Garter, having received the highest order of chivalry at the tender age of fourteen. The youth was now also given a commission of oyer and terminer, which were local courts, presided over by an assize judge, designed to hear and rule on serious cases including treason. In this capacity, Richard was now responsible for condemning Lancastrian traitors. He was also a signatory on the document whereby Edward offered his Burgundian brother-in-law, Charles the Bold, the Order of the Garter and was still closely connected with Warwick, being recorded as welcomed with him into the City of York. When Richard left his mentor's household at Middleham for Westminster by February 1469, he may have been aware of Warwick's increasing dissatisfaction with Edward's regime.

Perhaps the earl concealed his feelings from the king's brother or perhaps his criticism lay behind the young man's departure. By the time Richard was appointed Constable of England that October, the breach between the earl and the Yorkists was impossible to ignore. In fact, Richard was soon dispatched to Wales as a temporary figurehead to restore order, where one of his tasks was to recover territories from Warwick's rebellious supporters. When it came to his family, there was no doubting the young duke's motto of '*loyaulte me lie*'.

Warwick's allegiances had been changing for a while. Even as the Burgundian match had been secretly concluded, late in 1467, Edward continued to allow him to pursue a French alliance in competition with the Wydevilles' ambitions. When the earl was disabused of this policy, it must have been an unpleasant reminder of the deception the king had previously practised over his own marriage. After the treaty was formalised in February 1468, according to Croyland, Warwick 'conceived great indignation' and loathed the queen's family with 'a most deadly hatred', feeling that, once again, they had been preferred over him. While liaising with Louis XI, both men had made a number of attempts to sabotage the marriage and, now, the discovery finally drove Warwick into the arms of the French. To discredit the union, he attempted to harness the hostility and fears of London tradesmen by planning an attack by his retainers on Flemish merchants in the city, although the plot was discovered and the riot prevented. Louis armed Jasper Tudor, Earl of Pembroke, who then laid siege to Harlech Castle in the hopes of prompting the return of Henry VI. As a result, though, Tudor was stripped of his title, which was bestowed upon the Lancastrian William Herbert, then the guardian of Tudor's nephew, Henry.

In retaliation, Edward arrested several Lancastrian lords but wider hostility to Edward's reign was growing and Warwick's dissatisfaction chimed with the national mood. Londoners were angered by the large enforced loans the king had not repaid and many felt he had failed to halt the general lawlessness which he had criticised back in 1461. The same year, rumours reached Edward of Warwick's increasing sympathy towards the Lancastrian cause: London chronicler Robert Fabyan recorded that 'many murmurous tales ran in the city atween the Earl of Warwick and the queen's blood'. The king summoned his old friend to court to refute the allegations but Warwick chose not to appear, replying instead in writing, dismissing the accusations. He was not seeking to join the Lancastrians, he wrote; his loyalties still lay with the House of York. In secret, though, he was already considering siding with another powerful figure, also dissatisfied by the rapid rise of the Wydevilles; in this, he had not deceived Edward. Still declaring his Yorkist leanings, he transferred his sympathy between brothers, turning now to the impulsive George, Duke of Clarence, for support as the king continued to promote his in-laws. It seemed a further deliberate insult to the earl when, in 1469, Anthony, Earl Rivers, was promoted to the significant post of Lieutenant of Calais and Captain of the King's Armada, giving him the control of the seas which Warwick had once enjoyed.

A further cause for Warwick's dissatisfaction related to his elder daughter. At eighteen, Isabel was already past the usual age of first marriages among the nobility and as the first child of the leading magnate of the country, she could expect a prestigious match. Yet there were precious few young men of equal or higher rank to provide her with a suitable partner. Warwick had already conceived of a match between her and the nineteen-year-old George, Duke of Clarence, at least as early as 1467; although this may date back to the loss of Henry, Duke of Buckingham, as a potential spouse. He had been matched at the age of nine, against his wishes, with Katherine Wydeville, one of the queen's sisters. Clarence was next in line to the throne after Edward and the young man's increasing annoyance with the dominance of the Wydevilles made him an ideal co-conspirator and son-in-law to the earl. 'Seemly of person and well visage', Clarence was an attractive, if slightly visceral figure, who saw in Warwick an outlet for many of the frustrations he was feeling at being passed over. When the match was proposed, Edward had firmly rejected it, perhaps due to the closeness of their family relations, but more likely to prevent the union of two malcontents whose power would be increased though the connection. Queen Elizabeth had yet to bear a son and the prospect of Clarence fathering a male heir created a significant alternative figurehead behind which rebels could gather and attempt to depose the king. His refusal only inflamed Warwick further, who then sent Edward's own representative to negotiate with the Pope, resulting in the necessary dispensation, which was dated to 14 March 1469. Aware that the king may still try to prevent the ceremony from taking place, the earl secured a further licence from Cardinal Bourchier, allowing the marriage to take place in Calais.

For Isabel and Anne, politics aside, this was a momentous personal occasion. The education of girls of all ranks of medieval society was geared towards their eventual roles as wives and mothers. The attainment of a suitable husband could be a matter of negotiation between families for years and often resulted in the unions of young girls with older or unappealing men. To be united with a young, influential and attractive man was a significant triumph, even for a girl of such high rank as Isabel Neville. On a political level, it was the best match she could make, becoming the wife of the heir to the throne. Illness, accident or death on the battlefield could easily remove Edward at any time, allowing the young couple, or any son Isabel bore, to inherit. There is no doubt that Isabel was aware that this was a factor in the match: it would have been perfectly natural for the eighteen-year-old to have imagined herself as queen, picturing her Coronation and the court she would create at Westminster.

The couple were already known to each other and close in age; there may well have been a degree of attraction, if not affection, on her side. This would have been an added bonus in an era when companionate unions were not the norm for those of the Neville girls' class. In the sequestered world amid which the daughters of the aristocracy were raised, a good marriage offered the life they had anticipated for years, with the opportunity to run their own household, the fulfilment of physical relations, the birth of children and increased social respect. Isabel's match satisfied all the criteria she could have hoped for, even if it was controversial and needed to be conducted out of the reach of her future brother-in-law. There were precedents for royal forgiveness in such cases though, with the queen's own parents marrying against the wishes of Henry VI and later being welcomed back into court circles. While she probably knew that they were defying Edward, it is unclear to what extent Isabel was aware of the insubordination underpinning her father's and husband's co-operation, which would result in treason. As she, her mother and sister began the preparations for the match, sewing and preparing her linen and dresses, the occasion was more the significant step in a young woman's life cycle than an act of political defiance. That spring they sailed for Calais from Sandwich, excited at the prospect of the celebrations and the new life it offered.

The marriage took place on Tuesday 12 July 1469. It may have been celebrated at the Calais church of Our Lady, the Église Notre-Dame, which still stands in the town today. A rare survivor, with its twelfth-century foundations, the majority of the remaining building was developed during the fourteenth century. Alternatively, they may have become man and wife in the chapel dedicated to the Virgin Mary, within the walls of Calais Castle itself. Wherever they spoke their vows, the union was marked by conspicuous festivities and pageantry. Warwick wanted to contrast the occasion with the clandestine nature of the king's own nuptials, staging the advent of an alternative Yorkist royal family to replace Edward, whose legitimacy he had questioned. Thus, he planned several days of splendour suitable for a royal wedding, to which he invited those leading dignitaries who dared attend, including five knights of the garter. The ceremony was conducted by George Neville, Archbishop of York and Cecily, Clarence's mother, may have been present. She was recorded as being with them in Canterbury, then in Sandwich, before the party departed, although this may represent an attempt to dissuade them from going ahead with the union against the king's wishes, rather than her personal endorsement.

Anne played a leading role in both the preparations and ceremony of the day. The girls would have been dressed in their finest; as new members of the royal family of York, they needed their attire to proclaim their enhanced statuses. While wedding dresses were not yet the standard white, the occasion provided them with the opportunity to deck themselves in cloth of gold, jewels and perhaps even the white rose emblem that Clarence's wife would be entitled to wear. Warwick was known for his generosity in his London town house; no doubt the feasting would have rivalled that the girls had experienced at their uncle's enthronement in 1465. However, Isabel may have been disappointed by what followed. There was to be no extended honeymoon; Chronicler Waurin suggests there were only two days of festivities and few guests. Five days later, Warwick and Clarence returned to England, leaving the new bride behind. Perhaps Isabel regretted that the first few days of her married life were cut short or that her new husband hurried away so soon. Perhaps she realised the match had been designed primarily to strengthen the ties between her family and his on the eve of rebellion. On the other hand, though, she may have understood the political expediency of the moment and, as did many wives of the medieval nobility, recognised her dynastic role within the context of the conflicts of the day. After all, like her sister, she was Warwick's daughter. No surviving evidence suggests that she was in any way a victim or a pawn. Now she was a wife, the Duchess of Clarence, married to the heir to the throne. Her situation also elevated her sister's. With her elder sister married, Anne's own future came into sharper focus: who would she marry and what path would she take?

6

Queens in Waiting
1469–1470

And look to thy daughters that none of them be lorn
from the very time that they are of thee born
busy thyself and gather fast for their marriage
and give them to spousing as soon as they be of age[1]

The next few months were to prove turbulent ones for Anne and Isabel. Their father's determination to seize control of the English throne would redefine his daughters' status, as much by his relentless audacity as by his apparent moments of indecision. Warwick was a shrewd opportunist, but through the rapid changes of the coming months, he may not have fully realised the consequences of restoring Henry VI to the throne. 'Kingmaking' was a feat he had already accomplished back in 1461, and now, for personal reasons, he set about reversing that process. Of course, his reasons for originally removing Henry had not changed. Then, he had been able to exercise considerable influence over the young Earl of March. Now, the rise of the Wydevilles placed him at a remove from the crown and he saw that, by contrast, the weak Lancastrian would be easier to manipulate. The rebels knew they were taking a huge gamble in attempting to topple a strong king, as Edward IV had none of the unstable, pacifist tendencies of his Lancastrian predecessor. By 1469, though, the appeal of the handsome, 6-foot-4 son of York had been clouded by lawlessness, nepotism and debt. When an independent pocket of discontent broke out in the North, his enemies seized the opportunity to stand against their king.

Warwick sensed the national mood had turned sufficiently to prove a serious threat to Edward's reign. In Richmondshire, his supporters rose simultaneously with rebels rallying under the leadership of a mysterious Robin of Redesdale or Robin Mend-all. Although his identity is still disputed, the folkloric Robin was probably one Sir John Conyers, or his brother William, to whom Warwick was related by marriage and who was acting at his prompting. Edward travelled north to disband their armies, leaving the capital vulnerable, just as the Kingmaker had hoped. This left the way clear for Warwick and his troops to land on the Kent coast, a region notoriously prone to dissent, where the earl had already incited sailors using the Sandwich–Calais route. Heading west, they received a warm welcome at Canterbury and gathered more troops for the entry to London. The capital had initially enjoyed a good relationship with Edward, welcoming him in relief in 1461, and although the king's pro-Burgundian stance had brought trading benefits, the city merchants had been angered by his habit of extracting money from them by enforced loans. Warwick's and Clarence's manifesto placed the Wydevilles at the heart of national dissatisfaction and called for their removal, a preventative measure to protect them from the charge of treason, although their secret intention was to replace Edward with Clarence. Aware of their approach, the king awaited them at Nottingham, while William Herbert, Earl of Pembroke, and Humphrey Stafford, Earl of Devon, raised their own armies and headed to join Edward's forces, hoping that a combined royalist army would defeat the traitors.

However, the rebels missed the king, clashing instead with the royal reinforcements which were coming up from the South. In a brief skirmish, Warwick's cousin, Henry Neville, was killed and the armies regrouped to meet again to force a decisive victory the following day. Having taken the initial advantage, Pembroke and Devon then disagreed and separated, fatally dividing their troops and leaving Pembroke without the essential archers that often played such a significant part in defending foot soldiers during battle. The following day, 26 July 1469, the rebels won a decisive victory at the shambolic Battle of Edgecote, before the king could arrive at the scene. Pembroke's decision to take the initiative and advance without cover proved disastrous and, although he put up a brave defence, Devon's forces did not arrive until after midday. Seeing a part of Warwick's troops arrive, the royal army panicked and many fled the scene. Around 4,000 Yorkists were killed and Warwick was now in an unprecedented position of power. Shortly afterwards, Edward himself was taken prisoner, along with his queen's unpopular father and brother, Richard Wydeville, and his son, John.

Finally Warwick had his enemies in his hands. Now, however, he had to decide what to do with them. He had no compunction in sentencing the Wydevilles to death, executing them in Coventry and placing their heads on spikes on the city walls. Edward, however, was another matter and he temporarily imprisoned his former friend in Warwick Castle while deciding what to do. Commines asserted that Warwick thought Edward 'a little simple' and had behaved 'like a father' towards him, surrounding him now with new servants 'to make him forget' the old ones. Rumours flew around Europe predicting Edward's fate, many of which were wildly exaggerated. Sforza di Bettini of Florence, the Milanese Ambassador in France, wrote to the Duke of Milan that, following a huge battle, Edward himself was dead and 'everything remains in the hands of the said Earl of Warwick, the conqueror'. He had apparently been told this news 'very joyfully' by King Louis XI himself, which he thought would give the duke 'exceptional pleasure', as the English 'tart would be divided' between the 'masters of the country', Warwick and Clarence.[2] Louis and Bettini were wrong about the king's fate but right about the position of power Warwick had assumed. The current state of affairs was neatly summarised in a comment made by Governor of Abbeville to Louis that the English 'have two rulers, M de Warwick and another, whose name I have forgotten'.

The outcome of Edgecote proved significant for another of the children born in the 1450s. The Earl of Pembroke, William Herbert, known as 'Black William', had been a long-term ally of Warwick and Richard, Duke of York, but now found himself on the opposing side. He had been the guardian of the young Henry Tudor for the past eight years, raising him in his Marches home at Raglan Castle and intending to marry him to his daughter Maude. Herbert's wife, Anne Devereux, had been particularly kind to the young boy, to the extent that Henry would send for her to come to London when he took the throne in 1485. After Henry's mother, Margaret Beaufort, married Henry Stafford in 1462, Anne was the closest thing he had had to a constant maternal presence. Pembroke was executed after Edgecote and the family unit was broken up. Anne then took the twelve-year-old Henry, and her own children, to her family home, the Devereux manor in Bodenham, Herefordshire. Thus, the young Henry Tudor spent the summer of 1469 in the countryside of the Welsh borders, watching to see how the national picture unfolded. Henry was certainly old enough to understand his situation but perhaps still young enough to make the most of his bucolic surroundings. The manor was recorded in the Domesday Book of 1086 as being in possession of a large number of ploughs and, perhaps, on its bend of the River Lugg, a particularly large and fertile location. The river was navigable and particularly good for fishing, joining the Wye at Hereford. Perhaps he attended the Assumption Day fair, held at the manor every 15 August after a grant was issued to the Devereux family by Richard II in 1378. Yet it was a tense time. Henry could only wait and see what would follow: as the half-nephew of his namesake, Henry VI, his future was dependent on the next move of the Kingmaker.

The battle also proved significant for Anne Neville. Her father's success may have prompted Warwick to summon his countess and daughters to return to England. Only two weeks had elapsed since Isabel's wedding but the political scenery in England looked set to favour a change in the regime, either with the restoration of Henry VI or the accession of Clarence: as his new wife, Isabel had taken a step closer to the throne. Assuming the match had been consummated in France, she already conceived the child she would deliver the following April; if not, she and Clarence must have been reunited pretty promptly, perhaps as her father and husband debated their futures and that of their royal prisoner. Edward was in their power. For a moment, they could shape the future of English history. Yet Warwick failed to push his advantage. Rarely one to hesitate, a number of issues now stayed his hand. He may have reconsidered his former friendship with Edward, or the consequences of treason, or Clarence's mutability under the influences of his mother and younger brother, Richard. He may have been reluctant take the decisive step of ordering the imprisoned king's death. Something caused the earl to pause and release his prisoner, or at least to turn a blind eye when he escaped on a hunting trip that October. The momentum was lost and Warwick had failed to capitalise on his position. Clarence was forgiven by his brother after a show of contrition orchestrated by the Yorkist women. Now the earl was left embarrassed, out in the cold, as Edward headed back into his capital for a temporary family reconciliation.

Apparently 'pardoned', Warwick retreated from court to one of his northern properties, either Middleham or Warwick Castle itself, with the countess and Anne. The pregnant eighteen-year-old Isabel and Clarence set up home together, with ordinances dating from December that year, outlining provisions for their household at the monastery in Waltham, Essex. It is unclear whether they inhabited part of a religious house or another property within the complex, which stood on the edge of Epping Forest. They are likely to have divided their time between several rural properties and their town house in central London. This may have been the old Warwick property, the Erber, just to the north-east of St Paul's and below Newgate, which went with the title Clarence had inherited, or else Coldharbour House, which they were known to use later. Isabel and Clarence may have been present when Edward celebrated Christmas with his family at Westminster but Warwick stayed away.

The reconciliation came slowly. In January, Edward's eldest daughter, the three-year-old Princess Elizabeth of York, was engaged to George Neville, the young son of the Earl of Northumberland, Warwick's brother, as a reward for his continuing support for the Yorkists. Temporary peace settled over the country while each side waited to see what the other would do next; Warwick was fuming at his son-in-law's desertion and the failure of their plans, while Edward watched his brother cautiously, wanting to believe in his declarations of loyalty. As the daughter of a traitor, even a forgiven one, Anne's position was again uncertain, but soon a powerful new match would bring her closer to the throne than her sister had come. Warwick may have failed to capitalise on his alliance with the Lancastrian rebels but, in the year to come, he set his sights higher, on another royal family.

With Henry VI in captivity since July 1465, Queen Margaret and her son were still in exile in France. She had originally fled to the court of her father René, living 'in great poverty' as her loyal Chief Justice, Sir John Fortescue, described, 'but yet the queen sustaineth us in meat and drink, so as we beeth not in extreme necessity'. Through the 1450s, Margaret had seen the Duke of York and Warwick as her bitter enemies. They, in turn, had fought against her warlike influence on the docile Henry VI and the undue power wielded by her favourites, Suffolk and Somerset. Gradually, though, the earl was coming to the realisation that Clarence was too unreliable a figure to prove a trustworthy replacement for Edward and that a union with his former enemies and the restoration of the Lancastrian line may represent his best chance. After all, Margaret had a son and the earl still had another daughter. Her poverty and their combined need might make them necessary bedfellows. Through the disturbances of 1470, it is likely that he considered France and Margaret as his safety-net in the eventuality of defeat, which was to prove fortuitous for him and decisive for his daughter Anne. Convincing Margaret of the value of this alliance would not be easy, though.

In the New Year, Warwick used his previous method of inciting rebellion in the North in order to draw the king out of London. Once again, Edward reacted promptly to the threat and Warwick was able to reconnect with his son-in-law. Although Clarence had been forgiven, the political landscape had changed little in the last twelve months and the unpopular Wydevilles were as dominant as ever. Chafing under his dislike of them, Clarence listened to the earl's persuasion and defected to his side. Hearing rumours of their intentions, Edward summoned them both to refute the allegations but neither attended. Finally convinced of their duplicity, Edward moved swiftly against them, summoning troops to deal with the combined threat once and for all. The sides clashed at the Battle of Empingham, on 12 March 1470, in an encounter which also came to be known as Losecoat Field. As the rebel armies fled, they shed their coats of Warwick and Clarence's liveries, leaving no doubt about who lay behind the uprising. This time the victorious Edward denied their request for a pardon and their open treachery left little option but flight.

The obvious haven was Calais. As they had on his appointment as Constable, Anne and the countess would accompany the earl. Warwick probably went via Middleham to collect them on his way south, while Isabel was with Clarence in Exeter. Heavily pregnant, she must have already been making plans for her imminent lying-in, even though the future looked uncertain. Now a frantic dash followed to pack and escape, with Edward's troops in hot pursuit. Warwick attempted to reach his newest ship, the *Trinity*, which was expected to arrive shortly at Southampton and could carry them across the Channel. The ship never managed to dock, though, being repelled by Earl Rivers. An alternative ship and port were needed. The family then travelled down to Dartmouth, from whence they embarked on 7 April in a ship offered to them by a supporter. As they pulled away from land and watched the coast recede, Warwick and his family must have breathed a sigh of relief. Perhaps Isabel, approaching her due date, went below deck to rest from the journey. Anne may have gone with her for company or else stood on deck, watching England disappear and wondering when, or if, she would ever return. The women would have anticipated Isabel giving birth to her child in her old childhood home at Calais, which they sighted on 16 April. However, Edward's orders had travelled faster than the earl. Having crossed the Channel safely, in sight of the harbour and castle, Warwick's ship was unexpectedly denied entry to Calais by his deputy, Lord Wenlock, acting under express royal orders which had arrived only shortly before the rebels.

It was at this point that Isabel went into labour. Nine months after her marriage, she may well have reached the natural point of delivery, or else her labour was brought on prematurely through stress and the rigours of the journey. As the ship plunged and rolled, her screams reached the sailors awaiting their orders. Childbirth during the late fifteenth century could be perilous at the best of times on dry land, with the benefit of herbal remedies and the wisdom of local midwives.

The countess was experienced in the delivery room, according to John Rous, but there was little else to offer the expectant mother in terms of relief or support. Warwick pleaded for permission to land and, although sympathetic enough to send the party two flagons of wine and suggest they land further round the coast, Wenlock dared not openly disobey the king. Not even the family's own domestic servants, still resident at the castle, could help them. Sources disagree about the gender of the child Isabel bore on board ship but there is no doubt about its fate: the mother survived but the baby was lost. It was either taken ashore at Calais or buried at sea. For the family this was a personal tragedy borne out of political conflict. Isabel may well have delivered a stillborn or weak child had she followed the usual protocol for delivery in the comfort of her own home, yet the circumstances of the death of her first child must have been a particularly bitter blow for herself, her mother and Anne. No doubt they recognised the necessity for their exile but it must have flown in the face of long-established oral traditions of female wisdom regarding childbirth, which provided a month of retirement and inactivity for the expectant mother. Nothing suggests that they resented Warwick or Clarence; as products of their class and time, a belief in the divine order and the existence of fate would have encouraged a pragmatic response. The exhausted and bereaved party finally landed safely in Normandy on 1 May.

Edward IV reacted swiftly. The Milan archives contain information from an 'English Knight, on his way to Jerusalem' that the king had 'publicly outlawed' Warwick and Clarence. According to this traveller, Edward sent his retainers to seize the property and lands of the traitors but 'the people rose and would not receive them'; an interesting indicator of the loyalty felt towards the Neville family, if it is true. It was also rumoured that one of Henry's half-brothers, which at this date would have been Jasper Tudor, was preparing lodgings in Champagne for the use of Edward, Prince of Wales.[3] Tudor was also uncle to Margaret Beaufort's son, Henry, now aged thirteen, who was now the strongest Lancastrian claimant left in England. His mother had attempted to regain custody of him, through letters and visits, but Edward had blocked her application. After Warwick's execution of his guardian, Henry Tudor had little cause to love either side in the conflict now and he probably remained in Herefordshire for the time being.

Now in exile, Warwick sought assistance from his old ally. Louis XI of France was known as the 'universal spider' for his many dealings, including any way of undermining any regime which favoured his enemies in Burgundy. Commines relates how he had ordered the Bastard of Bourbon, Admiral of France, to protect the fugitive's fleet against attacks from the Low Countries, whose navy was much feared. He received Warwick and Clarence in 'honourable and distinguished manner' at Dengen, near Torsi, riding three or four leagues to meet them. He was accompanied by all his principal lords, who approached the fugitives honourably on foot and embraced them 'in the most friendly way', according to Bettini. Louis then took them to be greeted by his queen, Charlotte of Savoy, before proceeding to his chambers in the castle, where they remained for two hours 'most privately and great familiarity', engaged in 'long discussions'. Louis entertained his guests with feasts, 'tournaments and dancing and everything else that distinguishes'. A few weeks later, Bettini wrote that Louis was still 'closeted and in secret councils ... about these affairs of Warwick'. According to the ambassador, Louis was trying 'by every means in his power, to get him to return to England', even offering ships and troops for the fight against Edward. A new Lancastrian leader was now suggested, young though he was. One rumour claimed the earl would cross the Channel with the sixteen-year-old 'Prince of Wales, son of King Henry, and will take the part of that king to see if, in that way, he will enjoy better success than he did in the other'.[4] It was Louis who officially proposed an alliance between the old enemies. While Warwick awaited Margaret at Vandoma, Clarence and the ladies went to Normandy: Anne was mentioned specifically among them as the 'other daughter, the future princess'.[5] By 8 July, they were at Valognes, near Barfleur, a fortified stronghold dating back to Roman times, which had been occupied during the second half of the Hundred Years' War by the English.

As defeated traitors, Warwick and his family were now reduced to the same penurial exile as the ex-queen Margaret and her son Edward of Westminster. Reputedly a bloodthirsty young man who spoke constantly of beheadings,[6] the Prince of Wales had been at his mother's side for the duration of the civil war. Now he was being named as a suitable husband for Anne. If the idea had originated with Warwick, he needed Louis to be his ambassador with his former enemy, so the French king now formally made the suggestion. It is unlikely Anne knew about the proposal at this stage, being removed from the scene at Barfleur, but her compliance was assumed. This does not mean she was forced into a match against her will, or that she was the manipulated pawn of legend. As a scion of the greatest noble family, she had been raised for this and her destiny went hand in hand with her father's.

Languishing at the bottom of the wheel of fortune, neither side had much to lose now, except their pride. To join forces might represent a significant threat to the English throne, no matter how great a U-turn this represented in their previous allegiances. The ex-queen did not embrace the connection easily at first but Warwick was a clever diplomat who recognised that his future depended upon whatever he could make of the current situation. It has been suggested that such a match had previously been mooted, as early as 1468, through Margaret's exiled chancellor, Sir John Fortescue. If this is true, it predates the earl's breach with Edward IV and was unlikely to have come to fruition. It also implies Margaret's approval, possibly her instigation. By 1470, though, matters had changed. Louis arranged the reconciliation and offered to fund an invasion, inviting both parties to visit him separately, where Warwick made the proposal to Margaret, in exchange for her pardon. According to *The Maner and Guyding of the Earl of Warwick*, the ex-queen was furious and 'right difficult' at the prospect of an alliance with her bitter enemies, until Louis persuaded her it was the best chance she had of restoring her husband's throne and securing a future for her son. Margaret also claimed she was anticipating a match between the prince and Edward IV's four-year-old daughter, Elizabeth of York. It was to be expected that she would not capitulate at once and, after famously keeping Warwick on bended knee for a full quarter of an hour, she allowed him to present a mutually beneficial arrangement, once he had retracted all his previous 'slanders'. As Vergil wrote, the discussions were lengthy: 'Many moe condytions wer entreatyd upon emongst them, which both the reason and weyght of the cause requyryd.' So much history had passed between the two, and each held the other personally responsible for various losses they had suffered, that they would never be easy bedfellows. Their children, though, could be.

Initially, Margaret could see 'neither honour nor profit in it' but was persuaded into the union on the advice of her father René, King of Naples.[7] It was, in fact, an extremely profitable match for Anne, but for Edward, as potential Prince of Wales with the possibility of a future foreign alliance with a princess of royal blood, it was a mark of his mother's fall from grace and desire to recapture her position. The speech Shakespeare gives Margaret in *Henry VI, Part 3*, albeit at an earlier stage of her history, summarizes her necessity of making the most of her misfortune.

> I was, I must confess,
> Great Albion's queen in former golden days:

> But now mischance hath trod my title down,
> And with dishonour laid me on the ground;
> Where I must take like seat unto my fortune,
> And to my humble seat conform myself.

Fortune and her 'humble seat' were responsible for the alliance the ex-queen now made with Warwick. Chronicler John Warkworth, Master of Peterhouse College, Cambridge, claims that an omen was responsible for what happened next, which he describes in almost Biblical terms:

> Whenne the seide Duke of Clarence and the Erle of Warwyke were in Fraunce here apperede a blasynge sterre in the weste, and the flame therof lyke a spere hede, the whiche dyverse of the Kynges howse saw it, whereof thei were fulle sore adrede. And thanne in Fraunce whenne the seide lordes where, thei toke there counselle qwhat was beste for to do; and thei coude fynde no remedy but to sende to Quene Margaret, and to make a maryage betwex Prynce Edwarde, Kynge Herry sonne, and an other of the seid Erle of Warwykys doughters.

The inclusion of this blazing star appears to lend a divine purpose to the match, to which the superstitious and ambitious Warwick and Clarence could find 'no remedy', yet whether they even saw this phenomenon, let alone allowed it to influence their decision-making, is unknown. Perhaps it was a physical manifestation of that 'fortune' alluded to by Shakespeare, or perhaps simply poetic licence.

Presumably this 'other' daughter, the fourteen-year-old Anne, now knew about their discussions, although she was excluded from them. Having witnessed her sister's recent experiences, she understood the role to which she was born and that any personal feelings must be set aside. Additionally, any affection that may have existed between her and Richard, Duke of Gloucester, was now complicated by his loyalty to his brother, making him theoretically her enemy. Two weeks later, on 25 July 1470, Edward of Westminster and Anne Neville were formally betrothed in the cathedral at Angers, making their oaths upon a 'piece of the true cross'. The subsequent marriage and consummation were to be conditional upon the earl proving himself in battle against Edward, so a few days after the match, he set sail again for England with 2,000 troops financed by Louis XI.

On 31 July, Margaret, Edward and fiancée left for Amboise, the favourite residence of the French royal family, situated on a spur overlooking the River Loire. Among its magnificent surroundings,

Anne was now in the company of those strangers she had long been accustomed to consider her foes; her own mother was also present, and possibly Isabel, whose whereabouts at this time are unclear. She knew little of her betrothed but could not have escaped hearing much of the queen and her warlike nature. Now this formidable woman was her guardian, soon to be her mother-in-law, as well as her companion over the coming months. At the age of forty, the ex-queen had been a driving force through the recent decades of conflict and was considered to be aggressive and volatile. Her deep-seated hatred of the Duke of York had transferred to his offspring and, in her company, Anne would find no sympathy for her childhood friend, Richard. There is nothing to suggest, though, that Margaret felt any hostility towards her son's young wife. It is quite likely that the necessity of civil conflict had bred a sense of expediency in the resourceful queen, who now welcomed the young girl as the future mother of her grandchildren, whom she hoped would in turn inherit the English throne. Margaret had herself been a bride at only fifteen and understood much of what Anne must have been feeling, as well as being aware of the benefits the union brought to the Lancastrian cause. From this point forward, Anne's welfare would be her mother-in-law's concern. Rumours that Margaret wished Anne ill, or even that she attempted to have her poisoned, are unsubstantiated and would have achieved nothing. She had nothing to gain by alienating the young woman and only delayed the actual marriage ceremony until the necessary paperwork had arrived and Warwick had proved his loyalty in England by restoring Henry VI.

Little is known about Edward of Westminster, Prince of Wales. Born amid his father's main bout of instability, he had not been recognised by Henry VI until he was almost a year old. Three years Anne's elder, much of his life had been spent on the road, in flight from the scenes of battle, a witness to the barbarities and harsh justice of medieval warfare. As a small child, he had been invested as Prince of Wales, then disinherited in favour of the Duke of York, suffering the change in his fortunes before he was old enough to understand them. In October 1458, around the time of his fifth birthday, Italian Rafaello de Negra described the prince in a letter to the Duchess of Milan, as 'a most handsome boy' who, in common with the rest of the court, 'always go on their knees' when addressing the queen.[8] After the accession of Edward IV forced them into exile, Margaret had used him as a figurehead to rally support, handing out little silver badges of his personal device, the swan, which she had taken from his grandfather Edward III, to their supporters and using his presence to soften the hearts of outlaws and thieves.[9] The most commonly quoted anecdote of Edward's early life is that of a child issuing the death sentence on his enemies following the Second Battle of St Albans in 1461. It represents little more than a seven-year-old trying to please his mother and punish those who had failed to protect his father and cannot be taken as symptomatic. He was a more complex individual than this suggests but he had learned the realities of his situation early. Experiences of conflict and fluctuating fortunes had shaped him to the degree that the Milanese Ambassador named him the 'God of battle' but the chances are that, as a fifteenth-century prince, he was also pious, courageous and chivalrous. The rumours of his illegitimacy in the 1450s, such as those recorded in letters by Coppini, which had ascribed his paternity to the unpopular Duke of Somerset, remain only rumours.

What Anne made of her betrothed on a personal level is not recorded. She and Isabel were young women of their time and, while marriage itself raised their status significantly, they were probably more pragmatic about it than some historians and romantic novelists have given them credit for. The introduction to the Rous Roll claims it was Anne's 'unhappy destiny to be made the pivot on which turned more than one state intrigue', yet there is no evidence that Anne was unhappy, or anything but complicit in these 'intrigues'. Rather than being the exploited pawns of an ambitious, ruthless father, the girls were more likely to have been willing participants in his schemes. The earl's motives overlapped their own, imbued as they were with the sense of family and loyalty, which Richard of Gloucester was to demonstrate in his personal motto, *'loyaulte me lie'* or loyalty binds me. Teenage noblewomen did repudiate the matches their parents attempted to arrange for them and find their own husbands, the most famous contemporary example being Margaret Paston in 1469. The future Henry VIII also rejected his father's arrangement for him to wed Catherine of Aragon in 1505, although he did actually marry her four years later. The significant age was fourteen. At that point, a young person was considered to be capable of knowing their own mind and rejecting an undesired spouse. Anne had reached that age and chose to marry Edward. Whether the young pair maintained a formal distance or attempted to forge a more companionate connection during these years of waiting is unknown. Anne was not blessed with hindsight but she did have an imagination: now a future unfolded before her in which she and Edward were partners for life, as King and Queen of England. It must have been an attractive prospect.

Marriages were often conducted among the nobility when the spouses were in their teens and pregnancy could follow soon after consummation, as in Isabel's case. Both Edward and Anne were past the age of consent and the act of betrothal itself, rather than the marriage vows, frequently marked a transition to physical intimacy, even full sexual relations. It was customary for one party to reside in the household of another from an early age and now, at sixteen and fourteen, the young couple were almost man and wife. However, Margaret had made it clear that the finality of their match was dependent upon events in England; closely watching Warwick's next move, it is unlikely she would have allowed her son to sleep with Anne yet and it is doubtful that the teenagers would have had the will or opportunity to initiate relations behind her back. It seems unlikely, therefore, that this final step was taken during 1470. The period of waiting allowed Anne to spend time with the young man who was to become her husband and possibly her king. Edward certainly had qualities which suggested he could be a successful ruler: some accounts paint him as driven and ruthless: of course, he was still only in his teens, but his namesake, Edward IV, had led victorious armies into battle at a similar age. The pair, along with their mothers, passed the summer months in the beautiful castle at Amboise, with its gardens overlooking the Loire, waiting to hear what the future might bring. The news from England seemed promising.

In fact, the kingdom had fallen all too easily. Warwick's brother-in-law, Lord Fitzhugh, had reignited rebellion in Yorkshire, drawing Edward north and allowing the rebels to march unimpeded into London. On arriving, according to Vergil, Warwick had issued a proclamation calling all men to arm themselves against Edward IV who had, 'contrary to right and law usurpyd the kingdom', upon which thousands of armed men flocked to his side and marched to the capital, where, the Milanese Ambassador reported, he was actually received 'in most friendly fashion'. Warwick proceeded to the Tower and released the bemused Henry VI, whom he then paraded through the streets in a 'shabby blue gown', 'crowned and proclaimed through all the town of London with the greatest festivities and pomp as the true king and lord of England'. Yet he was ruler in name only and Warwick, the 'Kingmaker', had not finished yet. Word soon reached Edward of plans for his own arrest, leaving him in little doubt that his old ally would show him no mercy. With the Lancastrian regime restored and the capital occupied, he decided the only option was flight and headed for the East Coast, along with Richard of Gloucester, only reaching the safety of the Netherlands after terrible weather conditions and offering the coat off his back in payment to the captain of the merchant ship that agreed to carry him. Commines relates that, along with 700–800 followers, the brothers escaped 'without a penny between them' in three small boats. As Bettini reported in October, Warwick had 'practically the whole island in his power' and Edward IV was a fugitive in exile.[10]

It is at this point that the Burgundian chronicler, Commines, was himself sent on a diplomatic mission to France and visited Calais, giving a portrait of the town Anne knew so well at the point of a change in allegiance. In the spring of 1470, it was in turmoil due to the unsubstantiated and conflicting reports of what had just happened across the Channel: Lord Wenlock had been rewarded handsomely by Edward for repelling his former master but his sympathies had always lain with Warwick, later switching sides with him to the Lancastrian cause. Wearing the Duke of Burgundy's signet ring for protection, Commines received Wenlock's grant of safe conduct, proceeding without event to the castle, which had been Anne's home. Everyone in the town was wearing Warwick's livery of red jackets embroidered with ragged staffs and on the door of the ambassador's lodgings were pinned 'more than a hundred' white crosses and rhymes asserting the unity between King Louis XI and Warwick. Invited to dinner with Lord Wenlock, Commines found him wearing the earl's emblem as a badge on his hat. His host confided that when the messenger had brought news of their master's latest success, the entire place had switched liveries, from York back to Warwick, 'so hasty and sudden was the change'. Commines was then shocked to find how those previously supportive of Edward 'were those who threatened him most violently'. This episode reveals just how 'unstable' the situation was and how swiftly circumstances and loyalties could change. The 'treachery' of which many key figures had been accused during the war, including Margaret, Clarence, Warwick, Stafford, Wenlock, Montagu and Northumberland, was, in fact, little more than necessity. Allegiances determined the survival of an individual and their family; backing the right side was important. At that moment, the Kingmaker was the man to back.

For Margaret, Prince Edward and Anne, it seemed that Warwick had fulfilled all his promises and they could return to England and claim their rightful positions. Yet they did not leave at once. Bettini recorded that 'the Queen of England and the Countess of Warwick, with their children, are still here, as although his Majesty took leave of them some days ago for them to return to England, yet he has changed his mind, and it is thought that he will detain them until a reply has come from his ambassadors who have gone to England, who left about twelve days ago. It is thought that they will leave immediately the reply arrives.'[11] It was November when Margaret and her party arrived in Paris with a guard of honour, where she was received as a queen, with tapestries hung out, flags and banners and lodged in splendour at the palace.[12] Bettini recorded their departure: 'the queen of England and the Countess of Warwick, with the prince and princess their children, have left and returned to England, to the unspeakable satisfaction and content of his said Majesty [Louis]'.[13] Yet the ambassador's comments were premature as, the following March, he wrote that Margaret 'has delayed crossing up to the present, but now she is going over in God's name, and it is reckoned that at this moment she has either crossed, or is on the sea in the act of doing so. She would have gone earlier still if the escort to take her had come sooner, for she took leave of the king at Amboise more than three months ago.' The reasons for the delay are unclear. Warwick's success had already peaked by the time the royals-in-waiting left France and, as a result, they missed their chance. In their absence, Clarence was made heir to the Lancastrian line in the event of Prince Edward dying childless and Henry VI was very clearly only a puppet, allowed to make few decisions. To all intents and purposes, the country was being ruled by Warwick, which was not the outcome either side had desired. The presence of Margaret and her son would have added a legitimacy and authority to the new regime in which people could believe. More Lancastrians would then have rallied to their cause, instead of being deterred by the power of Warwick, against whom many had recently fought. It was to prove a fatal delay.

One reason that Margaret may have remained in France was her uncertainty over her son's marriage. Edward and Anne shared a common ancestor in John of Gaunt, which required a formal dispensation before the union was allowed to proceed. Louis made it his business to facilitate the paperwork, dispatching his own man to Lyons in July and even urging the couple to go ahead and wed without permission. He considered Anne to be the wife of the prince, receiving her as such at his court from August onwards, after the Pope had issued the first of three dispensations. However, the final one did not arrive until 28 November, after which preparations began in earnest. The ceremony took place at Amboise on 13 December, attended by Margaret and the Countess of Warwick, a small-scale affair in comparison to Isabel's in 1469. By this time, Anne's husband was no longer a stranger. If the match had not been consummated until then, it would have been that night or soon after, just as her sister's had been. Only this act would make the marriage legitimate and without it, Anne could be vulnerable to being discarded, should her father's cause not go her way. Conversely, it also removed her own escape clause, if Warwick and the Lancastrians should ever part company again.

Commines was not alone in thinking 'this was a strange marriage', given that Warwick had 'defeated and ruined' the Prince's father. The Croyland Chronicler claimed that the match was made so that Warwick and Margaret's 'reconcilement and good faith towards each other might appear in the eyes of future ages the more undoubted'. Yet Warwick had never lacked ambition and was clearly driven by dynastic desire for the throne, having placed both daughters in marriages with two prospective heirs to the throne. By December 1470, when the wedding of Anne and Edward was finally conducted, the situation had changed again. The birth of a son to Edward IV displaced Clarence in the line of succession and Warwick was finding it increasingly hard to trust his son-in-law. Therefore, the Lancastrian marriage gave him the best option of having a grandchild to sit on the English throne. Isabel had lost her first child and would not conceive again in her father's lifetime. If Anne could fall pregnant now, her baby would pose a powerful threat to the Yorkist heir, now that regime appeared to have fallen. The teenage couple passed their wedding night at Amboise and, forty-eight hours later, had departed, heading north.

The readeption of Henry VI was also good news for the thirteen-year-old Henry Tudor and his mother Margaret Beaufort, now Stafford. After the death of Lord Herbert and the family's flight to Herefordshire, Margaret had tried unsuccessfully to regain custody of her son, whom she wished to have live with her at Woking, but the rapidly unfolding events soon brought them together again. With Edward in exile, the way was clear for a reunion and, when Jasper Tudor returned to England, he took his nephew to London. The Tudors received significant financial rewards from Henry and Warwick but the boy was unable to inherit the title of Earl of Richmond, which had been given to Clarence. However, mother and son were reunited at the new Lancastrian court for about six weeks in October and early November, where they dined frequently with the king. After Henry VI's own Prince of Wales and his half-brother Jasper, Henry Tudor was next in line to the throne and was treated as such. The magnificent feasts at Westminster that autumn must have seemed to usher in a new era of optimism for Margaret and her son.

7

Lancastrian Princess
1471

In granting your love you shall purchase renown,
Your head shall be crowned with Englands crown
thy garments most gallant of gold shall be wrought
if true love with treasure with the may be bought.[1]

In March 1471, Edward IV landed in Yorkshire. The initial response from his subjects was not warm but he managed to gain access to the City of York by claiming he was only interested in the restoration of his dukedom. Richard of Gloucester had been by his side during his exile and now, Clarence, the prodigal brother, returned to the fold again. Marching south and gathering troops intended for Warwick, he had succumbed to the influence of his mother, uncles and sisters and was reconciled with the king. However, he did then seek to act as an intermediary, urging Edward to pardon his father-in-law. Isabel, who was also in England and perhaps in communication with her father, must have found her loyalties seriously compromised, as were those of many wives and mothers at the time, especially her mother-in-law Cecily. According to the *Historie of the Arrivall of Edward IV in England and the finall recouerye of his Kingdomes from Henry VI*, Clarence knew himself to be held 'in great suspicion, despite, disdeigne and hatered' by those who were 'adherents and full partakers' of the Lancastrian cause. Through the arbitration of family members, the brothers were brought to a 'parfecte accord', whereby Clarence was 'full honourably and trwly acquitted' of his treachery.[2] For Warwick, this desertion must have represented a significant blow. However, Edward extended a gesture of forgiveness as a result of Clarence's influence, presenting him with a kind of Hobson's choice, as he was forced to reject one of his daughters in favour of the other. If

Warwick had accepted and united again with the Yorkists, Clarence and Isabel, it would have left Anne and the countess ostracised and friendless with their enemies in exile. On the other hand, to refuse the king's beneficence would protect Anne, but estrange him from Isabel and lead to the inevitable conflict that must result in the defeat and probable death of either the earl or the king.

Warwick refused Edward's pardon. The *Arrivall* suggests he may have 'dispaired of any ... continuance of good accord betwixt the Kynge and hym, for tyme to come, consyderinge so great attemptes by hym comytted against the Kynge', or else he could not break the vows he had made in Angers Cathedral, on the 'fragment of the true cross', without terrible consequences. He sent Lord Wenlock to accompany the countess, Queen Margaret, Prince Edward and Anne back to England, planning for them to embark from Honfleur on 24 March. Treacherous conditions in the Channel delayed them though, with 'great stormes, wyndes and tempestes'[3] preventing the fleet from sailing until mid-April. While Margaret's party waited in France for the storms to abate, King Edward entered and retook London, welcomed back by the city whose trade had been threatened by Warwick's anti-Burgundian agenda. The city merchants were also keen to receive the loans the Yorkist still owed them and, according to Commines, were persuaded by their wives, who still held the attractive man in great affection. Edward was reunited with his queen and introduced to the young son she had borne in sanctuary the previous November, the future Edward V, elder of the Princes in the Tower. Timing had played a crucial role in the king's return: the popular Warwick was only a day behind him and had expected the city to remain loyal to him.[4]

The Lancastrian party finally arrived at Weymouth, 'aftar longe abydyng passage', while Anne's mother, in a separate ship, landed at Portsmouth. As the shores of England had come into view, each must have been exhilarated at the prospect of returning to a land newly conquered in their name, a land over which they could expect to rule and be received as royalty. No doubt they anticipated a triumphant procession to Westminster, lauded as they rode through the streets of London, before their reunion with Henry VI and instalment in the rich apartments of the Palace of Westminster. The following day was Easter. It dawned mistily and, while they prepared their celebrations, news arrived of a terrible battle being fought at Barnet, a small town north of London. Vergil described the slaughter: 'Many wer slane every wher, whose rowmes fresh men dyd ever of new supply.' Anne's father was among them. According to his account, Warwick was impressive to the last, having 'great confydence and hope of victory' and 'vehemently

encoragyd and hartyly desyryd his soldiers, thowghe very weary, yet
now to abyde this last brunt with valyant corage', until he was 'thrust
thoughe and slane … manfully fighting … having almost the victory
in his hand'. Although some accounts cite that Edward had asked for
Warwick to be taken alive, Commines places the blame for his death
at the king's feet, as part of a wider policy of slaughter because 'he had
conceived a deep hatred against the people of England for the great
favour which he saw the people bore towards the Earl of Warwick'.
While it seems unlikely that the 'great hatred' was directed against his
subjects, Edward may well have understood the necessity of removing
such a popular alternative leader. One or other of them had to die.

For Anne the dream was quickly shattered; amid the thick fog,
confusion had led to chaos. The Great Chronicle of London estimated
that 15,000 had been killed although Hall and Holinshed put the
figure closer to 10,000: either way, the majority of losses had been
sustained on the Lancastrian side. The encounter also marked the
eighteen-year-old Richard of Gloucester's first engagement in battle,
fighting against a man under whose roof he had lived as a youth,
whom he had considered a friend and mentor. Regret must have
mingled with relief when he heard the day had been won. Perhaps
he spared a thought for Anne, her father and the days they spent at
Middleham, which must have seemed very distant then, although they
were in reality only a couple of years past. One romantic story, dating
from a Victorian biography, claims that Warwick encountered the
young Richard on the battlefield and spared his life out of affection for
him.[5] What is more usually recounted is the earl's break from his habit
of remaining on horseback, in order to support his brother Montagu
on foot, rendering him incapable of escape when the fighting turned
against him. On Easter Saturday, 14 April 1471, the Yorkists' smaller
force had emerged victorious and, in spite of Edward's supposed
instructions, Anne heard that Warwick had indeed been slain.

The triumphant Yorkists now returned to London, where the
bodies of Warwick and Montagu were 'layid nakid' on public display
at St Paul's Cathedral, to 'prevent newe murmors, insurrections and
rebellyons among indisposed people',[6] before being handed over to
George Neville, Archbishop of York, and laid in the family vault at
Bisham Priory in Berkshire. The tomb no longer exists, having been
destroyed during the Reformation, but the earl's reputation was not so
easily forgotten. Not even the public display of Warwick's naked torso
could completely dispel the belief that such a legendary figure and
competent military leader could have met his mortal end. Rumours
flew around Europe and even Louis XI himself was the recipient of

incorrect reports of the aftermath of Barnet. Christofforo de Bollate, Milanese Ambassador to France, recorded that 'yesterday evening, his Majesty had a letter from the Queen of England, saying that the Earl of Warwick was not dead, as reported, but he had been wounded in the fight with King Edward and had withdrawn to a secret and solitary place to get well of his wounds and sickness'. If such a letter existed, it suggests that Margaret, and by association Anne, still held out vain hopes for Warwick's return. The second part of the letter, though, 'contains not truth, as the women would well have known'. It stated that the Prince of Wales, King Henry's son, was 'in London with a very large following of men and with the favour and assistance of the greater part of the common people and citizens',[7] when he was actually still with his mother and wife in the west. It is more likely, then, that Margaret and Anne had to swiftly accept the news that the earl had been lost. Perhaps Anne was not alone in her personal grief; the *Arrivall* describes Margaret as being 'right heavy and sorry' at the news.

On hearing the news, the Countess of Warwick, who had by then reached Southampton, fled into sanctuary at Beaulieu Abbey, which the *Arrivall* claims was done 'secretly' as an act of defection, because 'she would no farther goo towards the Qwene'. If this is the case, she was also turning her back on her daughter Anne, which may explain their later cool relationship. Vergil claims that Margaret actually 'swownyed for feare … distrawght, dismayed and tormentyd with sorrow', lamenting the 'calamyty of the time, the adversity of fortune, hir owne toyle and mysery'. She may have allowed herself to indulge her grief initially but Margaret quickly recovered her resolve and led her son and daughter-in-law to Cerne Abbey, a tenth-century Benedictine monastery in Dorset, where they could reassess their plans. Little remains now of the extensive abbey, which dominated the area in the fifteenth century, yet the South Gate House and Guesthouse would be recognised today by Anne. Here, amid such tranquil surroundings, she watched as the stalwarts of the Lancastrian cause began to arrive, including Edmund Beaufort, the Duke of Somerset, second son of Margaret's former favourite, whom Warwick had killed at the First Battle of St Albans. His elder brother had been executed after a minor battle in 1464. Beaufort had been Warwick's cousin but it is unlikely he had any sympathy now for the dead man's daughter. Also present were key Lancastrians Dorset, Devon, Exeter and the Bishop of Ely, John Morton, who had been educated at Cerne Abbey and may have suggested the location. It was Morton who had led the Parliament of Devils which passed the act of attainder against Anne's family.

For the fourteen-year-old girl, no matter how brave and strong she felt, with her loyalty transferred through marriage, such company must have inspired mixed emotions and no small amount of fear. It is understandable that those who had been loyal to Henry VI for years despised the marriage his wife had forged for their son and did not wish to see Anne Neville sharing the throne with Prince Edward. Ironically, it may well have been her status as Princess of Wales which secured her position and her safety. Perhaps they made the young wife swear oaths of allegiance, perhaps they simply dismissed her as a child or considered her only as the bodily vessel by which the dynasty could continue. Later historians and dramatists have made much of Anne's supposed 'defection' to the Yorkist side when she remarried, but, as she waited at Cerne Abbey with her former enemies, she may well have longed to welcome her childhood friends with open arms.

Margaret now listened to Somerset's advice: they could proceed without the earl and reclaim London, under the leadership of the determined young Edward of Westminster. Commines claimed they had 40,000 troops at this point, and, although this figure is exaggerated, more supporters kept arriving. A letter from Zannotus Spinula to his father, now in the Milan archives, related that many Lancastrians did not consider the earl's death to be detrimental to their cause, as they had never really trusted him in the first instance: 'there are many who consider the queen's prospects favourable, chiefly because of the death of Warwick, because it is reckoned she ought to have many lords in her favour, who intended to resist her because they were enemies of Warwick; Northumberland among others'.[8] Warkworth notes that the loss of Clarence was also 'distruccion' to them although, perhaps, his absence was less mourned than railed over by those who had put their trust in him. As news of Margaret's arrival spread, more lords began to rally to the Lancastrian banner, as the party headed for Exeter, and on via Glastonbury, to Bath. Among her father's former enemies, Anne may well have feared for her own safety.

The Lancastrian force arrived in Bath at the end of April. From there, they hoped to unite with Jasper Tudor, Earl of Pembroke, who had been recruiting in the family stronghold of Wales, in order to give them the advantage over the king's army. Meanwhile, Edward IV had heard of the scale of desertion. Knowing this could only prove disadvantageous to his cause, he decided to seize the moment and engage the forces of the queen and prince before Tudor could come to their assistance. Now it became a race against time. Both sides were determined to find Tudor first. With the king in pursuit, Margaret ordered her party to flee north, gathering up what they could and taking to the roads as soon as possible. Did Anne look over her shoulder as they rode at breakneck speed through the English countryside? Their ride took them through Gloucester, which remained loyal to Anne's childhood friend, now its duke. More Yorkists prevented the party from crossing the River Severn, forcing them to divert their route up to Tewkesbury, arriving on the afternoon of 3 May. There, Anne was at least on familiar territory, as her mother was a patroness of the abbey and it was the final resting place of her grandmother. Perhaps it was even she who suggested her family's nearby manor house as a suitable place to stay.

Standing to the south-east of the modern town of Tewkesbury, Gupshill Manor had been built in 1438 and originally stood in a small hamlet of twenty houses. At the time, it was known as Gobes Hall. Now a restaurant, the black-and-white timbered building comprises three sections which retain many of the original features that Margaret and Anne would have seen when they stayed there for the night before the fighting took place. Other Lancastrian wives, including the Countess of Devon, who were captured with them after the battle, may also have kept them company there. It was here that Anne took leave of her young husband, wondering under what circumstances they would meet again. Perhaps they prayed together with Margaret, led by Bishop Morton, mindful of the possible outcomes of the impending clash. Either the Lancastrian family would be restored, and Anne would accompany her victorious husband on a triumphant march to Westminster as a princess and eventually inherit the throne or, alternatively, all would be lost. Probably none of them slept well, if at all. As the dark hours of the night began to lighten, Edward rose and said his final goodbyes to his wife. This was the closest Anne had ever come to conflict but, with her father's recent fate in mind, she must have feared for the safety of the tall, determined seventeen-year-old as he disappeared from sight.

That morning, Somerset led out his Lancastrian force of 6,000 men from the direction of the abbey, south of the town. Waiting for them were 5,000 Yorkists, headed by Edward, flanked by Clarence, Gloucester and Hastings. Vergil claims that the duke was overhasty, 'drawing his men' forth 'against th'advice of th'other captaines', because he knew that Edward IV was approaching. It meant that the armies engaged before the arrival of Tudor's reinforcements, which may have proved decisive. The fighting took place on uneven ground, among the surrounding 'evil lanes' and fields, with the legendary 'bloody meadow' visible from the manor house window although, by then, there was no one there. Anne and Margaret had fled the scene and did not witness the battle. When the first reports came back of defeat, they were being sheltered by a family living at Payne's Place in Bushley, before going on to Birtsmorton Court, where Margaret's chamber still stands.⁹ From there, they proceeded to Malvern Priory in Worcestershire, where they were safer. Thus, Anne did not see that King Edward had entrusted his eighteen-year-old brother Richard to lead a division of the army, in the only battle where Anne's two husbands faced each other on the field. Richard's section of the army came into direct conflict with that of Somerset, who was hampered by a stream running through his position, and beat him back towards the River Severn. Writing in 1904, American historian Jacob Abbot has Margaret witnessing the battle from a distance and attempting to rush onto the field to rescue her son, 'frantic with excitement and terror' from which her companions found it 'almost impossible to restrain her' until she swooned and was 'borne away senseless' in a carriage to a convent. It is not difficult to imagine such a scene, with Anne attempting to restrain her mother-in-law, but no evidence exists for it. The women probably retreated early and did not see the escaping Lancastrians being shot down by the archers Edward had placed in nearby woodland. Nor did they witness the moment when the fortunes of battle turned in favour of the Yorkists and Edward of Westminster, Prince of Wales, lost his life.

Exactly how Anne's husband met his death is unclear. Literary and dramatic sources have presented a range of possibilities, implicating various Yorkists in differing degrees. Of the contemporary chroniclers recording the scene without being present, Commines agrees with the Croyland and Benet chronicles, which clearly state that he fell on the field of battle, while the *Arrivall* observes, 'And there was slain in the field Prince Edward, which cried for succour to his brother-in-law, the Duke of Clarence.' Even having sworn allegiance to him less than a year before, Clarence clearly did not feel sufficiently moved to show the prince pity, stating in a letter to Henry Vernon that the prince was 'slain in playn bataill', differentiating his death from the 'execution' of Somerset also described in the correspondence. Warkworth agrees that the prince 'was taken fleeing ... townwards, and slain in the field', perhaps heading back for the safety of the abbey, or 'poor religious place', where his wife and mother waited. Tudor historian Andre Bernard, writing in 1501, also stated that the prince was slain in combat, even though, at that time, it would have been in his interests to slur the reputations of the Yorkist brothers.

The alternative story of Edward's murder began to gain credence soon after his death. Weeks after the battle, Bettini wrote to the Duke of Milan that the Yorkists had 'not only routed the prince but taken and slain him, together with all the leading men with him'.[10] As early as 1473, one French chronicle, the *Histoire de Charles, dernier duc de Bourgogne*, claimed he had been surrounded and murdered in cold blood by his enemies. Vergil's account has King Edward asking the 'excellent yowth' why he took up arms against his sovereign, to which the prince replied bravely that it was to free his father from miserable oppression and regain his usurped crown. Then Edward waved him away to be 'cruelly butchered' by his brothers, which is repeated by Hall and Holinshed. Based on this, local tradition still points out a house in Church Street, Tewkesbury, nearly opposite the marketplace, as that in which the young prince was stabbed in the presence of the king. Predictably, Shakespeare has Gloucester himself wielding the sword, in *King Henry VI, Part 3* Act 5 Scene 5. The prince declares to his enemies,

> I know my duty;, you are all undutiful:
> Lascivious Edward, and thou perjured George,
> And thou misshapen Dick, I tell ye all
> I am your better, traitors as ye are:
> And thou usurp'st my father's right and mine.

However, in *Richard III*, written around the same time, the killing has already taken place before the action begins, as it is an earlier part of the same cycle. Now, though, Richard denies his involvement to Anne, stating instead that the prince was 'slain by Edward's hand'. In response, Anne cites her witness, Queen Margaret, who saw his 'murderous falchion smoking in his blood'. The dramatic irony of Richard's admission of guilt to the audience once Anne leaves the stage is a timely reminder of the duplicitous nature of public denials and that those responsible were hardly going to advertise the fact.

Fabyan, a London chronicler of 1516, describes the murder as having taken place in the presence of the king, in no way singling out Richard of Gloucester. Edward, he says, 'strake him [the prince] with his gauntlet upon the face, after which stroke, so by him received, he was by the king's servants incontinently slain'. The seventeenth-century George Buck, 'on the authority of a faithful contemporary manuscript', asserts that when the bloody attack was made on the young prince, 'the Duke of Gloucester only, of all the great persons, stood still, and drew not his sword', giving rise to the theory that Richard was unwilling to participate in the murder of Anne's husband, because of his existing affection for her, 'whom he loved very affectionately, though secretly'. Shakespeare goes one better and has Richard try to convince Anne that it was for the sake of her beauty that her husband was slain, bereaving her of him in order 'to help thee to a better husband'. At least one later historian has suggested that the murder, if it was murder, was in retaliation for the death of the seventeen-year-old Edmund, Earl of Rutland, the fourth Yorkist brother, who had been killed alongside their father at Wakefield in 1460. This is not impossible. The question of his death is something of a historical misnomer though. All noblemen participating in battle could expect to be killed during the conflict or in a brief trial in the aftermath, as had been established since the First Battle of St Albans. Violent death was no stranger to those who vied for the throne, particularly since the death of the Duke of Suffolk in 1450, followed by that of the 1st Duke of Somerset in 1455, which had set the tone for the wars. Of course Edward would be killed if he were taken. To expect otherwise, to hope for some sort of leniency in view of his youth or status, would have been naïve. Death was death, whether it happened in the thick of fighting or came at the end of an axe or dagger in the midst of the enemy camp. However Prince Edward died, and the plaque in the abbey states he was 'slain in battle'; the result was the same for Anne, who was left a widow at the age of fourteen. Now she and Margaret were at the mercy of the York brothers.

Edward was not the only significant casualty of the battle. As the Lancastrian army scattered, Somerset turned on Warwick's ally, Lord Wenlock, and, according to Hall, killed him with an axe for 'holding back'. Somerset's younger brother, John Beaufort, was also slain in the fighting, and the duke, along with many of the defeated lords, took shelter in nearby Tewkesbury Abbey. There, the Yorkists offered prayers for their victory and gave Abbot Strensham their word as permission for the dead to be buried and for the sheltering Lancastrians to be pardoned. However, something changed in the following days. Only two days later, on 6 May, Somerset and the others were dragged out of the abbey and beheaded. A fifteenth-century depiction of this scene in a late Ghent manuscript appears to exonerate Richard and his brothers from actually carrying out the deed, as it depicts King Edward watching the executioner, who stands on a block to wield the axe and is a clearly older man, sporting a little pot belly. As a result of the violence, the abbey had to be cleansed and reconsecrated a month later. Edward, Prince of Wales, was interred within its walls and, today, his final resting place is marked by a plaque on the floor. Also losing out at Tewkesbury were Jasper Tudor and his nephew Henry, whose brief hopes for the restoration were dashed, sending them both into exile. It marked the beginning of a fourteen-year separation between Henry and his mother, Margaret Beaufort. Her second husband, Henry Stafford, had been so badly wounded after Barnet that he would die of his injuries that October, leaving her a widow for a second time. She would not see her son again until he was a grown man at the head of an invasion army in 1485, but for another mother, her namesake, the battle at Tewkesbury was to have the worst possible outcome.

At some point, probably late in the day of the conflict itself, the terrible news was carried to the women waiting in the convent. Thomas Stanley may have been the messenger, as suggested by John Abbott, as he had been married to Warwick's sister and would soon take Margaret Beaufort as his second wife. Thus, Anne heard the news from her uncle. Their defeat was absolute, for Margaret as a mother as well as a queen: Vergil describes the remainder of her life as being lived in 'perpetuall moorning'. However deep their grief, Margaret and Anne were themselves in danger and fled to a church near Tewkesbury, where they were arrested two days later by another Stanley brother, William, who conducted them to King Edward at Coventry. Anne's own grief would have been determined by the extent of her feelings for her dead husband. Even if love had not blossomed between them, they had been in each other's company for the past nine months and shared the mixed fortunes of exiles. Anne had thrown in her lot with the Lancastrians, with the possibility of a future at Edward's side in Westminster: she had known and shared his aspirations – and probably his fears and determination – before the battle. There is no evidence that she welcomed his death, as some historical novels have suggested; in fact, as his wife, she had every reason now to expect harsh treatment from his enemies. As she rode with Margaret in captivity towards Coventry, her emotions must have been turbulent, wondering just how lenient the king was prepared to be. Her age and gender were on her side, as was the past she had shared with both King Edward and Richard. How far would that go towards saving her now?

On 11 May, Margaret and Anne appeared before King Edward at Coventry. Given Margaret's later humiliating return to London, driven imprisoned in a chariot for the baying crowds to see, there was probably little sympathy for the ex-queen. Alison Weir alleges that Margaret screamed abuse and curses at Edward to the extent that he considered ordering her execution. Having witnessed her grief, Anne may well have felt compassion for her mother-in-law, although, as Warwick's daughter, she was aware that it was now a battle for individual survival. She could not ally herself with Margaret now, as her future did not lie with her. It would not have been clear exactly where that future did lie but if she was wise, Anne would have tried to tread a careful political path and wait to see how events would unfold. Once again, her youth and gender probably served her well in this. It was likely that her arrival at Coventry as a prisoner also marked her brief reunion with Richard of Gloucester, now cast in the role of victor. A romantic interpretation of the meeting would stress the resurfacing of old affections, as their eyes met across the room, full of assembled war-weary lords. On a practical level, it was probably a painful and difficult encounter, given the distance that the last two years had placed between the childhood friends. In the aftermath of battle, Anne's widowed status was undeniable, making her available for remarriage, but if Richard conceived any intention of making her his wife at this stage, it was purely theoretical. The proceedings of that day were likely to have been formal and practical, to determine arrangements for the prisoners. Richard may not even have been present, or only briefly so, as he went south fairly soon after Tewkesbury in order to deal with an uprising among Kentish rebels. The ex-queen then began her journey south to the Tower on 14 May, where Henry VI was still housed, while Anne was released into the custody of her sister and Clarence. Vergil narrates a little anecdote in his 1513 history, whereby Margaret had foreseen her husband's death after the Battle of Barnet: 'she bewayled the unhappy end of King Henry, which now she accountyd assurydly to be at hand'. She was quite correct that the loss of her son removed the safeguard to her husband's life. While Prince Edward had lived, his father's death would only have transferred his claim to a younger, more competent man, but the extinction of the Lancastrian line sealed the old king's fate.

The same night that Margaret arrived at the Tower, her husband lost his life. It is unlikely that they were reunited first.

Popular legend has him praying on bended knee at midnight in the Wakefield Tower when the unknown assassin struck. Edward IV was re-crowned the following day and Henry's bleeding body was carried through the streets and lain on the pavement outside St Paul's Abbey, where it continued to 'blede newe and fresche', according to Warkworth. While the Fleetwood Chronicle states that 'of pure displeasure and melancholy, he died' and the *Arrivall* agrees that his end was hastened by grief on hearing of the death of his son, others lay the blame for the deed at the feet of the Yorkists. There were precedents for such descriptions, euphemistically used for the demise of the usurped Richard II in 1399. Writing about three weeks later in mid-June, Bettini asserted 'King Edward has had him put to death secretly … he has in short chosen to crush the seed'.[11] Rous' second, post-Tudor version of events takes relish in personally implicating Richard, who 'as many believe, [killed] with his own hand, that most sacred man King Henry VI'. This is repeated as fact by Commines: 'Immediately after this battle, the Duke of Gloucester either killed with his own hand, or caused to be murdered in his presence, in some spot apart, this good man King Henry,' making the first mention of the weapon, apparently a dagger, although how he was so certain of these details is unknown, being at the time in France. Fabyan echoed the idea of popular belief in helping to ascertain guilt. 'Of the death of this prince,' he says, 'diverse tales were told, but the most common fame went that he was stykked with a dagger by the hands of the Duke of Gloucester.' Vergil confirms that common report attributed the crime to Gloucester. 'Henry VI,' he says, 'being not long before deprived of his diadem, was put to death in the Tower of London,' adding that the weapon of choice was a sword, while More says of Richard, 'he slew … with his own hand, as men constantly say, King Henry VI, being prisoner in the Tower'.

These accounts influenced the most famous depiction of the king's death, where Shakespeare has Richard brutally interrupt Henry's long speech:

King Henry: The owl shrieked at thy birth, an evil sign;
The night-crow cried, aboding luckless time;
Dogs howled, and hideous tempests shook down trees;
The raven rook'd her on the chimney's top,
And chattering pies in dismal discords sung.
Thy mother felt more than a mother's pain,
And yet brought forth less than a mother's hope;

> To wit, an indigest deformed lump,
> Not like the fruit of such a goodly tree.
> Teeth hadst thou in thy head when thou wast born,
> To signify thou cam'st to bite the world;
> And, if the rest be true which I have heard,
> Thou cam'st...
>
> Gloucester: I'll hear no more. Die, prophet, in thy speech. [Stabs him.]

There is no evidence that Richard was the murderer of Henry VI; equally, there is no decisive evidence that he was not. Whoever wielded the sword was certainly acting under instructions from King Edward and Richard's position as a Constable of England would have made the execution of such duties his responsibility, either by his own hand or by delegation. It is possible that Richard was present in the Tower that night but he was more likely to have been at Westminster, celebrating his family's success. Thomas Rymer's *Foedera*, published early in the eighteenth century, claims that two esquires, Robert Ratcliffe and William Sayer, with no fewer than ten or eleven other persons, were appointed to attend upon the unhappy monarch. As a friend of Richard from Middleham days, Ratcliffe's presence could be interpreted as sinister but, on the other hand, it is to be expected that the Yorkists would man the Tower with men they could trust. The Warkworth Chronicle also places Richard at the scene when Henry was 'putt to dethe' between 9 and 10 o'clock at night, 'beinge thenne at the Toure the Duke of Gloucestre', but then goes on to add that 'many other' were there too. Just as with later reports of the deaths of the Princes in the Tower, common fame and later accounts continued to use Richard as a convenient villain.

After the threats to the Yorkist regime in the period 1469–71, Henry VI and his son were too dangerous to be allowed to live. Their removal was no more remarkable than the deaths of Richard, Duke of York, the Earl of Rutland, the Duke of Suffolk, both Dukes of Somerset and the Earls of Warwick and Montagu, which were shocking in their own way, yet were simply the realistic outcome of civil conflict. In each case, their killers, where known, have escaped the sort of censure reserved for the death of the Lancastrian king. The killing of Henry has captured the popular imagination because of the passive, saintly nature of the victim and his helplessness in the face of his supposedly ruthless enemies. If ever there was a pawn in the course of these wars, it was him. Considering that his half-nephew, Henry VII, later attempted to have him canonised, it is unsurprising that the majority of accounts, which were written after the advent of the Tudors, should seek to implicate the Yorkists. The Cousins' Wars were marked by acts of ferocity and brutality; increasingly it was a question of kill or be killed. In all likelihood, the unfortunate Henry was put to death by royal command, which is more significant than the identity of the servant who carried out the order. When Henry's tomb was opened in 1910 and the contents examined at Cambridge University, his skull was found to be broken and the remaining hair still matted with blood; there seems little reason to disagree with the archaeologists' findings that he suffered the 'violent death' that the majority of chroniclers describe.[12] Richard may have wielded the sword but ultimately, responsibility lies with Edward IV.

Henry's body was put on display at St Paul's, as Warwick's had been, in order for the public to view him and ascertain that he was, in fact, dead. After this, he was buried in Chertsey Abbey, with his body being later transferred to St George's chapel, Windsor in 1484, on the order of Richard, then king. These events would have been relayed to his one-time daughter-in-law, Anne, as she remained under the watchful eyes of Isabel and Clarence, probably at Coldharbour House. Into her mouth, Shakespeare puts a description of his 'murderer':

> O, gentlemen see, see! dead Henry's wounds
> Open their congeal'd mouths and bleed afresh.
> Blush, blush thou lump of foul deformity;
> For 'tis thy presence that exhales this blood
> From cold and empty veins, where no blood dwells;
> Thy deed, inhuman and unnatural,
> Provokes this deluge most unnatural.

Anne probably did not attend the funeral procession or burial of Henry VI. Her feelings towards her future husband, described here as an 'unnatural' 'lump of foul deformity', were far more complex than the playwright suggests.

Soon after the death of Henry VI, miracles were recorded in his name in a volume at St George's chapel, Winsdor. Typically they included curing the sick, saving the unjustly condemned and raising the dead. Edward IV attempted to quash these accounts but, interestingly, by the time of his reign, Richard himself became an advocate of the late king's sainthood. It was Richard who ordered

the removal of his body from Chertsey and the re-interment at
Windsor and who initiated the record which, by 1500, contained
174 stories. His personal effects were also put on display as relics
and his velvet cap was recorded by Stowe as being able to cure
headaches. It is ironic, then, that his cult was developed by the
Tudors in contrast to the later perceived 'villainy' of Richard
and, in tandem with reports of his role in the king's death, as a
foil for their favourite Yorkist villain. Richard has been ascribed
various motives for this, from cynical manipulation through to
genuine piety: all are unsubstantiated. Henry's canonisation was
advocated by his half-nephew, Henry VII, and by the 1520s, papal
representatives were seeking to verify the stories, although this was
abandoned with the Reformation.

Appearing as a ghost on the eve of the Battle of Bosworth,
Henry is given the following words, by Shakespeare, with which he
accuses Richard III:

> When I was mortal, my anointed body
> By thee was punched full of deadly holes
> Think on the Tower and me: despair, and die!
> Harry the Sixth bids thee despair, and die!

Thus admonished by an apparent saint, Richard promptly complied.

Anne
and
Gloucester

8

A Strange Courtship
1471–1472

But if I sang your praises
it wasn't out of love
but for the profit I might get from it
just as any joglar sings a lady's fame[1]

Anne had lost her father and husband in battle. Her mother had remained in sanctuary, beyond reach, while her sister was married to the enemy. She had been taken into captivity along with her mother-in-law, who was still a prisoner in the formidable Tower. Then her father-in-law, the king, had been murdered. All this had happened within the space of a few months, yet it was not the end for the teenager. Of course, she did not have the benefit of foresight to reassure her, but she was lucky to have come through recent events and now be in a position of safety, even optimism; as a survivor, and following her father's example, she was probably accustomed to seek out whatever opportunities might present themselves, however unlikely. In fact, far from being an end, it was a significant new beginning. A regime change at the top could mark a swathe of new allies and potential connections, particularly for a young, healthy and attractive woman. Anne has often been sidelined as a pawn amid men's more powerful games but there is no reason why her gender should exclude ambition, cunning and drive. After all, she had Margaret of Anjou as an example, albeit perhaps a negative one. Now, she knew she must adapt to the status quo and start to map out a future for herself.

Following the events of May 1471, Anne had been released into the custody of her sister Isabel and brother-in-law, Clarence, who had now inherited her father's title of Earl of Warwick. It was a situation which allowed for the widowed princess's return to society, giving her access to the court at Westminster and a degree of freedom suggestive of a hopeful future as a Yorkist ally. She was lucky not to have been entrusted to her mother, then still in sanctuary at Beaulieu Abbey,who, as the widow of a traitor, was considered legally deceased. Perhaps Anne was extended an element of choice in this. From this point forward, Anne de Beauchamp would play no significant role in the lives of either of her daughters or their husbands, who would fight over her inheritance. The sisters may have considered their mother's flight as an act of betrayal. Perhaps they had never been close; it is not difficult to cast Warwick as the dominant parent, also even the one who had inspired devotion, but this is speculation. Equally it was in Clarence's interests to keep his sister-in-law close, as he was currently in possession of the majority of the Warwick legacy and did not wish to divide that with whomever Anne should wed next. As she turned fifteen, barely months after becoming a widow, the subject of Anne's remarriage was already a sensitive one.

The duke and duchess were then resident at Coldharbour House in Thames Street, in the parish of All-Hallows-the-Less, or perhaps All-Hallows-in-the-Hay, named after an adjoining hay wharf, near where the London Brewery now stands. It was an ancient and important 'right fair and stately' house, according to John Stowe, originally two fortified buildings on the river-bank, which had been home to Henry IV in 1400 and to Henry V during his tenure as Prince of Wales. Following the attainder of Anne of York's husband, Henry Holland, the property came into the possession of the Crown and was used by various members of the York family. It is mentioned in a mid-seventeenth-century play by Heywood and Rowley as having twenty chimneys, was reputed to have a number of turrets built around a courtyard and was generally believed to be impregnable. In the 1460s it had been owned by the Lancastrian Henry Holland, Duke of Exeter, but was confiscated after his involvement in the Battle of Barnet. It would have been there that Anne was taken, under escort from the Tower, to be part of her sister's household.

It is possible to reconstruct a fairly full picture of what life was like under Clarence's roof in 1471, due to the set of surviving guidelines produced eighteen months before, for the running of his affairs during a stay at Waltham. Royalty had long been visitors to Waltham monastery, which was ideally located for hunting in the surrounding royal forest, now Epping Forest. Henry II had founded an Augustine priory on the site, which later became an abbey, one of the wealthiest of its order. Clarence's connection with the area was established in 1465, when Cheshunt Manor, just over the border in Hertfordshire, had been granted to him after the death of Elizabeth, Lady Say. Even as late as the eighteenth century, descendants of Clarence's daughter Margaret were listed as living at nearby Much Waltham. The *Stablishmentes and Ordinaunces made for the Rule and Guydinge*[2] for the household of Clarence at the monastery of Waltham, 9 December 1469, just six months after his marriage, shows the extent and expenditure of his home and the provisions made for his new duchess. It seems to owe something to the similar routine followed by his mother Cecily and that which Isabel herself had grown up under at Middleham, but although the new duchess had jurisdiction over her servants, her husband would have had the final say. The Waltham *Ordinances* clarify the standard of living that Duchess Isabel would have experienced in London and Essex and wherever Isabel went during the second half of 1471, Anne went too.

Embedded within the regulations is a paragraph reminding the household of the Clarences' then recent marriage:

> Be it knowen and remembred that the Tewesdaye, the xii day of the moneth of July in the castelle of Calais, the seid Duke tooke in marriage Isabell, one of the daughters and heires of Richard the seid erle of Warwik whiche that tyme was present there.[3]

Following this, the duchess's household, described in *The State, Rule and Governaunce of the Excellent Princess in the Standing Householde*, includes her personal servants of a baroness and five gentlewomen, each with their own staff and her own smaller version of the duke's household, with treasurer, chamberlain, almoner, chaplain, yeomen, servers, ushers, waiters and kitchen hands. She had yeomen of the robes and beds, a groom of the robes, clerk of the closet, pages of the chamber for water and other necessaries, a clerk of the jewels and lavandrie, or washers, of her clothing. The extensive stabling arrangements include carriages, chariots, palfreys, chairs and litters for her travel; no doubt Anne would have been collected from the Tower in one of her sister's vehicles, perhaps covered over to avoid attention. Isabel may well have made the arrangements herself, as she clearly had a degree of control over her own servants: 'All ladyes, gentyelwomen and chamberers attending upon the seid duchesse, take such fees, rewards and clothinge, as shall please the duchesse.'

The more general rules for the running of the Clarence household would have dictated Anne's daily routine. Typically for its time and status, it was a household concerned with appearances, respect and service. Individuals holding positions of importance, particularly those involved in the organisation of finances, charity and catering, such as the chamberlain, almoner, steward, treasurer, chancellor, controller of the household, marshall, ushers and servers, were to be worshipful, virtuous and honest. A range of fines, usually the suspension of a day's wages, existed for any who did not fulfil their duties, were disrespectful or wasteful. In summer, they dined at 10 a.m. and 5 p.m., while in winter, the hours shifted forwards to 9 a.m. and 4 p.m. Those in attendance must ensure the family were well and honourably served, or else suffer financial penalty and the loss of their daily meals. Livery must be worn by all employees to 'give good example to the court', for identification and to demonstrate allegiance, which was particularly important in an era of shifting loyalties. The Counting House was responsible for assigning all the household servants with livery, which in 1469 totalled 299 people, costing £188 13s 4d. Some servants were permitted to exercise their own judgement within reasonable limits. The almoner was to have 12d daily to distribute to the poor and, after each meal, would take the leftovers 'to be given to the most needy man or woman to his discretion', while the porter was to fetch wood, white lights and wax but 'no more than was reasonable'.[4]

While staying at Coldharbour House, Anne would have been well provided for. Having come from the royal court at Amboise, with Louis XI in residence, in full expectation of assuming the role of the Princess of Wales at Westminster, her life under Clarence's regime was not materially too far removed from that of Edward and his queen at Westminster. The projected total annual expenditure for the duke and duchess in 1469 had been a considerable £4,505 15s 10d. The ordinances list the different kitchen departments of bakehouse, pantry, cellar, buttery and picher house, spicery, larder, seething house, scalding house, scullery, saucer, hall, ewery, chandry and butchery, as well as all those who worked in and around them like the porters, servers and clerks. Bread was baked daily, with the small, fine, white payne-manes and manchettes produced for the table as well as loaves for the horses and hounds. The estimations for a year's consumption in 1469 included 650 quarters of wheat, 41 tons of wine and 365 tons of ales, 2,700 sheep, 420 pigs, 2 barrels of honey and a long, luxurious list of spices, including pepper, saffron, ginger, cloves, mace, cinnamon, nutmeg, dates, licorice, sugar, raisins, currants, figs and rice, totalling over £72. Over £30 was spent on sauces, £8 on white salt and £106 on wood and coal.[5]

Although Coldharbour House was reputedly impregnable, comprising what had been two fortified town houses, recent events had taught the Clarences that even strongholds like the Tower could fall victim to the attacks of marauding rebels. It is unsurprising, then, that the *Ordinances* emphasise the need for security. In summer, the gates were open between 5 a.m. and 10 p.m., changing in winter to 7 a.m.–9 p.m., but they were manned at all times. The porters were to wait at the gate and ensure no household stuff, such as silver plates and pewter vessels, was 'embezzled out' and no man was allowed to break doors, windows or locks on pain of losing wages. The security measures may also have been in place to prevent the Clarences' charge from escaping or being snatched from under their nose. Once it emerged that Richard, Duke of Gloucester, was interested in becoming Anne's second husband, his brother was keen to prevent the two from meeting. The romantic legend that he banished her to the kitchens, where she was dressed in the garb of a kitchen maid, may owe more to historical fiction, although there is the fair possibility that he sent her out of sight when his brother was visiting.

Shakespeare has Richard actively wooing Anne. An audience sees him confess his guilt and declare his intention to wed her by way of a challenge in spite of her 'heart's extremest hate, with curses in her mouth and tears in her eyes'. He initiates the wooing in Act 1, Scene 2 and she reacts with repulsion, before being won over by his false displays of affection. Yet there is no way of knowing now just how the marriage came about. It is reductive to Anne to assume the courtship had to be initiated by Richard, when she had just as much to gain from the match as he. Anne may well have seen Gloucester as an ally who would provide her with the status she needed for independence and the necessary assistance to take control of her inheritance. Clearly, she was the ideal wife for him, bringing with her the lands, revenues and reputation of her father that would allow him to assume the mantle of his old mentor. Anne was no fool; she knew her value and what she had to offer. Perhaps she suggested the match to him herself. The status of an independent widow would have been less attractive to a fifteen-year-old than, perhaps, to a woman of more mature years. Anne had been raised with marriage as her goal and there were few men equal to her in rank. She would gain a protector and he would share her portion of the Warwick estate; without his help, she could not even enjoy her inheritance and, lacking that, there was little chance of her making a better match. She was certainly capable of taking the initiative. From Clarence's custody, Anne wrote to Queen Elizabeth, her mother Jacquetta of Luxembourg and her daughter, Princess Elizabeth, requesting the chance to claim her own half of the Warwick estates in court.[6] It was denied. Quite cynically, uniting with Richard was a win-win situation and, ever the realist, Anne embraced it.

It is not clear what role the Clarences played in the negotiations, although Croyland's story about Anne's concealment, as well as the subsequent disputes arising over the Warwick inheritance, would suggest they were not overly keen for the marriage to go ahead. The legal settlement that followed certainly provoked an unpleasant breach between the brothers and consequently their wives. It would be romantically satisfying to believe in the theory that this was a love match; that mutual affection had grown between the young pair during their Middleham days, which survived the intervening conflict that placed them on opposing sides, in order to later reunite them purely for companionate love. Such a story provides the premature 'happy ending' for Anne that, with hindsight, the historian and novelist know she would not get. It is only human to wish to snatch a little bit of romance out of the jaws of battle and premature death. But it would also be as misleading to make this assumption as it would be to accept Shakespeare's version of events. There is no way of knowing whether one pursued the other, or which of them first conceived of the idea and somehow communicated it. Perhaps the idea was mooted by letter or in a whispered discussion in the corner of the Erber; perhaps Richard or Anne approached Clarence or Isabel, seeking their approval. Perhaps it was denied. Of course, it cannot be entirely ruled out that Richard did 'prove a lover' and swept his young childhood friend off her feet with the romantic words and promises at which his brother Edward was adept. It would be to underestimate Richard to assume he was not sincere or capable of this. The details of exactly how Richard and Anne came together may never be known.

What is more apparent is the rapid time-scale of the courtship. As Michael Hicks has pointed out in his biography of Anne,[7] Richard was much occupied during the latter half of 1471. Immediately after the Battle of Tewkesbury, rebels in Kent rose up in arms under the leadership of the Bastard of Fauconberg, an illegitimate son of Sir William Neville, and hence Warwick's cousin. Richard was in Sandwich that May to subdue them, then up in the North to quell other pockets of insurrection, where Fauconberg was apprehended and beheaded that September. Gloucester was also about his own business, issuing grants in the North on 30 August, 4 and 6 October, 20 November and 11 December, leaving little time for a lengthy courtship. Lisa Hilton[8] suggests the plan was hatched after Richard visited the Clarences at Christmas, which may be the occasion of Croyland's kitchen maid story, when Anne was disguised or sent out of sight. Anthony Cheetham[9] claims Richard already had Edward's permission for the marriage as early as the summer and that Edward warned Clarence not to interfere, hence the subterfuge. It would have been in the king's interests to allow the match to go ahead, in order to limit the degree of untrustworthy Clarence's inheritance. The more money his middle brother had, the more potentially dangerous he could be. Whenever it happened, an agreement was reached before 16 February 1472, when Richard 'facilitated' Anne's escape from Coldharbour House and her flight into sanctuary at the London church of St Martin-le-Grand. Did she climb out of a window, as Perkin Warbeck would do in 1499? Perhaps she lit a candle at midnight and watched for his dark shadow appearing on the lawns below. Whatever arrangements they made, Anne would have been waiting for him. Theories suggesting she was 'abducted' have failed to recognise that the majority of medieval cases involving heiresses use the term synonymously with 'eloped'. Did she disguise herself and creep out of the gates at night? Did Richard come for her while Clarence was at Westminster or while Isabel slept?

Established by William the Conqueror, the precincts of St Martin-le-Grand lay within the City's walls, but were not subject to its jurisdiction, allowing the inhabitants a degree of freedom. It had long been a controversial place, with citizens complaining in 1402 of thieving apprentices and servants who were living there on the profit of stolen goods alongside murderers and robbers, although it was not until 1448 that a sheriff visited and introduced some semblance of justice. By 1457, it was a slightly safer place to stay, as anyone arriving to take refuge there would first be stripped of all weapons and counterfeit goods, as well as being registered with the dean. On the outbreak of war, Dean Stillington supported the Yorkists, later being employed by Richard when he became king and may even have been the Robert Stillington, Archbishop of Bath and Wells, who was to play such a significant role in the fates of the Princes in the Tower, or else a relative of his.[10] There Anne remained until July, whence she emerged to become Richard's wife. Although the exact date of the ceremony is uncertain, 12 July 1472 has been suggested, based on the 1474 provisions in the event of their divorce and estimations that place the birth of their son in 1473. The twelfth was also the anniversary of Isabel and Clarence's wedding.

Anne has been accused of remarrying with indecent haste[11] but the interval of fourteen months was by no means atypical of an era when new matches were often arranged with rapidity. Margaret Beaufort had been widowed after Anne, in October 1471, when her third husband finally succumbed to wounds he had sustained at the Battle of Barnet. Her fourth wedding was conducted the following June, to a man who had previously been her enemy, Thomas Stanley, Lord

High Constable. This may well have been a marriage of convenience, as some historians have suggested, although it served Margaret and her son Henry Tudor well enough in 1485, and even if it was, its speed demonstrates how quickly mutually beneficial alliances could be forged across enemy lines. Equally, John Howard's wife, Margaret, had married him within a year of being widowed. The alliance of man and woman could supersede previous dynastic ties. If Anne and Richard recognised each other as their best possible match, then why wait to secure the union and the inheritance? It is anachronistic to suggest otherwise, especially as Anne's first marriage had been one of convenience. Michael Hicks writes that this unseemly 'precipitate haste' was not 'what was expected' at the time, accusing Anne of 'cynical and calculating materialism'. Yet this is underpinned by modern romantic sentiments and cannot be supported as indecent 'even by fifteenth century standards'. Rather, the proliferation of such connections, which Hicks acknowledges, cannot be ignored and is, in fact, probably the rule rather than the exception. Even Clarence would seek a Burgundian match for himself less than a year after Isabel's death. If Anne did act with 'cynical and calculating materialism', she was only embracing the best means of advancement, by which most of her contemporaries had survived.

Yet some historians, like Michael Hicks, have suggested that Richard and Anne should never have married. In *Anne Neville* (2007), he identifies a technical glitch which he claims should have prevented the ceremony from going ahead. According to the standards of the day, certain matches were forbidden because those involved were within degrees of affinity or relation, either through birth, existing marriages or spiritual connection. Hicks has rightly identified that the need for papal dispensations has been 'downplayed' by historians who regard the process as a 'curious technicality', a 'necessary mechanism to remove technical obstacles to what ought to have been perfectly acceptable'. The twenty-first-century mind may not find it strange to accept that the dispensation was required at the time but, rather, that like indulgences, it seems strange that a piece of paper can somehow wipe these 'impediments' clean away. With the English aristocracy drawn from such a limited gene pool, many matches required this action, including Anne's first marriage with Edward of Westminster and Isabel's union with Clarence. Then, as now, to wed without the necessary paperwork created problems. For the late medieval couple, an illegal and immoral marriage would not only be invalid in the eyes of the law, but any children born to them would be illegitimate, with all the repercussions for inheritance. In addition, both parties risked the very real medieval fear of eternal damnation. However, this did not have to prevent such a match and there were precedents of marriage between pairs of siblings. The impediment would only have applied if Anne had had relations with Clarence or Richard with Isabel. At any rate, it did not stop the Gloucesters. As a deeply religious man, Richard would not have countenanced making an invalid marriage; even with the ongoing dispute for Anne's inheritance; if further dispensations had been required, and there is no reason why they should not have been issued, the couple did not need to pre-empt them. As members of the aristocracy, they were well aware of the importance of legitimacy: neither would have risked the possibility of their future children's inheritances being called into question.

Marriages contracted without the relevant paperwork did sometimes attract attention but it was usually when one of the parties had a vested interest in doing so. Among the Vatican papers, a case exists from Ireland in August 1473, when an Ellen Cantwell petitioned that Richard Boteller contracted a union with her, 'solemnized it with banns and consummated it'. The pair had children and lived together for year until it emerged that he had previously been married to a close relative of his, named Cathelina Boteller, 'without having obtained papal dispensation'. The ruling upheld Ellen as his legal wife.[12] Similarly, in March 1485, John Yve of Derby and Emmota, widow or 'relict, of Roger Lyversiche', were given a dispensation to 'remain in the marriage' they had contracted 'in ignorance that the said Roger had been godfather to a child of the said John and the late Joan his wife'. If this was not enough, John had also been godfather to Emmota's child by Roger, but the union received the stamp of legitimacy 'notwithstanding the impediment of spiritual relationship arising'.[13] The papal records are full of such cases, contemporary with the alliance of the Gloucesters. The minimum paperwork they required was the dispensation to provide for the case of affinity stemming from the sibling tie between Richard's mother, Cecily Neville, and Anne's grandfather, Richard, Duke of Salisbury. The couple shared mutual ancestors in the same way that Anne had with Edward of Lancaster, so a similar dispensation would have been required to that of her first match. The paperwork was issued on 22 April 1472. It probably arrived in England around June.

It seems plausible that Anne and Richard's marriage was celebrated that summer. If there had been a large celebration, or if the occasion had been marked at Westminster, a record would have survived, which suggests they became man and wife in a small, comparatively private way. Richard was the sixth and final of Cecily of York's children to get married: she had disapproved of Elizabeth Wydeville as a daughter-in-law but may have been more receptive to Clarence's match with Isabel once that union had been accepted by the king. Her relationship with Anne was to develop into a close one, so perhaps she now proved a friend to the young couple. She may have offered her London home of Baynard's Castle as a venue for their marriage, where Edward had proclaimed himself king in 1461 and where Richard would do in 1483. Later, Richard would rent Crosby Hall, or Place, an impressive building of 1466 in Bishopsgate, but this did not happen until well after the marriage, when it was still in the hands of Anne Crosby, widow of its constructor. Shakespeare refers to it anachronistically in Act 1, Scene 2 of *Richard III*, when Richard, still as Gloucester, urges Anne to repair there after the burial of Henry VI although, in fact, he was not resident at the property until the late 1470s at the earliest. Alternatively, the church of St-Martin-le-Grand may have provided them with a convenient location for a quick ceremony, or they may have travelled north together to one of the chapels or churches associated with a York or Warwick property. As they were to spend most of their married life at Middleham, the nearby church of St Mary and St Alkeda, which Richard designated as collegiate in 1478, may have witnessed the nuptials. The wedding night would have been spent wherever was convenient after the ceremony and was likely to have been successfully consummated, as suggested dates for the arrival of the couple's son could place his conception early in the marriage. By the time she was due to give birth, Anne was settled as Richard's wife, Duchess of Gloucester, in her childhood home of Middleham.

9

Richard's Wife
1472–1483

With love founded on profit, pleasure and honesty
then shall true friendship reign among you.[1]

For the next decade, the rule of Edward IV went unchallenged. His queen, Elizabeth Wydeville, bore five more children to add to the existing five and, with the death of Henry VI and Queen Margaret effectively silenced, it looked as if the Yorkist regime was finally secure. Richard and Anne retreated to their estate at Middleham Castle, where they settled into the roles of a great northern magnate and his wife. The seals from surviving documents relating to Richard's activities indicate that he spent most of his time at the castle, which was their primary residence, although they also owned Sheriff Hutton, which was useful for its proximity to York and a number of other properties. Richard was to play an important role in government during this time, ruling the Earl of Warwick's old lands in the name of his brother. He regularly attended Parliament, travelling south in the autumn of 1472 for the first session since his marriage and leaving his young wife behind, although they were probably reunited for their first Christmas. Anne bore a son early in the marriage and established herself as the head of the Ducal household, even deputising for her husband in his absence. There was nothing to suggest the pair would not live out happy, quiet lives, raising their child among the rolling hills of Anne's childhood home.

Today it is possible to get a sense of the majesty of the couple's home, even though the building stands in ruins. Middleham was entered across a traditional defensive moat and drawbridge, either into the castle's east gatehouse or the gatehouse to the north. Both gave into a courtyard which was flanked by the chapel and the massive keep, where a staircase led up to the Great Hall. The chapel's surviving masonry gives an idea of the extent of the huge arches on third-story level and the little niches and pedestals that would have contained statues and devotional items. The impressive keep, with its reconstructed wooden steps, stood over the cellars, while the inner chamber was warmed by the kitchens below. Wooden bridges linked the upper levels to the garderobe or latrine block, the Lady's Chamber and Prince's Tower, where Anne is rumoured to have given birth.

The arrival of Edward of Middleham has usually been placed around 1473 or 1474, although Charles Ross has put it as late as 1476. His case has been based on the boy's investiture as Prince of Wales in August 1483, when he is described in one account as being around seven. Edward had certainly arrived by April 1477, when a licence was granted to the manor and church of Fulmere, Cambridge, for prayers to be said for 'the king's brother, Richard, Duke of Gloucester and Anne, his consort and Edward, their son'.[2] Then, in 1478, the boy was given Anne's grandfather's title of Earl of Salisbury. Anne may well have conceived just days after her wedding, as Isabel had, allowing for the first of the possible dates of delivery in the late spring or summer of 1473, while *The Peerage* gives December of that year as his birth month.

At seventeen, Anne was relatively young to become a mother, although a number of her aristocratic contemporaries had already done so by that age. When she was certain she was expecting, after the baby had quickened, she would have prepared linen and furnished her chamber in the tower with bed and cradle, making sure that draughts were excluded. Supplies would have been ordered and it would have been scrubbed thoroughly clean, perhaps even given a fresh coat of paint or plaster before her lying-in. Possibly it was Anne's pregnancy that prompted Richard to rescue his mother-in-law from her confinement in Beaulieu Abbey that May, sending Sir James Tyrell south to fetch her, even though Clarence was 'not agreed' to the arrangement. The Rous Roll stressed the countess's proficiency in, and fondness for, the birth chamber, so it is possible that she was present at Middleham for the delivery itself. A midwife and local women would have cared for Anne during those final months, as well as a physician, although the period of confinement was exclusively female. As she was on her home territory, there is a fair chance that some or all of them may have been part of the household since her infancy, perhaps even the nurses and governess of her own childhood. It is not impossible that Cecily Neville, Duchess of York, travelled from London or the nearby Fotheringhay to attend her daughter-in-law, with whom she

Right: 3. Edward III. King of England from 1327 to 1377, and common ancestor of the warring houses of Lancaster and York. Richard III's family were descended from his second son, Lionel of Antwerp, through the female line, while Henry VI derived his claim from the third son, John of Gaunt. Anne was his great-great-granddaughter and Richard was his great-grandson. (Author's collection)

Below: 4. Anne de Beauchamp. According to Pevsner, this fifteenth-century corbel in the nave of St Andrew's church, Chedworth, Gloucestershire, depicts Anne's mother, Anne de Beauchamp, Countess of Warwick. She was born in 1426 and bore Anne, her last child, at the comparatively advanced age of thirty. (Guy Thornton)

Above: 5. Warwick Castle. Anne was born here on 11 June 1456. One of the most wealthy and impressive in the country, there had been a castle on this bend of the River Avon since the eleventh century. Warwick inherited it and the title through his wife, after the death of the last Beauchamp earls in the 1440s. (Matthew Wells)

Left: 6. St Mary's church, Warwick. Anne was baptised here in June 1456, within days of her birth. Medieval babies were usually christened as soon as possible, to ensure their salvation, as cases of infant mortality were high. Anne's ceremony would have been arranged by her godparents, as her mother would not have yet emerged from her confinement. (Colin Sabin)

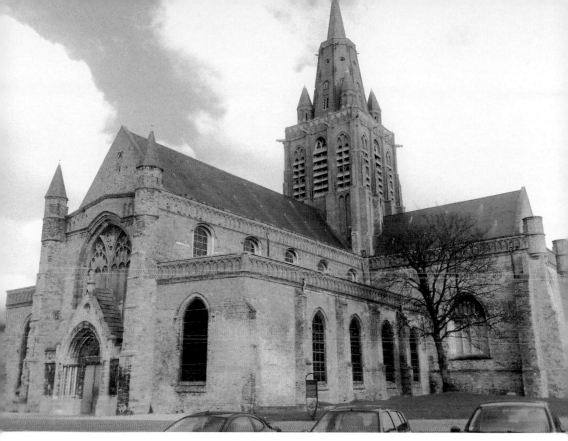

7. St Mary's church, Calais. L'église Notre-Dame, one of the few remaining landmarks in Calais that Anne would recognise from her childhood. Begun in the thirteenth century, building work continued throughout the English occupation of the Hundred Years' War, with its tower completed around 1500. (Matthew Reames)

8. Inner Court, Warwick Castle. The interior of Warwick, showing the extent of the inner courtyard. In Anne's day, this would have been bustling with activity. The crenelated wing, which overlooks the river, was designed by the Beauchamps as a symbol of strength and status. Retaining its original defensive features, steps had been made to make the living quarters more comfortable by the time of the earl's residence. (Matthew Wells)

9. Falcon and fetterlock. The House of York is best known for its device of the sun in splendour but the falcon and fetterlock was also among its early heraldic devices, featured here on a tower at Fotheringhay Castle. It may have come from the Mortimer family, of which Richard, Duke of York's mother had been a member. (Simon Leach)

10. St Albans. 'French Row', in St Albans, Hertfordshire; a narrow street just off the medieval marketplace and cross. With its origins in the thirteenth century, this, and other narrow lanes in the town, must have seen the worst of the hand-to-hand fighting in the battles of 1455 and 1461. (Steve Cadman)

Above: 11. St Albans Abbey, now Cathedral. From here, Abbot Whethamstede witnessed the battle of 1455, amid fears that the abbey would be sacked. After the death of Somerset, some of the Lancastrian lords sought refuge from Warwick's victorious troops, hiding their armour and disguising themselves as monks. (Steve Cadman)

Right: 12. Sandwich. The gateway from the town to the dock. One of the original Cinque Ports, the Kentish town was used as the main foothold into the kingdom by Warwick. Earl Rivers had amassed a fleet here with the intention of raiding Calais, but a pre-emptive strike in 1460 resulted in his humiliating capture and that of his parents as they lay in bed in the town. Now the port is silted up and only a narrow river flows past this gate. (Jane Ring)

Above: 13. Micklegate Bar, York. After Richard, Duke of York and his second son, Edmund, Earl of Rutland, were killed at the Battle of Wakefield on 30 December 1460, their heads were displayed on the gate for all to see. York's was dressed in a paper crown, as an allusion to the claim he had made to the throne that autumn. His youngest son, named after him, was eight at the time. (Mark Smith)

Left: 14. Angers Cathedral. It was here, in July 1470, that Anne Neville and Edward of Westminster were formally betrothed, in the presence of her parents and his mother, Margaret of Anjou. Their oaths were reputedly sworn upon a fragment of the true cross but the marriage wasn't solemnised until six months later. (Tjeerd Huisman)

15. Château d'Amboise. The imposing and beautiful château, favourite of the French monarchy, set on a bend of the River Loire. Anne and her mother arrived in July, along with Edward and her mother-in-law Margaret of Anjou, as guests of Louis XI. Together they awaited news of Warwick's attempt to restore Henry VI to the English throne. (Tjeerd Huisman)

16. View, Château d'Amboise. During the summer of 1470, Anne and her fiancé Edward passed the days at Amboise by walking in the surrounding gardens and watching the road for messengers. Here, the two young people got to know each other. With its breathtaking view across the river, the château must have seemed an idyllic place to start their lives together. (Tjeerd Huisman)

Left: 17. Margaret of Anjou and Prince Edward. Statue in the Jardin de Luxembourg, Paris, of Margaret of Anjou and her son, Edward of Westminster. The inscription on the base reads, translated, 'If you do not respect a proscribed queen, respect an unhappy mother.' Margaret and Edward appear to have been close and united in their ambitions; his loss was a devastating blow to her. (Deborah Esrick)

Below: 18. Tewkesbury Abbey. The armies of Lancaster and York met outside the abbey at Tewkesbury in Gloucestershire on 4 May 1471. As Anne and Margaret waited, the battle turned decisively against them. It was the first campaign of both Anne's husbands, Richard of Gloucester and Edward of Westminster. The young Prince of Wales was killed, either during the fighting or shortly afterwards. Some of the Lancastrian lords sheltering inside the cathedral were later extracted and beheaded, forcing the building to be reconsecrated. It is also the final resting place of Isabel Neville. (Simon Jenkins)

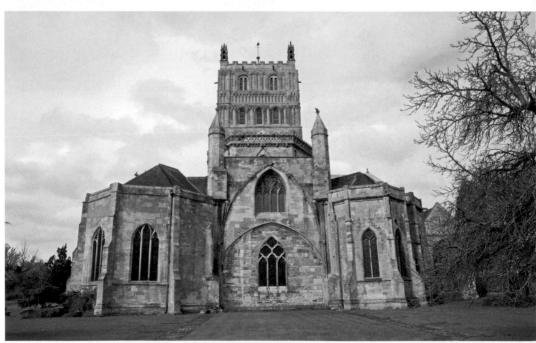

19. Cerne Abbey. It was to the beautiful abbey at Cerne, in Dorset, that Margaret of Anjou fled with Anne and Edward in April 1471. They had arrived in England expecting to be welcomed as its newly reinstated royal family, only to receive news of Warwick's death. Inside the peaceful walls of Cerne, they planned their next move. (Danny McL @ Flickr)

20. The Wakefield Tower. Built by Henry III, this part of the Tower of London was used to imprison Yorkists after the 1460 Battle of Wakefield, possibly giving rise to its name. The hapless Henry VI was incarcerated here and met his mysterious death within its walls, reputedly while at prayer. (Christopher Hall)

Inside the roundels (medieval script):

Prince
Edward son
to king henri
the vi first
husbond of
Anne

Anne
doughter
to the forsaid
Richard and
first wif to
prince Edward
to king
Richard

King
Richard the
iij Second
husbond to
the Anne

Opposite: 21. Warwick the Kingmaker. (David Baldwin)

Above: 22. Anne Neville (centre), her first husband Prince Edward of Lancaster (left), and her second husband Richard III (right). (Jonathan Reeve JR1731b90fp109C 14001500)

23. Richard III and Anne Neville. (*Richard, Duke of Gloucester, and the Lady Anne* by Edwin Austin Abbey. Yale University Art Gallery, Edwin Austin Abbey Memorial Collection)

Left: 24. Arms of Anne and Richard. A cigarette card dating from 1906, featuring the arms of Anne Neville surmounting those of Richard with its tusked boars. (Keith)

Below: 25. Middleham Castle. Exterior of the castle that was home to the Warwick family on their return from Calais in 1461. The thirteen-year-old Richard came to join them here in around 1465 to be trained as a 'henxman' in the martial and noble arts essential to his future role. Anne and Richard's friendship may have developed from this time. (Mark Wheaver, englishtowns.net)

Right: 26. The Great Hall, Middleham Castle. The Great Hall at Middleham, which was built over the cellars, for which the central pillars remain. This would have been the centre of castle life, where feasting and entertaining took place, business was conducted and the duke presided over a local court. After their marriage in 1472, Richard and Anne made it their home. (Mark Wheaver, englishtowns.net)

Below: 27. Inner Chambers, Middleham Castle. A statue of Richard III now stands on the ground floor where the kitchen was once located. Above it, on the second storey, were the Gloucesters' private rooms, the Great Chamber and Inner Chamber. (Mark Wheaver, englishtowns.net)

28. South Wing, Middleham Castle. The horse mill, centre, and oven, left, were installed in the sixteenth century. Before that, the first floor of the range contained four rooms known as the 'privy' (private), or lady, chamber. (Mark Wheaver, englishtowns.net)

29. St Mary's and Alkelda's church, Middleham. This was the local parish church for the Gloucesters, where Richard intended to found a collegiate college. He obtained the necessary grant from Parliament in 1478 but the plans were ended with his death. The stalls were named after the couple's favoured saints. (Karen Beal)

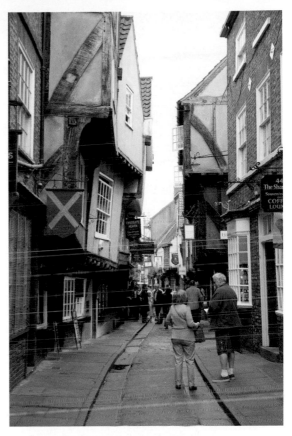

30. The Shambles, York. Anne would have been familiar with the winding medieval streets of York, where she could have purchased luxury items, which arrived in the markets from ships on the River Ouse. The central Shambles would have been at the heart of the city's trade since its first incarnation in the Domesday Book. Historically a street of butchers, the present fifteenth-century buildings recently earned it the title of 'most picturesque street in England'. (Steve Cadman)

31. York Minster. Anne and Richard's arrival at Middleham in the summer of 1472 came soon after the building had finally been completed. Dedicated to St Peter, it was the seat of Anne's uncle, George Neville, who had been enthroned as archbishop in 1465. The role it would later play in their reigns indicates the affection in which they held it. (Neil Melville-Kenney)

32. The white rose. A modern carving in the City of York evokes the long association of the city with Richard's family. The white rose was used by Edward IV, along with the sunburst image, as his personal devices. His daughter, Elizabeth, would have them embroidered on her clothing. This forms part of the design of a bridge spanning the River Ouse. (Mark Smith)

33. Sheriff Hutton. The remains of Sheriff Hutton Castle, Yorkshire, which Richard received in 1471, following Warwick's death. It was here that he based his 'King's Household in the North' and where his council regularly met. The castle was home to his nephews, Edward of Warwick and John de la Pole, from 1484 and it was here that he sent his niece Elizabeth of York, in the wake of rumours of his amorous intentions towards her in 1485. (Tom Blackwell, www.tjblackwell.co.uk)

34. Fotheringhay Castle ruins. Ruins are all that now remain of the northern stronghold of the York family, birthplace of Richard III in 1452. Thirty years later, he would be present when a treaty was signed with the Duke of Albany for an invasion of Scotland. Anne would have been familiar with the castle as a guest of her mother-in-law and great aunt, Cecily Neville. (Amanda Miller @ Amanda's Arcadia)

35. St Mary and All Saints church, Fotheringhay. Close to the York family seat of Fotheringhay Castle is this early fifteenth-century church. In 1476, Edward IV ordered the reinterment of his father and brother, Richard, Duke of York and Edmund, Earl of Rutland, following their deaths at Wakefield. Cecily Neville was also buried there on her death in 1495. (Amanda Miller @ Amanda's Arcadia)

Above: 36. Richmond Castle. The seat of the Tudors in Yorkshire, this twelfth-century castle made from the local honeystone had been confiscated and bestowed on George, Duke of Clarence. On his death in 1478, it was given to Richard and Anne. (Alan Taylor)

Left: 37. Window, Fotheringhay church. A modern memorial window at Fotheringhay, featuring the royal arms of York, including the falcon and fetterlock, sunburst and boar. (Simon Leach)

Above: 38. Penrith Castle. Once in the hands of the Neville family and set in a prestigious location near the Scottish border, Richard obtained it in 1471 and added a banqueting hall to its layout. (Stephen Woodcock)

Right: 39. Crosby Hall. By 1483, Richard had acquired this Bishopsgate town house from the original owner's widow; it was here that Anne stayed with him during the turbulent events of June 1483. Shakespeare mentions it at the time of Henry VI's funeral but it was not in Gloucester's possession at that time. In 1910, it was removed, brick by brick, to its present site in Cheyne Walk, Chelsea. (Jos)

40. Ludlow Castle. Edward, Prince of Wales, had been raised in his own household at Ludlow, on the Welsh borders, under the tutelage of his uncle, Earl Rivers. News of his father's death reached here on 14 April 1483. (Les D.)

41. Arms of Edward V. The arms of the twelve-year-old Edward V, who reigned from 9 April to 26 June 1483. (Keith)

Above: 42. Princes in the Tower. The young Edward V was conducted to the Tower of London to await his Coronation, and soon his brother, Richard of York, joined him. They were seen for the last time playing in the grounds in June 1483. This cigarette card dates from around 1924. (Keith)

Top right: 43. The White Boar. A modern version of Richard's motif located at Bosworth Field, surrounded by his motto '*loyaultie me lie*' or 'loyalty binds me'. Thousands of boar badges were made and distributed in York to coincide with the investiture of Edward as Prince of Wales of September 1483. (Mike Cox)

Bottom right: 44. Staircase, White Tower. The flight of steps leading to the chapel in the White Tower, Tower of London. Renovations in 1674 unearthed a box of bones which had been buried deep in the well under the steps, which were placed within an urn now in Westminster Abbey. The discovery of Richard III's remains has reopened debate about whether the bones in the urn will now be subject to forensic study. (Ann Longmore-Etheridge)

Above: 45. Lincoln. Richard was visiting the city in October 1483 when news reached him that Buckingham had joined the rebellion sweeping the South. It may have come as a surprise to Richard, as only four months earlier Buckingham had helped put him on the throne and given every appearance of loyalty. (Snapper)

Left: 46. Richard, Duke of York (d.1460), Richard III's father. Drawing of a statue formerly on the Welsh bridge at Shrewsbury. (Jonathan Reeve JR1577b4p548 14501500)

47. A hunchbacked portrayal of Richard III. (Jonathan Reeve JR1559folio5 14501500)

48. Nottingham Castle. It was while staying here that Richard and Anne received the terrible news about their son's death, in April 1484. They left at once for Middleham. It is rumoured that Richard referred to it afterwards as his 'castle of care'. (Tom Bastin)

Opposite: 49. Statue of Richard III. Richard is commemorated in a modern statue in Leicester Park. He stayed at the Blue Boar Inn on the night before the battle and rode out from the city to Bosworth Field on 22 August 1485. (James Nicholls)

Right: 50. Westminster Abbey. Anne died on 16 March 1485 amid an eclipse of the sun. She was buried in an unmarked grave in Westminster Abbey; if Richard had intended to erect a tomb to her, his own demise prevented it. In 1960, the Richard III Society put up a bronze plaque in her honour. (Steve Cadman)

51. St Margaret's church, Stoke Golding. Local legend suggests that the grooves made in this window-sill were caused by soldiers sharpening their swords before the Battle of Bosworth, fought nearby in 1485. (Lee Hutchinson)

52. Bosworth Field. On the night of 21 August 1485, Richard was supposedly plagued by bad dreams in which, according to Shakespeare, Anne appeared to accuse him of her murder. In the morning, though, he rallied his troops on the high ground, believing that God would vindicate his rule through a decisive victory. (Lee Hutchinson)

53. Bosworth Field Memorial. A modern-day memorial to those who fell in battle at Bosworth, or Ambion Hill, on 22 August 1485. (Mike Cox)

Above: 54. Bow Bridge, Leicester. This memorial plaque relates that a soothsayer predicted Richard's demise where his 'spur struck'. Tradition has it that he did just this, on the ride over the bridge out to battle on 22 August, and that as his corpse was carried back, his head also struck the bridge. (Snapper)

Right: 55. Henry VI. The king depicted on a screen in Ludham church in Norfolk. (Jonathan Reeve JR1721f14 14001500)

56. Margaret Beaufort, Christ's College, Cambridge. Henry Tudor was her only son, whom she bore at the age of thirteen. (Elizabeth Norton)

Left: 57. Henry VII by Holbein. (Elizabeth Norton)

Opposite: 58. Tudor-era stained glass depiction of Elizabeth of York. (Author's collection)

Elizabetha·R

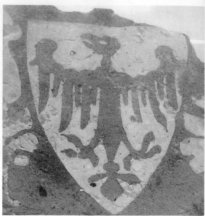

Above left: 59. Corner of a Leicestershire car park. One unkempt corner of the Leicester car park before the university dig began in late August 2012. The exact location of the Greyfriars church was unknown, but the discovery of stones under the tarmac soon established its perimeters. (Snapper)

Above right: 60. Medieval tile. This tile, with its heraldic motif, was found at the Leicester dig site in 2012, still located in the well-preserved floor of the Greyfriars church. (Snapper)

61. Greyfriars church, Leicester. In this section of the dig, the diamond-shaped indentations of the floor tiles are still visible within the church choir. (Snapper)

Above: 62. Greyfriars trench. The public were allowed in to view the long, thin trench in September 2012, which shows just how little space the archaeologists had to work with when seeking to locate the grave. (Snapper)

Below: 63. Burial site of Richard III. The location within the Greyfriars choir from which the bones of Richard III were exhumed in September 2012. (Jim Crowdell)

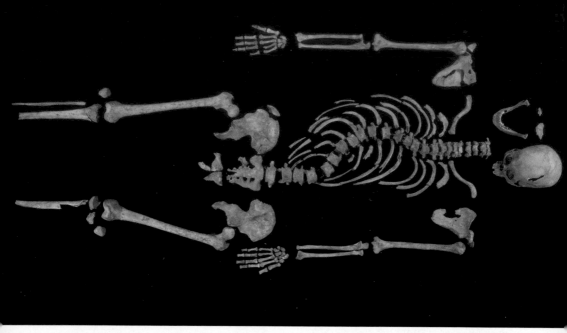

Above: 64. Skeleton of Richard III. The skeleton, minus feet, of Richard III, unveiled at the press conference of 4 February 2013. (University of Leicester)

Below left: 65. Skull of Richard III. Image released before the press conference on 4 February 2013. (University of Leicester)

Below right: 66. Spine of Richard III. Richard's spine, excavated in September 2012, shows signs of idiopathic adolescent onset scoliosis, forming the distinctive 'S' shape, which would have caused some discomfort. (University of Leicester)

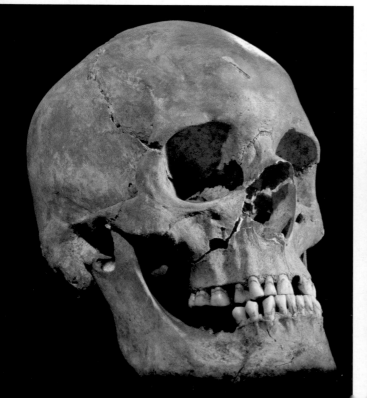

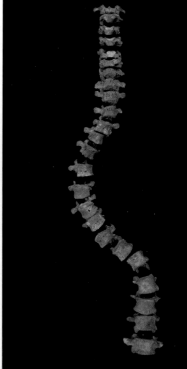

was reputedly on good terms. As her time approached, Anne took mass in the castle chapel and withdrew from the household routine, sequestering herself in the tower to await her labour. There was little to alleviate her pain beyond herbal remedies and the panacea of devotional objects. The risks were high, gynaecological understanding and standards of hygiene were poor, but Anne had youth on her side. Her son arrived safely.

Baby Edward had his own household staff and routine within Middleham Castle. The traditional association of one tower of the building with him may well have a basis in fact, suggesting his location of birth and the nursery that his parents established. A payment made in the Calendar Rolls of 1484 sheds a little light on the identities of those who cared for Edward, with an Isabel Burgh, wife of Henry, receiving from Richard 'an annuity of twenty marks' for 'good service' to his family.[3] The Burgh family's connection with Middleham went back even further. In 1471, an indenture was made between Richard and Squire William Burgh, allotting him an annual income from the nearby farm of Sleighholme in return for his loyalty.[4] Three years later, an Alice Burgh, described as Richard's 'beloved gentlewoman', was granted a £20 annuity for life from Middleham for 'certain special causes and considerations'. Michael Hicks suggests the Burghs were a local gentry family from Knaresborough, although the connection may have been even closer. In fact, they may have been related to the Yorks, if William's family was a branch of the Irish de Burgh family, from which Richard's great-great-grandmother Elizabeth came. Hicks also proposes that the 'beloved gentlewoman' with her 'special causes' was Richard's mistress.

The nursery was presided over by an Anne Idley, an Oxfordshire woman who had been widowed around the time of Edward's birth. When she left her home, Drayton Manor, for Middleham, her stepson refused to pay her the annuity they had agreed, leading Richard to intervene to ensure the debt was settled. Ironically, Anne's late husband Peter had written a book of manners, or education, for the rearing of boys, called *Instructions to his Son*. While Idley Junior may not have benefited from his advice, Edward of Middleham did. The text advised a son to:

> thy fadre and modre thow honoure
> As thou wolde thy son shold to the...
> And in rewarde it is geve vnto the
> The blessyng of thy fadre and modre.[5]

It is tempting to consider the *Instructions* as a manual which the widow Anne Idley and the duchess used with Edward. In it the boy was reminded that his 'fadre in age is, whiche now thy helpe is and favoure', which should serve as a reminder to negligent youth that 'after warme youth coometh age coolde'. Although many similar manuals existed, Edward's access to this text encourages speculation as to the lessons he was taught and, by projection, the man and king he might have become. Idley advocated discretion and consideration, keeping 'within thi breste that may be stille' and not letting the tongue 'clakke as a mille'. The avoidance of unnecessary conflict and the giving of offence are considered important facets of personal control:

> A grete worde may cause affray
> And causeth men ofte to be slain
> Thus tonge is cause of moche pain.[6]

In fact, wariness and secrecy were a constant theme in the book: Idley advocates a boy to 'keep cloos all thing, as thombe in fiste', and 'lete mekenes euer be thy Rayne', as 'many in this world wyde haue been cast adoun for their grete pride'. Also, 'while thy counceill is within thy breste, it is sure as within a castell wall', so a child should 'keep thy tonge and keep thy frende'. He should be lowly and honest to rich and poor, in both word and deed, respectful of his masters and superiors. Idley warned that games and japes were likely to backfire and that evil company could taint and bring a boy into mischief. Friendship was the greatest treasure the author could recommend, as more precious than silver or gold and that a man without friends was a man without a soul. He should not be too hasty in making promises to friends or foe, or too quick to take vengeance. Equally, he should not ask for advice when he was angry as 'it is harde than the trouthe to feele' nor accept it from those who were 'greene' or inexperienced.[7]

Some of Richard III's critics have accused him of being driven by ambition and avarice, in the Shakespearean model. Idley's manual contains advice for the boy to 'flee the counceill of a man covetous', whose desire for worldly goods could make a man 'leese both lande and house'. Some of the following lines sound almost like the Bard's presentation of Edward's father:

> He can shewe two facis in oon hode
> Many a traitour is of his bloode
> He causes other many theeves

A woman vicious in divers places
Men to be slayn in feldis and in greeves.[8]

Interestingly, as Edward's father would find, Idley warns 'a man may somtyme wade so depe, it passeth his power to turn ageyn'. The young boy at Middleham may have made a wise and cautious monarch, had he lived long enough to put Idley's advice into practice.[9]

If Edward arrived in the August of 1473, all three York brothers were the fathers of children who were born that month. At Shrewsbury, the queen, Elizabeth Wydeville, was delivered of Richard, Duke of York, younger of the two Princes in the Tower, while Isabel, Duchess of Clarence, had a daughter named Margaret, at Farleigh Hungerford Castle, in Somerset. It is difficult to know to what extent the inheritance dispute affected the relationship between the sisters; the battle had been fought between Richard and Clarence but Anne and Isabel may never have been fully reconciled. It is not even certain whether Anne visited London during these years, perhaps keen to keep away from the Wydeville family, whom her father had so disliked, and all the memories associated with his death. Geography provided a neat divide too, with the marriage settlement allotting land in the north to the Gloucesters while the Clarences were favoured with property in London and in the South, including Warwick's town house, the Erber. When Isabel's son Edward was born in February 1475, though, she was at Warwick, and less than a year later, she was pregnant again, going into confinement at Tewkesbury, where she had inherited the legacy of her maternal Despenser grandmother. She was delivered of another boy on the sixth, whom she named Richard. The choice may have been in memory of Warwick, although it might also indicate a reconciliation with her sister and her husband. By extension, Gloucester may even have been godfather.

Edward was to be Anne's only child, although later miscarriages and stillbirths cannot be ruled out. The documenter of her family, John Rous, would not have been aware of them in his retreat at Guy's Cliffe, near Warwick, and such losses were not always recorded retrospectively. In this, the Clare Roll that lists all Richard's lost siblings is a rare and unusual survival. No other record remains of the duchess experiencing any unsuccessful pregnancies, or losing children at birth. As Lisa Hilton suggests, Anne may have suffered from tuberculous endometritis, a symptomless disease that causes infertility and possibly also affected her mother and sister. Richard, however, was the acknowledged father of two children, with rumours of a third. Their ages suggest they were the result of liaisons conducted before his marriage, in the late 1460s or early 1470s. His son, John of Pontefract, or Pomfret, may have been borne by the Alice Burgh, who received a payment of 20 marks a year in 1474, according to Michael Hicks. She was probably a local woman, related to Edward's wet nurse, Isabel Burgh, which may date their affair either to Richard's late teens or the early years of his marriage. However, it is more likely that John's conception probably occurred during Richard's year-long residency at Pomfret Castle, from April 1471, making the boy twelve when was knighted at York in 1483. This would place his conception around the time of Anne's exile in France and marriage to Edward of Westminster, when Richard himself was eighteen. His mother was likely to have been a woman living in Pontefract, with whom the young duke sought solace. John was possibly under the guardianship of Robert Brackenbury, who was with him in 1484 when they stopped over in Canterbury, en route to Sandwich, and dined on pike, leavened bread and wine. In March 1485, he was made captain of Calais and there are indications that Richard would have considered him his 'spare heir'.

Richard also had a daughter, Katherine Plantagenet, who was married between March and May 1484 to William Herbert, Earl of Huntingdon, son of the Earl of Pembroke, Henry Tudor's old guardian. Although matches were made between aristocratic children, the illegitimate Katherine had probably reached the minimum age of fourteen, dating her birth, also, to the years preceding Richard's marriage. As king, he financed her nuptials and settled, on her and her heirs, lands worth 1,000 marks a year, although she would die three years later, possibly in childbirth. A third potential son, Richard Plantagenet, a stonemason of Eastwell, Kent, was reputed to have been born in 1469 and died in 1550, although he is now widely believed not to have been a son of York. The question of his identity was raised by the local parish register and impressive altar tomb in the ruined Eastwell church but if he was Richard's son, the king never publicly acknowledged him.[10] While the evidence suggests all Richard's bastards were conceived before the summer of 1472, it cannot be stated categorically that he was faithful to Anne, nor would standards of the day necessarily have expected it. Most famously, her sister-in-law, the beautiful Elizabeth Wydeville, had little choice but to turn a blind eye while King Edward pursued a number of other women.

It was not until after the birth of their son that Anne and Richard's marriage settlement was finalised, in 1474. Clarence had been loath to share Isabel's inheritance but the king ruled that Anne must receive her share of her mother's Beauchamp and Despenser legacy, so Parliament divided the Countess of Warwick's lands as if she were dead. Richard had liberated his mother-in-law from her confinement at Beaulieu the previous year and the forfeiture of her estates may have been her side of a mutually beneficial bargain. In July 1484, he would allocate her a yearly pension of £80, but ironically, she would go on to outlive both her daughters and sons-in-law. The settlement allowed Richard to step into Warwick's shoes and take over the loyalty of his retainers even though Clarence was to keep the title. Through his years under Warwick's tutelage at Middleham, as well as his birth at Fotheringhay, Richard was already known in the area. He took steps to consolidate this by assuming the mantle of the old earl's good lordship by creating ties of patronage and clientage. On 13 May 1473, he was at Nottingham to settle the long-running Percy–Neville feud, agreeing to be a 'good and gracious lord' to all those involved.[11] The following July he was at Alnwick Castle, where an indenture was drawn up between him and his cousin, the newly reinstated 4th Earl of Northumberland, Henry Percy. The earl had previously been imprisoned and stripped of his title, which had been granted to John Neville, following the death of his father, the third Earl, at Towton. Now, Percy petitioned the king for his inheritance to be returned, along with his estates. Richard oversaw this claim, making the new earl promise to be his 'faithfull servaunt ... at all tymes' and do him 'lawfull and convenient' service, as well as pledging his allegiance to Edward IV and his heirs. In turn, Gloucester would be his 'good and faithful lorde', to 'sustain' the earl in his rights and not challenge any grants he may receive from the king or the activity or offices of his servants.[12]

From the early 1470s until his succession as king, Richard established a network of obligations and endowments that made him the most powerful magnate in the North. His birth and childhood at Fotheringhay Castle, Northamptonshire, followed by an adolescence at Middleham, made him a man shaped by and committed to his geographical area. He had this in common with Anne and the pair would have travelled together in the region, establishing order and being familiar faces at ceremonial occasions. Sometimes Anne deputised for her husband, such as in 1475–76, when she represented him at York during his absence in France. This may well have involved arbitrating when it came to disputes and hearing minor court cases; she certainly corresponded with the Mayor and Aldermen of York. Once married, they made their permanent base at Middleham Castle and Richard secured a licence from Edward so the town could hold fairs twice yearly, as well as planning to endow a college there. Between them, they also held a number of properties across the North. Sandal Castle in Wakefield, West Yorkshire, had belonged to Richard's father and witnessed his death in 1460 but now Richard established it as another base of the Council in the North. Situated overlooking the River Calder, his improvements of the 1470s included a new tower, bakehouse and brewhouse, although its associations with the death of his father and brother cannot have been welcome.

In 1471, before marrying Anne, Richard had already claimed Penrith Castle, south of Carlisle, newly built to be a defensive post against the Scots, where he added a banqueting hall later that decade. The same year saw him acquire the Norman Pontefract Castle, in Wakefield, which had been his official residence for a year, as Steward of the Duchy of Lancaster. With Warwick's settlement of 1474 came the impressive Scarborough Castle, overlooking the sea, which Richard and Anne visited in June 1484 and, in the following year, they gained Barnard Castle in County Durham. Richmond Castle was also among their possessions, confiscated from the Tudors, which the duke had been promised back in 1462, although it had been granted instead to Clarence. The other main residence used by the Gloucesters during this time was Sheriff Hutton, conveniently located about 10 miles to the north of York. A long-standing Neville property, it had passed to Richard after the death of Richard Neville at the Battle of Barnet. Anne was probably familiar with it from her childhood and, after her marriage, was able to revisit it, along with the other Ducal properties. Travelling between and overseeing the administration of all these estates must have been almost a full-time occupation.

As Edward's representative on the Council of the North, Richard was a frequent visitor to York in the 1470s. The citizens presented him and his councillors with bread, rabbits and wine at the session of 1475, although this did not prevent the insurrection he returned to subdue in 1476, at the head of 5,000 men. The citizens also sought his help to resolve conflict in certain cases, such as the removal of salmon traps from the river, which was proving a hazard for shipping, and a case of vandalism and theft at the Holy Trinity Priory at Micklegate.[13] He would not have been present when the cathedral was reconsecrated after extensive repairs in July 1473 but both he and Anne would have visited at some point in the following decade. It was an important site of pilgrimage with its impressive Gothic transepts and beautiful glazed Great East Window, fitted at the start of the fifteenth century. Anne would have been accustomed to the bustling streets of medieval York, with its markets, hospitals and religious orders. Together, they may have joined the stream of pilgrims praying and making offerings at the shrine of the city's patron saint, William Fitzherbert. While visiting, they would stay in the Augustinian priory, the smallest of the city's religious houses. Richard would create Friar William Berwyck 'surveyour of our works' there in 1484; the friar would also be the recipient of boards left over from the staging of pageants to welcome the new king and queen in 1483, which were used to build a closet.[14]

York was also an important centre for trade, where Anne would have gone to make any special purchases, either in person or deputizing to a servant. At that time, the city's taxation records indicate the six main areas of activity: wool, leather, metal, construction, victuals and specialist craft workers. York was not what it had once been; the fifteenth century marked a period of decline for it, as it did for many urban centres. However, it still had the advantage of being a port, on the junction of the Rivers Ouse and Foss, so foreign ships regularly brought supplies of luxury items such as the rich spices that would have graced the dining table at Middleham. There was also a high proportion of goldsmiths, producing ceremonial and decorative items such as the Middleham jewel, an engraved, diamond-shaped pendant of gold, set with a large sapphire, unearthed by a local metal detectorist in 1985. Possibly a reliquary, an inscription on the border, indicates it may have also been used as an amulet to protect against the 'falling sickness' or epilepsy. The jewel dates from Anne's residency at the castle but perhaps it is going too far to suggest that young Edward may have suffered from this.

What constituted a good wife in the 1470s? One contemporary sermon on wives and widows stated that love founded on profit, pleasure and honesty would lead to true friendship and that 'the spouse you have is the spouse ordained for you by God'. There were practical jobs for a wife to carry out, or oversee, as a woman in Anne's position would have done. These included the running of the kitchen, granary, storage and supply of provisions, besides the usual sewing, knitting and spinning of domestic clothing and linen. Marriage was advocated as a blessing for single men, who were apparently incapable of keeping themselves clean and tidy, sleeping 'in a pit', with the 'sheets never changed until they are torn'. Equally, the bachelor's dinner hall floor was 'littered with melon rinds, bones and salad peelings', his cloth was laid with little care and 'dogs lick[ed] his trenchers [bread plates] clean'.[15] Luckily for Anne, a small army of servants would have ensured she never had to bend down and pick up the dropped bones!

Christine de Pisan also had advice for 'young women living on manors' whose husbands might be absent on courtly or administrative business. According to her 1405 *Book of the City of Ladies*, a routine was essential; a lady should rise early and busy herself about the house, to set an example to her employees. She should possess sufficient skills to be able to cope with the household accounts, not being too polite to ask how much her income is and how much revenue she gets from her lands. If her husband was reluctant to disclose this, she must use 'kind words and sensible admonitions' to encourage his confidence so that they could live within their means. When it came to administration, a wife must be thoroughly knowledgeable regarding land, law and rents, according to customs of the region, to avoid falling victim to deception and so that she could best represent her dependants. Good lordship was also, by extension, good ladyship, otherwise, according to Pisan, 'it would be a burden on the souls of her and her husband until they make amends for it'. A good business head must combine with empathy though, as the lady must be 'more compassionate than strict' towards the poor. With Richard so often away for sessions of the London Parliament and administering justice in the North, Anne must have been trusted with the necessary information and managed to run their home to his satisfaction.

Another source of wifely decorum, dating from the 1390s, the fictional manual *Le Ménagier de Paris*, advised a wife to translate her obedience and respect for her husband into practical care. She should keep him in clean linen, for he will 'go and come and journey hither and thither, in rain and wind, in snow and hail, now drenched, now dry, now sweating, now shivering, ill-fed, ill-lodged, ill-warmed and ill-bedded. And naught harmeth him because he is upheld by the hope that he hath of the care that his wife will take of him on his return.' When he returned home, he should 'be unshod before a good fire ... have his feet washed and fresh shoes and hose, to be given good food and drink' before being 'well bedded in white sheets and night caps, well covered with good furs and assuaged with other joys and desports, privities, loves and secrets of which I am silent'. There should be no fleas in the bed, so the good wife would strew it with alder leaves and bread soaked in glue and set a lighted candle in the middle to draw them out. In the bedroom, she should hang up sprigs of fern to ward off the flies or 'tempteth them with a bowl of milk and hare's gall', failing those, a raw onion and honey might just do the trick. According to the narrator 'husband', such services make a man love and desire to return to his home and see his goodwife. It was one of the strange anomalies of Anne's life that her position as a duchess could encompass the supervision of pest removal and the dispensation of justice.

In June 1475, Edward launched a joint attack on France with the Burgundians, with the intention of dividing the country between them. Richard went with him, bringing 1,000 archers and over 100 men-at-arms, mustered from his northern estates. However, the men were to see no fighting. Terms were quickly reached with Louis XI, resulting in a large pension for Edward and various gifts for Richard and Clarence, who dined with the French king on 31 August. Far from being cowardly, as some later writers have asserted, Edward had made sufficient gains without needing to spill a drop of his men's blood. Rather than being disappointed by this, Gloucester would have been pleased to spare his men, who were Yorkshire locals, known to him personally from the farms and estates surrounding his own and probably indentured to him. Anne may have spent the intervening time waiting in London, where the Gloucesters were reunited. She was certainly there between 3 and 6 December, when payments to city merchants were made in both their names. They could well have remained in the capital to celebrate Christmas that year.

The couple were regular visitors to London, dictated by Richard's seat on the royal council. On 9 November 1477, he attended a feast hosted by his nephew, Prince Edward, soon after his seventh birthday. On Clarence's demise, the following year, Richard and Anne came into possession again of the Erber, Anne's old childhood base in the capital. At some point between 1475 and 1483, the Gloucesters leased Crosby Place, a house built in 1466 in Bishopsgate. An extant floor plan shows how the building encroached into the space occupied by the Priory of St Helen, comprising a number of small chambers, rear garden, outer court, parlour and hall, which had a carved ceiling and minstrels' gallery. In disrepair by the twentieth century, the house was demolished and rebuilt, brick by brick, in Chelsea in 1910. According to More, Richard held informal council meetings at Crosby Place and it was there that his association with the Duke of Buckingham developed. The Gloucesters would also have had access to the London home of Richard's mother, Cecily, at Baynard's Castle and perhaps Coldharbour House, which remained in the family after Clarence vacated it.

In July 1476, all three York brothers attended the re-interment of their father Richard, Duke of York, and their brother Edmund, Earl of Rutland, in the mausoleum at the church of St Mary and All Saints, at their childhood home of Fotheringhay. The family had come a long way since their deaths at Wakefield over fifteen years earlier. The Chester Herald, Thomas Whiting, described how Richard, dressed in mourning, followed the funeral chariot, which was draped in black, up to the church door, where Edward IV and Clarence were waiting. Their father's body had been dressed in a suitably regal ermine furred mantle and draped with cloth of gold. Anne would have been waiting inside the church, alongside her mother-in-law Cecily and sisters-in-law Elizabeth, the queen, and Isabel, then six months pregnant. After masses were said, seven pieces of cloth of gold were laid to make a cross upon his body before it was interred in the choir. His son, Rutland, was buried in the Lady chapel. Around 5,000 local people came to receive arms and the following banquet, held in the king's pavilion, was rumoured to have fed 20,000, for which the bill was in excess of £300. It was probably the last time Anne and Isabel were together.

It was around Christmas 1476 when bad news arrived at Middleham. Two and a half months after giving birth, Isabel, Duchess of Clarence, had died at Tewkesbury, aged only twenty-five. The cause was probably complications following childbirth; perhaps some sort of delayed post-partum fever, an illness contracted during her period of recovery, or else consumption. It is likely that her two surviving children, the 3½-year old Margaret and Edward, not yet two, came into Anne's care at some point soon afterwards, perhaps at Sheriff Hutton, where Richard would establish a 'household' for them. If they did not arrive at once, they probably found their way there soon after the bizarre events that overcame their father. After his wife's death, Clarence's behaviour, always volatile and grandiose, became increasingly strange. In April 1477, he ordered the arrest of Ankarette Twynho, an elderly gentlewoman who had been in attendance on his wife and whom he now claimed had poisoned her. Dragged from her house, she was brought from Somerset to Warwick where, four days later, she was tried and sentenced to death. The jury heard that she had supposedly 'given to the said Isabel a venomous drink of ale mixed with poison, of which the latter sickened until the Sunday before Christmas'. Considering that this draught had apparently been administered on 16 October, ten days after Isabel delivered her last child, it took a long time to take effect. Regardless of this, the old woman was dead within three hours of her conviction, being hanged from the city gallows.

After this incident, Clarence became convinced that none less than King Edward himself was seeking to poison him 'as a candle is consumed by burning'. When three members of his household were arrested on the charge of 'imagining the king's death' and suffered the full fate of traitors at Tyburn, Clarence disrupted a meeting of the Privy Council and tried to petition them against his brother. For the king, who had forgiven his many various acts of treachery, this was the final straw. That July, Edward summoned him to Westminster, where he was charged with dangerous conduct and sent to the Tower. He languished there until January, when a Bill of Attainder accused him of plotting to usurp the throne and threatening the lives of Edward's family by spreading rumours that the king used witchcraft and that he was illegitimate. On February 16, Clarence met his end in the Tower. Richard was undeniably involved, as was every lord on the council who heard the evidence and passed the Bill. As with the death of Henry VI, the responsibility was ultimately Edward's. The legend that Clarence was drowned in a butt of Malmsey wine was first mentioned by Italian diplomat, Mancini, over a century before Shakespeare wrote his version. Edward had been very forgiving when it came to Warwick and Clarence's treachery: now, the duke had simply pushed his luck too far.

The year of Clarence's execution also saw Richard and Anne taking a step closer to realising their religious plans. The role of a leading local magnate and his wife had a crucial spiritual dimension, placing them at the forefront of local worship and as important observers of holy days of the Catholic calendar. The duke and duchess had a strong connection with their local church, the twelfth-century St Mary and Alkelda at Middleham, naming each of the stalls in turn after their favourite saints. Anne, no doubt, played a part in this and their choices may reveal something further about each of them, betraying a combination of military and domestic roles. As a seasoned commander of the recent wars, Richard would have been drawn to St George, England's national saint and a prominent military figure who was traditionally invoked before battle. Also, St Barbara, the patron saint of artillerymen and explosives, along with St Catherine, was thought to protect against sudden, unplanned death.

A more domestic note was struck by the inclusion of St Anthony, patron of lost articles, and St Ninian, a fourth-century Scottish saint associated with traditional healing miracles, including one where he healed a deformed boy after appearing to his parents in a dream. Richard's connections with Durham may have led to the selection of St Cuthbert, endowed with healing and insight, as well as for his charm and generosity to the poor. In the early 1480s, the duke may have followed the long-standing tradition of carrying the saint's banner into battle against the Scots. Also included was St Winifred, particularly associated with the Beauchamps, which Anne F. Sutton suggests was at the personal devotion and knowledge of Anne.[16] During 1483–84, Caxton would publish a life of St Winifred, possibly under Anne's patronage.

The Gloucesters also chose St Catherine, a popular saint of the day; the Cambridge college bearing her name was founded 1473. A princess, she had a large female following and was considered an exemplar for intercession, the mediatory role that was desirable in medieval wives, duchesses and queens. Pisan and other contemporary writers held Catherine up as an example of wifely virtue and a role model for young women. Like two other women included in the Gloucester's choices, she was esteemed for her virginity. St Mary the Virgin was another traditional choice, with probably the most powerful of all English saintly cults of the medieval period. She was also a sympathetic figure to mothers although, interestingly, the Gloucesters' selection includes none of the other saints that were commonly associated with conception and pregnancy. Anne can hardly have given up hope of conceiving another child by 1478, at the age of only twenty-two. The latest estimates for the arrival of Edward place his birth only a year before this, so perhaps the spectre of infertility had not yet raised its head.

Richard planned to establish chantry colleges at Middleham and Barnard Castle, where prayers would be said for the salvation of his kin and kind. In 1478, he received a grant to elevate St Mary and Alkelda to the status of college, with places for a dean and six secular priests. However, his premature death curtailed the development of these. Through the period of his marriage and into his reign, he was a regular visitor at Durham Cathedral which, in 1474–76 and 1478–79, recorded various lengths of cloth being required to furnish the table when he was fed. Anne would have accompanied him at that time, or when he made offerings, as king, on 16 May, leaving behind a gift of a robe of blue velvet, embroidered with large gold lions. In 1476, Anne became a lay sister of the eleventh-century Durham Priory. The priory's library had been considerably developed under Prior John of Washington, who collected documents about the establishment's history and also extended and repaired the buildings. Both the duke and duchess would also have been regulars at York Minster, whenever they visited the city, attending mass and making donations. Certainly Richard intended to be buried in York, for which purpose he intended to found a chantry chapel, where, customarily, Anne would lie beside him. When she predeceased him in 1485 though, those plans were forgotten or abandoned.

Richard and Anne were staying at Sheriff Hutton in autumn 1480 when they received news that the Scots were planning an invasion in retaliation for a raiding party he had led across the border that summer. By November, Parliament had made the decision to invade and preparations were begun for a counter-attack, with Richard receiving £10,000 to provide wages for his men. As the newly appointed Lieutenant of the North, it would have fallen to Richard to lead the offensive but Edward toyed with the idea himself, prolonging the actual invasion. In the meanwhile, a number of small skirmishes continued along the borders, during one of which the English unsuccessfully besieged the town of Berwick. Richard took an active part in these conflicts, fighting alongside his childhood friends, Richard Ratcliffe and Francis Lovell, whom he knighted for their loyal services, near Berwick in 1482. When Edward finally relinquished the idea of fronting the army, control fell to Richard. Here, the duke had another opportunity to prove his military prowess as commander of a major campaign. The brother and rival of King James III, the Duke of Albany, fled to England in the spring of 1482 and signed a treaty at Fotheringhay that June, supporting the invasion. In return, he would replace his brother as a sympathetic Yorkist ruler. By mid-July, a force of 20,000 men, largely gathered from the North, crossed the border under Richard's leadership. Berwick opened its gates, James III was taken prisoner and the English force occupied Edinburgh. At the point of success, Albany showed reluctance to assume the throne and Richard made him swear an oath of loyalty. The armies then returned to the border and disbanded. It was hardly an invasion that covered the duke in glory, even less successful than Edward's 1475 French offensive. Richard would have stopped over at Middleham on the way back, before proceeding to Westminster, to give his account of events to the Parliament that met that autumn. Anne must have been relieved to see him home, safe and sound. Perhaps she travelled south with him, to spend Christmas 1482 in the capital.

Some sources, like Croyland, claim the court was at Westminster for the festive season, while others place it at the extensively rebuilt Eltham Palace, where 2,000 people were fed daily by the new kitchens. According to Croyland, the forty-year-old portly Edward was still cutting a fine figure, 'frequently appearing clad in a great variety of most costly garments, of quite a different cut to those which had been usually seen heitherto [sic] in our kingdom'. Always interested in fashion, the 'full and hanging' robe sleeves, 'greatly resembling a monk's frock' and lined with fur, may have been the latest Burgundian look. The chronicler was not present, but it sounded as if he had spoken with someone who had been, who described the outfit as giving the 'elegant' king 'a new and distinguished air'. The phrase 'you might have seen, in those days', reminds us this was written retrospectively, after Edward's decease; in places there is a wistful nostalgia for the old regime, with 'the royal court presenting no other appearance than such as fully befits a most mighty kingdom, filled with riches and with people of almost all nations'.

Richard was in London for the session of Edward's last Parliament, which commenced sitting on 20 January 1483, in order to discuss the wars against Scotland and France. Taxes were granted for the protection of the realm, making an invasion of some kind appear inevitable. Following the Scottish campaign, the young duke could anticipate leading it, perhaps at the head of the 4,000 archers that were offered to Brittany in defence against France. Richard left London towards the end of February and arrived at York on 6 March. Presumably he was back at Middleham with Anne for Easter, which fell three weeks later. As events transpired, there would be no offensive against the French or Scots. The conquest of the English throne would be achieved from within.

10

Crisis
Summer 1483

We largely shewed our trewe entente and mynde in al such thinges[1]

Three months in the spring and early summer of 1483 were to propel Anne from her quiet Middleham estate back into the centre of national politics. While the events following the death of Edward IV and accession of his son, the twelve-year-old Edward V, have been well documented and analysed, Anne's role in them is less clear. Historians are divided over her husband's intentions and motivation but Anne's understanding of the process which made her queen is just as mystifying. Perhaps, at the time, she was not required to understand. However, it remains that Anne did accept the throne, whether or not the exercise of personal choice lay within in her control. Some may see her as complicit in all that Richard did, while others may judge that she was carried along on the wave of his changes. Did she, for example, know what happened to the Princes in the Tower? Did she wonder about the death of William Hastings? How did she resolve such questions in her mind, or in discussion with Richard? Should she share any of the 'guilt' that tradition has ascribed to her husband?

Anne was not in London for the months of April and May. She remained in Yorkshire after Richard had left and did not arrive until three weeks before he was proclaimed king and she, by extension, queen. Much had changed during that time, possibly including her husband's goals. How did he explain to her that her position was about to alter so drastically? It is impossible to determine how she viewed his actions, without ascertaining exactly what those actions were. Many interpretations of that summer's events assume that the steps Richard took were 'wrong', and that his acquisition of the throne was an act of 'usurpation'. This cannot simply be accepted without further exploration. To state the obvious, while Richard's behaviour may be analysed, his motivation can only be cause for speculation. His potential subterfuge makes it difficult to pinpoint the turning points of his ambition, yet secrecy had been expedient to the kingmaking activities of his mentor Warwick and those of both Richard's elder brothers. Anointed monarchs and teenage princes had lost their lives in the dynastic struggle: enemies were executed without legal trial and brother turned against brother. Richard's coup must be considered in the context of their struggles for control of the country: were any of his 'crimes' significantly worse than theirs?

Ultimately, one question comes to dominate all others: was Richard motivated by personal ambition or a sense of genuine entitlement? Was he a ruthless opportunist who employed violence and exploited the weak in order to seize the throne? Or, with an unblemished record of loyalty to his brother, did his belief in his nephew's illegitimacy dictate the changing course of his duty? His actions in 1483 appear to be out of character, unless he genuinely believed he was in danger from a Wydeville plot. Was he driven by the need to remove his enemies and prevent a return to the instability of civil war, or he had previously concealed his true nature? Even then, we cannot know how far the husband confided in his wife; how much was explicitly stated and how much was understood? Only one person knew the extent to which Richard shared his motives with Anne; that was Richard himself.

For Anne, it all started on 16 April 1483. The spring flowers were already starting to brighten the surrounding fields and buds on the trees were bursting into bloom when a letter arrived at Middleham Castle. King Edward was dead. In fact, he had been dead for a week, soon to be buried in the splendid chapel he had left unfinished at Windsor. It was only Lord Hastings, veteran of so many battles at Richard's side, who had chosen to write to him and break the news. Official word had still to come from Westminster, although arrangements were being discussed for the succession of Richard's nephew, the twelve-year-old Edward. It has been suggested that the Gloucesters were surprised to learn that the king had died on 9 April, a week ago, yet word had not reached his son in Ludlow until 14 April. Considering that the distance from Ludlow to the capital is around 150 miles, in comparison with the 240 miles from Westminster to Middleham, the extra two days delay, for even the fastest of horseback riders, appears reasonable. There may have been no intention to exclude Richard. More unexpectedly, it transpired that, on his deathbed, Edward had named his brother as Protector. As the son of Elizabeth Wydeville, raised in Ludlow Castle by her brother Anthony, the young prince would automatically have come under the control of his Wydeville relations. In the days leading up to his death, knowing that his end was imminent, the king had attempted to bring about a reconciliation between his unpopular Wydeville in-laws and other members of his household, including his close friend Hastings. For Edward to have entrusted his son to Richard spoke volumes about his concerns regarding the influence of the queen's family. As the final surviving son of that Yorkist generation, Richard would have at once risen to the challenge of defending the inheritance.

The death of Edward IV had been unexpected. At forty-one, he was no longer the youthful, athletic figure who had dominated the battlefield and years of indulgence had significantly increased his girth. At some point in late March or early April, according to Mancini, the king had been fishing on the Thames, after which he had caught a cold. This was unremarkable in itself, as the river was the main thoroughfare of London and frequently used for travel by the royal family. When he returned home, though, the illness worsened and he took to his bed. A number of suggestions have been made regarding the causes of his decline and death. The French chronicler Thomas Basin stated that the king had upset his digestive system by eating a surfeit of fruits and vegetables. Commines believed it was due to Edward's disappointment regarding the breakup of the intended marriage between his daughter Elizabeth and the Dauphin, but this had happened the previous year. Virgil described the illness as an 'unknown disease' and Dr John Rae, in 1913, suggested pneumonia because contemporaries say that Edward lay on his left side. Commines also said that Edward had a stroke. Whatever claimed his life, it set in motion a chain of extraordinary events.

It is interesting that a false report of Edward's death had already reached York on 6 April, 'in so authentic a form that no doubt was entertained of its truth'.[2] At this point, there were three days still to go before Edward actually died. According to the municipal records, the mayor received a message from the dean on a Sunday, inviting him and the aldermen to attend a dirge on Monday in the minster and a requiem service on Tuesday. However, a mistake in the dates or the translation must have occurred, as 9 April fell on a Monday that year, so if the message was dispatched on a Sunday, it must have been on Sunday 8 April. This is probably not as sinister as has been suggested and may have been an exaggerated report of his illness or else a result of the fifteenth century's imperfect communication networks. On 10 April, Edward's body was carried to the chapel of St Stephen for eight days of obsequies, after which it was taken to St

George's at Windsor and buried on 19 April. It was not until after this that Richard ordered a funeral mass to be performed in York Minster, on 21 April. The eighteenth-century Ricardian and Prime Minister, Horace Walpole, wondered whether Richard would have 'loitered in York' if he intended to seize the throne; in fact, Gloucester was already on his way south.

Richard had only 'loitered' a little in the North, awaiting official instructions and planning his next move. Hastings' letter probably informed him that Anthony Wydeville, Earl Rivers, had been instructed to bring the young Edward V to London by 1 May. Although it was essential to secure the safety of the new king, for Richard, this may have confirmed Edward's last-minute concerns of Wydeville domination. The Coronation of Edward V was being treated as a matter of urgency, perhaps in order to minimise Gloucester's power, which was commensurate only with the period of preparation. Once the crown had been placed on his nephew's head, Richard would be marginalised, then no one would be able to challenge the Wydeville hegemony. Surely it is not unreasonable to speculate that, at this point, he and Anne discussed the matter and she had given her opinions on the clan which her father had so loathed. The Wydevilles had been one of the key reasons for the rift that had opened between Warwick and Edward IV, so Anne had little reason to love them. Still waiting at Middleham, Richard wrote letters of condolence to the London Council, to the queen and to her brother, Earl Rivers, who had been the boy's guardian at Ludlow Castle. Then it was a matter of waiting for the reply. Hastings had urged him to travel south and 'secure the person' of the new king but no official word had come from Westminster. The Gloucesters were both still in Yorkshire while the old king's funeral went ahead, which is perhaps what prompted Richard to arrange a service in York, for 21 April, as a comment on his exclusion. Then another letter arrived, from the Duke of Buckingham, who also bore ill will to the Wydevilles, having been forced into a child marriage with the queen's sister. Buckingham offered his troops and services, so Richard agreed to meet him on the march south to join with the king's procession from Ludlow to London.

First, though, Richard went to York for the ceremony. As his duchess, and Edward's sister-in-law, Anne must have gone with him to pay her respects. Only ill health would have excused her from missing such an event. On 20 April they rode out from Middleham, accompanied by 300 men, and the following day Richard led the nobility of the region in swearing an oath of loyalty to Edward V. Anne would also have pledged her loyalty. Two days later, Richard left York for

Nottingham, where he planned to meet Buckingham and travel south. Anne probably returned to Middleham, to pack up her household in advance of her journey to London. What exactly had Richard confided in her at this point? What exactly was there to confide? Based on his behaviour, purely on external appearances, she would have anticipated attending the imminent Coronation of her nephew, Edward V, not that of her husband and herself. Richard's private intentions can only be a matter of speculation at this point. If he had already conceived any doubts concerning the future rule of Edward V, one indication of this may have been the size of the army he raised. Elizabeth Wydeville had agreed to the council's suggestion that her son be accompanied to London by a minimal number of troops; by planning to intercept them with more men, Richard must have either considered this to be inadequate provision or already intended to overrule them. At Middleham, packing up the necessaries for her journey, how long did Anne anticipate remaining in London? By the time she arrived in the capital, on 5 June, her husband's motives had already been called into question.

When Anne arrived in London, she and Richard retired to Crosby Place. No doubt she was soon apprised of recent events – if he had not already communicated with her by letter – and must have quickly grasped what the implications were for her future. Richard explained how he had met with Buckingham on the way to London. There, something passed between them that either changed or confirmed his attitudes towards the Wydevilles. Perhaps he became convinced they were attempting to prevent him from accepting his role as Protector or else minimise his influence. Perhaps their vision for Edward V's reign did not contain him. After spending what appeared to be a routine evening with Anthony Wydeville, Earl Rivers, Richard had ordered his arrest the following morning. He had then intercepted and assumed charge of the royal procession, which he conducted to the Bishop of London's Palace, summoning key citizens to swear loyalty to his nephew. Elizabeth Wydeville had fled into sanctuary with her children, which publicly demonstrated the depths of her mistrust of her brother-in-law. There is little indication, though, that any bad blood had existed between the queen's family and Gloucester prior to this. In fact, it was with Anne's family that they had, historically, been at odds. As the wife of the Protector, the Wydevilles may have feared she would seek to restrict their control of the boy king, as vengeance for her father's death, or even to seek to punish those she blamed.

Soon after arriving in London, Richard had met with the council, which had voted to move Edward V to the Tower of London and had confirmed his sovereign power, 'just like another king'. The peers of the realm had been summoned to the capital for 18 June, in plenty of time for the Coronation, which was scheduled for four days later. It was then that Richard had begun to meet with various councillors at Crosby Place, where he was now imparting this news to Anne, while the others lords continued to meet at Westminster. Did Richard take this step because he distrusted some of the members, or was he trying to cause a division among them? It was probably both, and, unsurprisingly, when the secret meetings became public knowledge, they aroused suspicion. Paul Kendall described how 'unease, restlessness, and doubt' gathered 'like mist at Westminster and the Tower. It is a thing of dark corners and the rustle of whispers, insubstantial but pervasive.' To discover Richard's intentions, Edward IV's old friend, Lord Hastings, had employed his lawyer, William Catesby, to attend his Crosby Place meetings and report the content to him. Some had even begun to suspect Gloucester of conspiring against the king and doubted his trustworthiness. A surviving fragment from the commonplace book of a London merchant indicated that 'divers imagined the death of the Duke of Gloucester', and Hastings' name was rumoured to be among them. In turn, Richard had used Buckingham to test Hastings' loyalty and, according to More, had discovered that the lord would accept Richard as Protector, but not as king, responding 'with terrible words'. This time-scale implies that Richard had already made his decision to seize the throne before Anne arrived in London. The explanation her husband gave her on the night of 5 June 1483 was determined by the nature of their marriage. If it was a strong partnership, equal as far as the times permitted, Richard would have been open with her as far as he could. If not, it may be going too far even to suggest he confided in her at all. Her presence and silent complicity may have simply been all that he required. But, if he actually told her, at this point, that he intended to become king, what impression did that make on her? Did she question his right? Or did she, at once, set her mind to helping overcome certain obstacles? Unfortunately, it is impossible now to know.

Anne was at Crosby House during the dramatic events of June 1483. About a week after her arrival, Lord Hastings paid the price of his loyalty to Edward V. As late as 20 May, he had been confirmed in his role of Chancellor and Richard, as Protector, had promoted him to Master of the Mint. There is no doubt that Richard was very good at 'keeping his powder dry', thus it was a surprise to Hastings when, summoned to the council meeting of 13 June, he found himself accompanied by an armed knight. The meeting was most famously portrayed by More and Shakespeare but the truth behind that morning's strange events is still baffling. At 9 o'clock, a smiling Richard entered the Tower, where his councillors were assembled. In conversation, he remarked that he would like some strawberries from Bishop Morton's Holborn garden, which were sent for. He soon left, but returned at about 10.30 a.m., his manner completely changed, claiming that witchcraft had been used against him and ordering the arrest of Hastings, Morton and Rotherham, Bishop of York. All sources agree that Hastings was executed within minutes; the Great Chronicle stated that it was carried out 'without any process of law or lawful examination', while Croyland said that innocent blood had been shed, 'and in this way, without justice or judgement, the three strongest supporters of the new king were removed'. Explanations for these events vary. On one side, Richard is accused of inventing a plot against himself in order to remove a man who would block his route to the throne. Hastings had employed spies against Richard and would not support his claim over that of Edward V. Therefore, Hastings had to go.

However, Richard may well have genuinely believed that witchcraft was being used against him. During the course of the morning, he began to feel its effects. It is possible that the dish of strawberries, brought from Morton's garden, produced a genuine allergic reaction which caused Richard's arm to wither and other physical symptoms to develop. Bizarre as this may sound, allergic reactions caused by the proteins in strawberries can produce tingling limbs, breathing difficulties and red, puffy, itchy skin. These symptoms usually occur within two hours of eating the fruit, beginning with swelling of the lips and tingling in the mouth. More's account has Richard fretting, frowning and 'knawing at his lips'. Food allergies can emerge even after an individual has eaten a particular dish for years. When the body's tolerance level is reached, the symptoms are triggered. Strawberries would have been seasonal, and therefore a rare treat. It is quite possible that Richard had a latent allergy to the fruit which emerged that June, causing the sudden physical responses in his body which he could only explain as witchcraft. Fifteenth-century people of all classes were deeply superstitious and believed that magic could be used to good and evil ends. Elizabeth Wydeville and her mother had both been accused and cleared of sorcery in 1469–70. More recently, Clarence had claimed that his brother Edward was conspiring against him through the medium of magic. It cannot be ruled out that, anticipating attacks from the Wydeville clan, Richard believed himself to have fallen victim to poison or enchantment. He stated that witchcraft had 'wasted his body'. Perhaps he genuinely believed it had. The usual targets for such accusations were female. Richard had pointed the finger at Morton, Hastings and his mistress, Jane Shore, the one-time love of Edward IV. However, only Hastings lost his life.

The intended day of Edward V's Coronation came and went. Soon afterwards, Dr Ralph Shaa, brother of the Mayor of London, delivered the sermon 'Bastard Slips Should Not Take Deep Root' at St Paul's Cross. As relayed by Mancini, the word spread across London that the 'progeny of King Edward should be instantly eradicated, for neither had he been a legitimate king, nor could his issue be so'. Anne may have accompanied her husband and Buckingham to St Paul's Cross to hear the sermon and her mother-in-law, Cecily Neville, may even have been with them, having come to London to attend her grandson's Coronation. How did she react, when forced to choose between her son and her grandson? Were the women surprised at what they heard or was this a secret from the family closet? It was certainly in Richard's interests that Edward V should be removed; the boy would have reached his majority within a few years and may have sought revenge on Richard for the death of his guardian Earl Rivers and other uncle, John Grey. One person with whom Richard had been consulting in his private meetings at Crosby Place was Richard Stillington, Bishop of Bath and Wells. Some time that May or June, the bishop had 'unburdened his conscience' to Richard, stating that in the early 1460s, Edward IV had been pre-contracted, if not actually already married, to Dame Eleanor Butler, *née* Talbot, who was now conveniently dead. The result was the legal confirmation that Edward's children could not inherit the throne: 'All the issue and children of the said king ... be bastards and unable ... to claim anything by inheritance.' This made Richard the next direct Yorkist heir.

Most subsequent evaluations of Richard's character have rested on the integrity of Bishop Stillington. The credibility of his word determines whether Richard is seen as a dutiful son of York or a manipulative and murdering usurper. The report of Edward's pre-contract was in keeping with what was known of his character; after all, he had married Elizabeth Wydeville in secret and bedded many other women on the basis of unsubstantiated promises. If Stillington had held on to this information for twenty years, what prompted him to publicise it now? There was another possible source though, dating from a more recent scandal. The bishop had been closely associated with the Duke of Clarence, even spending time with him in prison in 1478. During this time, the duke may have passed on this information, either as a genuine family secret, or part of his unstable accusations against his brother. Ironically, then, Richard's replacement of Edward's heirs was perpetrated by Clarence from beyond the grave. On the other hand, the whole story may have been concocted one night at Crosby House. Richard and Stillington had hit upon the single weapon that would bring the late king's family down, by exploiting the vices in which Edward was known to have indulged. The story had credibility. Did Anne play any part in it? Was she tucked up in bed asleep or sitting at the fireside, listening as they plotted? Did she contribute any fine details? If the story was an invention, then it was on the bishop's shoulders that the unlawful reign of Richard and Anne would rest.

After Dr Shaa's sermon, events moved quickly. Buckingham spoke for an hour and a half to the Mayor and Aldermen of London at the Guildhall, explaining the pre-contract and stating that kingship was 'no child's office'. When the council was recalled to Westminster, Mancini relates that it was still in the expectation of Edward V's imminent Coronation. Instead they met Buckingham, armed with three reasons for the invalidity of Edward's marriage to Elizabeth Wydeville. Firstly, it had been made without the consent of the lords and through witchcraft; secondly, it was conducted in private without the edition of banns and, finally, it was bigamous, since Edward had already made a pre-contract with another woman. There were also rumours, once employed by Warwick, that Edward IV himself had been the result of an affair his mother had conducted with a Norman archer. The dates provided to support such a view are not conclusive, given the variation in individual terms of pregnancy and there seems little reason to suspect that a woman of Cecily's breeding and stature would jeopardise her family bloodline.

Now Richard moved against the Wydevilles. At Pontefract, Richard Ratcliffe, his friend from Middleham days, had assembled Elizabeth Wydeville's brother, Earl Rivers, her son Thomas Grey and Thomas Vaughan, loyal to Edward V. On 24 June, they were condemned to death, without trial, for plotting against Richard. None were allowed to speak in their defence and they were executed the following day, to the universal condemnation of all contemporary writers. The Croyland chronicler observes that 'innocent blood ... was shed on the occasion of this sudden change'. According to Rous, they were 'unjustly and cruelly put to death, being lamented by everyone, and innocent of the deed for which they were charged'. Thomas More states that their only fault was in being 'good men, too true to the king', while Polydore Vergil says that their only offence was to stand in the way of Richard's ambitions. This act remains hard to defend. Richard may have believed in a plot against him, or else, by this point, the rapid removal of his enemies was expedient under any charge.

Anne was probably at Richard's side in Barnard Castle, the home of her mother-in-law, when Parliament came to petition him to accept the throne. Once again, queenship was within her reach, closer than it had ever been. Was she excited by this? Back in 1471, she had played a critical role in her father's royal ambitions. Her marriage to Edward of Westminster had made her Princess of Wales and could have resulted in her rule at Westminster. Did she now scheme along with her husband in order to achieve the same goal? She had no love for the Wydevilles, whose father had been her deadly enemy, and may have viewed them as the justifiable casualties of a three-decade-long war. Did she see that moment in June 1483 as the culmination of everything her father had worked for? Was she even impatient with her husband? Richard did not accept the throne at once. When the lords returned the next day, he 'reluctantly' agreed to become king. Did Anne 'reluctantly' celebrate becoming queen? In reality, was she closer to a Lady Macbeth figure than the pathetic pawn some novels have portrayed her as?

The version of events presented by later chroniclers upholds the villainous, murderous Richard who is familiar from Shakespeare's play. Like the Bard, the majority of writers date his ambition from the decease of Edward and attribute it to the classic character flaws of tragedy. Vergil wrote that, as soon as the news reached Middleham, he 'began to be kyndlyd with an ardent desyre of soveraigntie' and 'determynyd to assay his purposyd spytefull practyse by subtyltie and sleight'. Maybe as early as the middle of April, Richard and Anne were already plotting their route to the throne, considering whom they might trust and who needed to be removed. According to true dramatic convention, Vergil's Richard's 'owne frawd, wicked and mischievous intent, his owne desperate boldenes, maketh him frantyke and mad'. Perhaps Anne was also consumed by this driving ambition, seeing a final chance to achieve what her father had aimed at for so long. The Croyland chronicler was in no doubt regarding the identity of 'the sole mover at London of such seditious and disgraceful proceedings', but had these moves already been carefully rehearsed at Middleham? Fabyan emphasised Richard's duplicity, as he was able to behave 'so covertly in al his matters, that fewe understode his wicked purpose', although who else but Anne would have numbered among those 'few'? This view of Richard is well known and hardly needs repeating. As an interpretation of his wife, Lady Macbeth-like, it is fairly unsubstantiated, although motivation and behaviour are hard to substantiate when sources do not survive or never existed. As his wife, Anne's duty was to support Richard in all his endeavours, even if they ran contrary to legal or moral codes. Still the question remains of whether these 'crimes' should be considered as such. If Richard initially acted in good faith and was loyal to his nephews before receiving news of their illegitimacy, then he committed no crime. If he responded to a perceived threat from the Wydevilles, again, no law was broken. It would have been reprehensible if he had invented the witchcraft and pre-contract stories in order to bring about his enemies' swift defeat. Fabricating these pieces of 'evidence' to condemn others for his own personal advancement would be criminal indeed. If Vergil is correct regarding his ambition, then his actions in the summer of 1483 did constitute a usurpation. Yet if Edward's marriage had been invalid, perhaps a usurpation was exactly what was needed.

This was nothing new. Usurpation had been a vital skill in the Kingmaker's repertoire. The most recent precedent had been in 1399, when Henry of Bolingbroke usurped and probably murdered his cousin, Richard II, giving rise to decades of conflict. In Gloucester's lifetime, his own brother and Warwick had deposed Henry VI, before the earl tipped Edward off the throne and reinstated the Lancastrian, followed by the Yorkist restoration and Henry VI's death. If Richard had usurped a fully grown man, he would not have been the target of such contemporary and subsequent opprobrium. However, the two obstacles that blocked his path to the throne were children. His nephews, Edward and Richard, were aged twelve and nine in June 1483 when they disappeared in the Tower. What did Anne feel about this? A twenty-first-century response may begin with Anne's motherhood: surely, as a mother she could not condone the incarceration and murder of her nephews, barely older than her own boy? Yet this is to transpose modern values onto past events, to apply culturally constructed stereotypes, such as the 'mother', to an ambitiously driven aristocracy, with a unique standard of conduct. It does not follow that a royal mother of the fifteenth century would behave in the same way as a twenty-first-century 'mum': the acquiescence of Elizabeth Wydeville to Richard III demonstrates that. Perhaps Richard told Anne some acceptable lie regarding the boys; perhaps she chose to believe it. Maybe she guessed at their fate, or was even fully aware of it. Just as Margaret of Anjou fought like a lioness for the rights of her son, Anne may have recognised that certain obstacles had to be removed if her own boy was to become king. This possibility may be difficult to accept, yet it would make Anne a typical queen of her day. She cannot be retrospectively assigned the scruples of a modern woman in order to please modern sensibilities.

Rumours of the boys' death began to spread almost at once. While gossip is notoriously unreliable, it can give an indication of popular beliefs and opinions about the king and whether people believed him capable of the act. Mancini, author of *The Occupation of the Throne by Richard III*, may have got some of his information from a fellow Italian, Dr Argentine, who was in attendance on Princes Edward and Richard in the Tower. According to his account, the elder boy 'like a victim prepared for sacrifice, sought remission of his sins daily, in confession and penance because he believed that death was facing him'. This was also believed by Fabyan, who wrote that 'King Richard … put to death the two children of King Edward, for which cause he lost the hearts of the people', and was repeated in Weinreich's Danzig chronicle of 1483 and the speech of Guillaume de Rochefort at Tours in January 1484. Later, Croyland would write that 'the people of the south and … west … began to murmur greatly, to form assemblies … many were in secret, some quite open' about the princes' fate. More described people weeping in the streets when they thought of Edward V and his brother. One easy way to dispel these reports would have been for Richard to produce the princes and prove his innocence. Alternatively, he could have claimed they had died that summer or autumn from some illness or accident, which would at least have made their deaths palatable, even if it had been a lie. Given the extent of Richard's intelligence and abilities, it is surprising that he failed to address this directly. However, he cannot have known the sympathy that the boys would evince and may have assumed that a general acceptance of their illegitimacy would quash public interest in their fates. In this he was mistaken.

No modern court of law would convict Richard of killing the Princes in the Tower. The jury in a televised mock trial of 1984, examining the evidence presented by expert witnesses, returned a verdict of not guilty. As there is no conclusive source to ascertain his guilt or innocence, the balance of probabilities suggests they met their end soon after their last sighting, in the late summer. It seems most likely that they were put to death in the Tower during Richard's absence in the North; perhaps he deliberately removed himself from the capital for that purpose. It is also possible that he did not issue a direct order but that a servant of his understood that the boys needed to be dispatched and acted independently, presenting the king on his return with a *fait accompli*. Richard's servant, Sir James Tyrell, was at the Royal Wardrobe at the start of September, to collect clothing for Edward's investiture and, according to More, made a confession in 1501, perhaps under torture, that he was responsible for their deaths.

The investiture of his son Edward as Prince of Wales on 8 September was certainly seen by Elizabeth Wydeville as incontrovertible proof that her sons had been killed. More describes her grief when the news was broken to her in his usual melodramatic terms, yet the elevation of Richard's son was fairly decisive. There is no doubt that the innocent boys' murders were tragic. It would be wonderful to believe in one of the romantic tales of their escape and for decisive evidence to prove they lived long, fulfilled lives in some remote European court. Lambert Simnel and Perkin Warbeck, the pretenders to the throne who emerged under the reign of Henry Tudor, were not of the royal blood. They both made verifiable confessions of their own humble origins and the circumstances that propelled them into the public eye. Those contemporary heads of state who welcomed and 'recognised' them did so out of political expediency and personal inclination. No convincing report of the princes' survival has ever been found so it would seem most likely that they died. The box of bones uncovered under the staircase of the White Tower in 1674 probably represents their hasty burial. The blame lies with Richard. Whatever his role in their demise, he was their king, uncle and protector, but he failed to protect them. As king, having given the orders for their incarceration, he had ultimate responsibility for their welfare, whether he gave the orders personally or not. If he ordered their deaths, Anne probably knew it.

Queen
July–December 1483

Kingdoms are but cares,
State is devoid of stay,
Riches are ready snares,
And hasten to decay.
Pleasure is a privy prick
Which vice doth still provoke;
Pomp, imprompt; and fame, a flame;
Power, a smoldering smoke,
Who meaneth to remove the rock
Out of the slimy mud,
Shall mire himself, and hardly 'scape
The swelling of the flood.[1]

Less than a month after her arrival in London, Anne was anticipating her Coronation. Events had moved very quickly and, for many, unexpectedly. Thomas More's stinging comment, over twenty years later, was that she and Richard were wearing borrowed robes; 'that solemnitie was furnished for the most part, with the self same prouision that was appointed for the Coronacioun of his nephew'.[2] More's criticism has both metaphorical and literal resonances, in a vein rather similar to the funeral 'baked meats' that Hamlet observes to re-emerge at his mother's wedding. Even if the existing arrangements that had been made for Edward V's ceremony were adapted, the seamstresses at least must have worked in considerable haste, sewing flat out to produce the royal robes, after Peter Courteys, Keeper of the Great Wardrobe, received their orders on 27 June. This allowed nine days for their commission before the Coronation day arrived, although it was not until 3 July that Richard and Anne exchanged gifts of 20 yards of purple cloth of gold decorated with garters and roses.[3] Alice Claver, an experienced silk worker and mantle weaver from London, was paid handsomely for her work on various Coronation pieces; she was paid 63s and 2d for making laces of Venetian gold and purple silk, with tassels and buttons, for the king's and queen's robes and a further 60s and 7d for the white silk and gold lace on Anne's mantle.[4] On 4 July, Richard and Anne travelled by barge from Westminster to the Tower, where they settled into the royal apartments. Security was tight, with Londoners forbidden from carrying arms and a curfew imposed of 10 p.m. This would have meant that Richard and Anne were present in the Tower at the same time as their nephews, the princes, who, if they were still alive at that point, may have been aware of the sudden flurry of activity.

The following day, 5 July, Anne and Richard rode out through the London streets to Westminster, followed by what Holinshed describes as a huge procession of earls, knights and dukes, although the chronicler was wrong when he stated that their son Edward rode with them. Anne's ushers, William Joseph and John Vavasour, preceded her, guiding the way for her litter, borne by two palfreys draped in white damask. The litter itself was also of the same material, with white cloth of gold garnished with ribbon and hung with bells. Inside, Anne sat with her hair loose, her head crowned in a gold circlet set with pearls and other precious stones. She wore white cloth of gold, with a cloak and train furred with ermine and trimmed with lace and tassels. After her 'henxmen' came four carriages carrying her waiting women: twelve great ladies and seven ladies of the queen's chamber. Anne was no stranger to bravery. In the midst of the exiled Lancastrians in France, and later at Tewkesbury, she had proved her mettle, but she had never before been on such public display. Now, as she watched the upturned faces that lined her route, she knew she would never again be able to escape the responsibility, scrutiny and dangers that her new role brought. She may have been reassured to see the loyal Northern soldiers stationed at key points throughout the length of their journey. Outside St Paul's, the procession paused while she was presented with a gift of 500 marks from the city, before continuing to Westminster, where she joined Richard to partake of wine and spices in the Great Chamber. This was probably the King's Chamber, later known as the Painted Chamber, lined with impressive Biblical wall paintings and with a state bed headed by a gilded panel depicting the Coronation of St Edward the Confessor. The image of the eleventh-century king looked out over the scene as Richard and Anne prepared to emulate the ritual.

That night, Anne slept alone. Richard was to carry out the traditional pre-Coronation ceremony of dubbing Knights of the Bath; the arrangements for Edward's Coronation had included forty-nine knights but the surviving documents for Richard's day mention only seventeen. When these details were drawn up in advance, the officer who committed them to paper was unclear about the final arrangements, including the king's intended whereabouts at the time. There may have been some doubt about the time-scale or how long he would stay at Barnard Castle[5] but, in the end, protocol was observed by Richard and Anne staying in the Tower, before proceeding to Westminster. This is again indicative of the haste of the occasion, even the uncertainty over whether it would go ahead. First, these knights served dinner to the royal couple, which was fish as it was a Friday. The menu consisted of two courses, comprising nine and twelve dishes each. The first contained salt and seawater fish dishes while the second was more ceremonial, with freshwater fish and set pieces in 'foil', decorated in silver and gold leaf. Many were served in sauces coloured red and yellow by saffron and other spices. That evening, Richard 'took a ceremonial bath', which was lined and draped with 22½ ells of linen, in order to prepare spiritually, along with vigils and prayers.[6]

The morning of 6 July 1483 dawned warmly down the Thames. As Anne woke in her chamber overlooking the river, she must have felt a thrill of excitement, tinged with surprise at the rapidity of the recent changes that had brought her to the capital in her husband's wake. Perhaps her mood was also coloured by uncertainty. Did she have questions of her own about how she had been catapulted from her quiet Middleham existence onto the centre stage of English politics, or the role her husband had played and the implications for the lives of her nieces and nephews? After she rose and dressed, she was a few short hours away from the ceremony that was to mark the pinnacle of her achievement and her father's long-cherished aim. What were her thoughts that morning, and in the hours before she was due to be crowned as England's queen? Her son, Edward, was too ill to be with them; did she know that on that special day, the Mayor and Aldermen of York rode out to Middleham to present the boy with food and wine? By 7 o'clock, the Coronation party assembled in Westminster Hall. Anne wore a royal surcoat and mantle, made from 56 yards of rich purple velvet, adorned with rings and tassels of gold, and a second gown in crimson, furred with ermine. As a duchess, she would previously have been entitled to wear a mantle of only 13 yards. She was barefoot and her hair hung long and loose.

Richard was keen to involve as many of his kinsmen and extended family in the day's proceedings as he could. As she processed with her husband along the special carpet of ray cloth, their Coronation robes matching, Anne would have recognised many familiar faces. Richard's transition from protector to king had been so swift and unexpected that it was wise to surround themselves with allies, fulfilling the ceremonial roles of the day and enjoying the feasting and celebrations that would follow. At the head of the procession trumpets sounded the way, followed by the heralds of arms wearing colourful tabards that depicted the Yorkist arms. Following them, the Bishop of Rochester, Edmund Audley, carried the cross, himself a grandson of Constance of York, who was Anne's maternal great-grandmother.[7] Next came Henry Percy, Earl of Northumberland, barcheaded and carrying the pointless sword naked in his hands, which signified mercy. Percy had been married to Maud Herbert, intended as a wife for the young Henry Tudor during his time as her father's ward. Percy was related to both his new rulers: his maternal aunt was Richard's mother, Cecily Neville, who was sister to Anne's grandfather, the Earl of Salisbury. After Percy came William Herbert, the Earl of Huntingdon and Pembroke, Maud's brother, who would marry Richard's illegitimate daughter Catherine in 1484. He was also brother-in-law to Richard through his first marriage to Mary Wydeville, sister of Elizabeth, Edward IV's wife and queen. He bore the gilt spurs signifying knighthood.

Following Huntingdon came the Earl of Bedford, carrying the holy relic of St Edward's staff. This title had previously been held by George Neville, the young nephew of Warwick, who had received the title on his engagement to Princess Elizabeth of York in 1470, although he was deprived of the title in 1478 and had died two months earlier. Next came Thomas Stanley, Earl of Derby. Having survived the council meeting of 13 June where Hastings had lost his life, he was now bearing the mace of constableship. Originally married to Warwick's sister, Eleanor Neville, he had been steward of Edward IV's household before marrying the Lancastrian Margaret Beaufort. Three ceremonial swords were carried out next. The first was in the hands of Edmund Grey, 1st Earl of Kent, who had married one of his sons to Elizabeth Wydeville's sister Anne, and another to Joan or Eleanor Wydeville, making him Richard's brother-in-law twice over. The second was borne by Richard's childhood friend from Middleham, Francis, Lord Lovell, with the third carried by Thomas Howard, Earl of Surrey. In the mid-1460s Howard was a 'henxman' under Edward IV, possibly training with George, Duke of Clarence, not at Middleham with Richard. Following them was the Duke of Suffolk, Richard's brother-in-law by his marriage to his sister Elizabeth, holding the sceptre of peace, and then his son, John de la Pole, Earl of Lincoln, with the ball and cross of monarchy. Finally, came the Duke of Norfolk, John Howard, who carried the crown in his hands.[8] For all this impressive array of family, the conflicts of their youth had made Richard and Anne very aware that blood ties did not equate to loyalty. After all, the surviving aristocracy of England were already assembled in the capital in expectation of a very different Coronation.

After his kinsmen came Richard, wearing his robes of purple velvet, with a canopy carried over his head, flanked by bishops and barons. Buckingham followed, carrying the king's train and a white staff for the office of Lord High Steward. Anne followed her husband, also under a canopy, dressed 'like to the king', and 'on hir head a rich coronet set with stones and pearle'.[9] She had her own train of earls, viscounts and dukes carrying the ceremonial sceptre and rod with the dove. Anne's crown was carried by the thirteen-year-old Earl of Wiltshire, Edward Stafford, whose mother was another Anne Neville, Richard's great-aunt and Anne's great-great-aunt. After him came 'manie fair gentlewomen': Margaret Beaufort, Countess of Richmond was the first, bearing the train, then the Duchesses of Norfolk and Suffolk, as well as Anne's aunt Alice FitzHugh, Warwick's sister and her daughter, Elizabeth Parr. There was also Lovell's wife, Anne; Katherine Neville, the queen's great aunt; Elizabeth Talbot, mother of Anne de Mowbray; Elizabeth de la Pole, the Duchess of Suffolk, who was Richard's sister; Lady Scrope of Masham and Upsall and Lora, Lady Mountjoy. The Coronation records also list ladies from aristocratic northern families including Anne's illegitimate half-sister Margaret Huddleston, who was, perhaps, around her own age or a little older. All had changed the blue gowns they had worn during the procession for the crimson velvet required by the ceremony.

The procession passed through the palace and into the abbey at the West End, while 'divers solemn songs' were sung as they headed to the altar. Many of those assembled to witness the day had taken part in the recent decades of conflict, many fighting on the opposing side, and had travelled to London in anticipation of seeing the twelve-year-old Edward V making the same journey. The rapidly made robes that had been created especially for him were hanging in a wardrobe somewhere in one of the palaces, never to be worn. Did any of those assembled wonder where he was or question his right? If they did, no one spoke up and interrupted proceedings. At the altar, Richard and Anne were 'shifted of their robes' and anointed. Then as king and queen they changed into cloth of gold, with Anne's train furred with ermine and miniver, comprising 56 yards of material. A stage had been erected, covered with red worsted, where two empty thrones sat waiting. Richard's was central but Anne's was to the left and slightly lower: it was the first time in centuries that a king had succeeded to the throne who was already married. Together, they took their seats alongside the Archbishop of Canterbury, Thomas Bourchier, in whose household Richard had spent time as a youth. Anne was given sceptre in her right hand and the rod with a dove in her left, while a ring was placed on the fourth finger of her right hand. They knelt to hear the mass sung and share one consecrated host, which was divided between them before making offerings at the shrine of St Edward.[10]

The formal proceedings over, Richard and Anne were officially king and queen. He exchanged Edward the Confessor's crown, Fabyan's 'regal diadem', for one of his own before they processed outside and entered their new chambers in Westminster Palace. Here, for a moment, the pair had a rare moment of privacy. What passed between them? Were they excited at this, the high point of their lives? Were they relieved that the proceedings had passed off without a hitch, that they were now the anointed monarchs of the realm? Perhaps it would be straying into the territory of the romantic novelist to suggest they embraced and called each other 'king' and 'queen'. Quite possibly, they had little time to celebrate: there was much to be done and Richard was a man of action. No doubt, as a pragmatist and realist, Anne was busy at his side straight away, as they prepared for the next stage of the day. They may have changed their clothes or taken refreshment, even rested for what would be a long night ahead.

However they used that brief window of time, Anne was now officially Queen of England. It was a position she had once thought to attain by her first marriage to Prince Edward but had then believed lost to her forever. Now she had come to it by accident, through circumstances of fate and the choices made by her husband. As Warwick's daughter, no doubt she had ambition and pride. As wife and consort to Richard, she would have been more than equal to the moment, standing at his side. She had already been Princess of Wales and the sister-in-law to a queen. She may not have actively sought the crown but it would be naïve to think that Warwick's daughter would not have welcomed it, even if she had any private reservations about what it may entail. Only hindsight warns us of rebellion, her impending death and that of her son and husband. Too many accounts of her life had taken a 'doom-laden' approach, suggesting her weakness and ill health. In reality though, she may not have been experiencing any symptoms of the illness that would claim her life, as many of the

contemporary chroniclers agree it was of a short duration. Because of
the way her husband succeeded, she may have anticipated challenges
but the potential opponents were few: the Lancastrian line had been
effectively wiped out, with their best candidate, Henry Tudor, still in
exile in France. The news of Richard's coup would be as much of a
surprise to him as the fact that his mother, Margaret Beaufort, had
borne Anne's train. The other Yorkist claimants, sons of Edward IV
and Clarence, were still children. In July 1483, at the age of twenty-
seven, Anne could look forward to potential decades on the throne,
with her son continuing the Yorkist dynasty.

The ceremonies continued when the Duke of Norfolk entered the
Great Hall at Westminster. In his office as High Marshall, he entered
on horseback, draped to the ground with cloth of gold, and tapped
his rod on the floor to empty the hall. About four in the afternoon,
the king and queen entered for the feast. Richard took his place at the
middle of the marble table with Anne seated to his left. A countess
waited behind her on each side, holding up a cloth when she wished
to drink and all the other ladies were seated together in the middle of
the Hall. The dishes were carried up from the kitchens and handed
over to the aristocratic servers who were taking over the role for
the occasion. In order to underline differences in status and promote
deference, those accustomed to be waited on were responsible for
the smooth running of the feast. The Dukes of Norfolk and Surrey,
Stanley, treasurer Sir William Hopton and King's Controller Thomas
Percy all served the king with dishes of gold and silver, and Anne with
dishes of gilt. The Bishop of Durham was served on silver, with Lord
Audley as carver and Lord Scrope as cupbearer.[11]

It has been estimated that around 3,000 people were fed at the
Coronation banquet, sharing 1,200 messes or portions. Various
reports stated that it lasted for five and a half hours. In the kitchens
extra cooks were hired, new brooms bought and special 'hutches' to
lock away the spices.[12] The menu was comparatively simple, including
roast capons, royal custards, veal, pike, roast quail, egret, little chickens,
fresh sturgeon with fennel, 'crabbes of the sea' and other plain dishes
besides the usual dressed peacock.[13] The 1465 enthronement feast
of George Neville, Archbishop of York, had already set the standard
for an age, which Edward IV had equalled with a lavish feast at the
Garter ceremonies of 1472. In comparison, Richard's cooks would
have needed to produce luxurious and inventive dishes in order to
supersede it in the memories of the king's contemporaries but they did
not appear to try and rival it. Perhaps this was due to the lack of time
or the king's personal taste. Another feast menu, served up in 1455 by

the Count of Anjou, suggests the inventive extravagance of the era, by combining the business of eating with the theatricality of the medieval monarch. First, a huge centrepiece was set up in the middle of the table, comprising a hollow silver fortress which contained small birds with gilded feet and 'tufts', sitting on a lawn of grass surrounded with branches, sweet-scented flowers and peacock feathers. At the lawn's corners sat huge pies topped with further smaller pies like crowns, their crusts silvered and gilded, filled with many different types of meats. Later delicacies included red and white jellies decorated with the heraldic crests of the diners and plums stewed in rosewater. After the first course of the Coronation banquet, Richard's champion, Sir Richard Dimmocke, threw down the gauntlet to challenge any who disputed the king's honour. No one spoke up. Perhaps, as Fabyan suggests, 'the people [were] rather not repyning for feare than allowing therof'. After dinner, the Mayor of London, Edmund Shaa, served Richard and Anne with sweet wine; John Lamplew was paid £7 19s for 53 gallons of hippocras, and the royal kitchens £4 10s for red wine. By the time they had finished, 'all was doone, it was darke night'.[14] No doubt the drinking and entertainment continued but, after all the guests had gone, Richard and Anne remained at Westminster, as king and queen.

Two weeks after the Coronation, Richard and Anne left the capital to go on progress, initially heading west through the Thames Valley. Elaborate pageantry marked each stage of their journey. The route was carefully planned to impress and engage the affection of his subjects, whose financial gifts he declined along the way, stating he would prefer to have their love instead. Richard's subjects turned out in great numbers to see him and, according to Vergil, 'the day of generall procession was at hand, wherin ther was great confluence of people, for desire of beholding the new king'. Anne travelled with him from Greenwich to Windsor, where the newly interred body of Edward IV was lying among the incomplete renovations he had been making to St George's chapel. The pair probably visited his tomb and offered prayers there, although they may have been less likely to do so at the chapel of St Stephen, where Hastings had recently been interred. Anne then stayed at Windsor Castle while Richard continued on through Oxford, Tewkesbury, Gloucester, Worcester and Warwick. The reasons for this are unclear; perhaps she needed to recuperate after the last few weeks, although the couple's separation need not imply any weakness on her part. It was usual for a king to go about official business independently of his queen. It was a century since Edward III's renovations had transformed Windsor using the proceeds of the Hundred Years' War. A number of luxurious rooms were at her disposal, from the Rose Tower to the Upper Ward. In 1472, the chamber used by Elizabeth, Edward IV's queen, was the largest in the castle, while the beds in the guest rooms had coverlets of cloth of gold furred with ermine and curtains of white sarcanet. There were also extensive hunting grounds, a little park, a garden and 'vineyard of pleasour'. A herald's account of 1506 describes one room as being hung with rich cloth of gold bordered with crimson velvet, another as the king's dining or 'secret chamber' and an 'inner chamber' opening from it, which was used by the ladies. The private closets, where mass could be heard, may have appealed to Anne more than the indoor tennis court, although she may have watched games from its gallery. Here Anne may have enjoyed a brief retreat, being treated – literally – as a queen, before travelling north to join her husband at Warwick.

Richard arrived at Warwick on 8 August; Anne probably joined him soon after, along with her ladies. They stayed for a week at the castle, Anne's birthplace, where they were joined by her nephew, Isabel's son, Edward, who currently held the Warwick title. While there, they visited the family chronicler, the septuagenarian John Rous, at Guy's Cliff about a mile out of town, where he presented Anne with the first version of his *Roll of the Earls of Warwick*, with its sixty-four illustrations and descriptions of her ancestors. The images of Anne and Richard shed little light on them as individuals, being generic enough, along with their coats of arms and the heraldic bear and boar. Anne holds the sceptre and orb, while descending hands from the heavens offer her the two crowns that represent her marriages. Facing her, Richard wears full armour, with orb and sword in either hand, his crown lined with ermine. The illustration of their son, Edward, is identical to that of his father, only smaller. Faced with his portrait, Anne was aware that she would see him again soon. It was while his parents were in Warwick that the Spanish Ambassador proposed a marriage between Edward and one of the daughters of Ferdinand of Aragon and Isabella of Castile. This may have been the thirteen-year-old Isabella or the four-year-old Joanna; the couple's final and most famous daughter, Catherine of Aragon, would not be born until the end of 1485, after Richard, Anne and Edward were all dead.

They left Warwick on 15 August, travelling through Coventry, Leicester and Nottingham before staying in Pontefract Castle, which is possibly where Richard's illegitimate son, John of Pontefract, or Pomfret, joined them, along with Edward of Middleham. From there they proceeded to York, arriving on 29 August. To mark the occasion, 13,000 badges of Richard's white boar badge were commissioned.

The family were met outside the city and watched a series of pageants on their approach, which Hicks has implied may have featured the story of John the Baptist, whose feast day it was. Then they attended a service and retired to the Archbishop's Palace. This had been the see of Anne's uncle, George Neville, whose enthronement the couple had attended as teenagers; he had died in 1476 and the present incumbent was Thomas Rotherham, Edward IV's Lord Chancellor and Keeper of the Great Seal, who celebrated the king's funeral mass at Windsor. His loyalties, though, had remained with Edward's offspring and the Wydevilles. After he surrendered the seal to Queen Elizabeth, he had been deprived of his office and had been arrested on the same day that Hastings met his death. Rotherham, though, had been more fortunate, being released after a short spell in the Tower. Weeks later, he was playing host to Richard's family in his capacity, of five years' standing, as Archbishop of York. In past visits, Richard was accustomed to stay in the Augustinian Priory but, on this occasion, the guests may have been housed in Bishopthorpe Palace, or even Cawood Castle, which would have been familiar to Richard and Anne from her uncle's inauguration of 1465. It was during these days in late summer 1484, in the epicentre of support for the new king, that Richard and Anne would experience the pinnacle of their popularity and power.

At York, though, Edward was to take centre stage. On 19 July, he had been appointed as Lieutenant of Ireland for three years but, on 24 August, the boy was invested as Prince of Wales. Fabyan states that Richard repeated his Coronation and elevated his son to this status 'with a wreath upon his head and the insignia of the gold wand as after shall appear'. Vergil's account is more detailed, having Richard 'adornyd with a notable riche dyademe and accompanyd with a great number of noble men'. Anne followed 'also with a crowne upon hir head', leading her son by the hand 'crownyd also with so great honour, joy and congratulation of thinhabytants' and Edward is described as being about nine. Lisa Hilton states, though, that Edward was already so ill at this time that he had to be carried into the cathedral on a litter. The ceremony in the chapter house was followed by the 'most gorgeous and sumptuous feasts and banquets, for the purpose of gaining the affections of the people',[15] who responded by rejoicing. Edward's cousin and namesake, the young Earl of Warwick, was also knighted at the occasion. After mass at the cathedral, Richard made a gift to the city of twelve gilt figures of the apostles, before the family attended a banquet in their honour. Richard, Anne and Edward sat in state, possibly on some of the 13,000 cushions embroidered with boars, wearing their crowns for four hours, which led Croyland to call the occasion another Coronation. While the rites of anointment were not performed again, the performance of such ritual outside the capital was unprecedented and speaks volumes about the loyalty felt for the new king on his home ground. Around mid-September, Anne travelled back to Middleham with Edward, while Richard continued his progress through Pontefract and Lincoln.

Richard's choice to process north was an interesting one. After years spent living at Middleham, along with his other local connections and the Scottish campaign, he was already known and well respected there. Even the initial leg of the journey, through the Thames Valley, played to his existing strengths, as it was an area associated with his friend since childhood, Francis Lovell. The West Midlands, where he would venture next, had long been loyal to Warwick and his family. If Richard needed to secure his popularity, it was in the South and the capital, where rumours of dissent indicated that rebellion was already brewing. It may appear that the new king was prioritising his existing power base, to display his new status and reward his loyal subjects. In that sense, the purpose of the visit would have been to consolidate an existing stronghold, but there was more to his decision. Richard was undoubtedly an intelligent and talented leader, having proved himself in battle and service to the throne. It was not his people in the North he needed to impress; rather, he needed their loyalty to demonstrate the extent of his power before the southern lords and bishops in his company. Royal secretary John Kendall wrote ahead to the City of York that 'there come many southern lords and men of worship ... which will mark greatly your receiving their graces'. It was in this city that Richard's popularity was at its height. Vergil recorded how the people showed the new king 'great honor, joy, and congratulation' and that 'in shew of rejoysing they extollyd king Richard above the skyes'.[16] This progress was designed to display the full extent of his support outside the capital, as a deterrent for any potentially rebellious Southern lords. When the threat did come, it was from closer to home.

In Lincoln, unexpected news reached the king. Less than three months into the new regime, rebellion had broken out across the South of England. Behind it lay none other than Lady Margaret Beaufort, who had recently carried Anne's train in Westminster Abbey, and the Lancastrian Bishop of Ely, John Morton, with whom Anne and Margaret of Anjou had sheltered with before the Battle of Tewkesbury. In another remarkable alliance spawned by civil conflict, Margaret Beaufort, like her royal namesake, had realised an opportunity to promote the interests of her son by getting into bed with the enemy. Now she sent her physician to Edward's queen,

Elizabeth Wydeville, in sanctuary at Westminster, to discuss a marriage between her son, Henry Tudor, and Edward IV's eldest child, Elizabeth of York. Dissatisfied individuals also began to murmur in favour of Henry and a plan was soon afoot to replace Richard with the exile, now aged twenty-six. Croyland expresses the extent of the threat, involving 'people in the vicinity of the City of London, throughout the counties of Kent, Essex, Sussex, Hampshire, Dorsetshire, Devonshire, Somersetshire, Wiltshire, and Berkshire' who were determined 'to avenge their grievances' and spoke widely of the young Tudor. Two embryonic plots had been discovered and thwarted back in June, to release the Princes in the Tower and send the Yorkist princesses abroad for their safety. There were still a few voices raised in favour of the princes as late as September, but the fact that the main emphasis had shifted away from the restoration of Edward V in favour of Tudor was an indication that the general public believed the princes were no longer alive. Several chroniclers claim this was what prompted the involvement of Richard's close ally, the Duke of Buckingham.

Having been instrumental in placing Richard on the throne, Buckingham now quickly shifted his allegiance. He had been in communication with Henry and Jasper Tudor, as well as Margaret and Bishop Morton, but his motives remain unclear. It was too early in the reign for him to feel aggrieved at any sense of being unrewarded by Richard, whom he had proclaimed in public at St Paul's Cross at the end of June. It has long been speculated by historians that Buckingham was privy to some information that prompted his change of heart. Croyland says it was in reaction to news that the Princes in the Tower had been killed, which Richard may have confided in him during his progress. Others have laid the charge for their deaths at Buckingham's feet, who now saw himself as something like a latter-day Kingmaker. Perhaps, with Edward's heirs out of the way, he wanted to assert his own claim to the throne, with Tudor's help. Buckingham had not been present at York; he had left the progress at Gloucester to go to his Welsh estates, where he had made the decision to join the rebels and was raising an army in Brecon. Now, news reached Richard that his former friend's treachery was no longer in doubt.

Just how far did this come as a surprise to Richard and Anne? They must have been anticipating some sort of response to the sudden events of the summer, especially after the plots uncovered that June. Croyland claims the plot was 'perfectly well known' to Richard by a network of spies, who, with the 'greatest activity and vigilance', contrived that 'armed men should be set in readiness around the said duke, as soon as ever he had set a foot from his home, to pounce upon all his property' and 'in every way to obstruct his progress'. If this was true, Richard's spy network was extensive and had been very quickly established. It also meant he was taking a risk by remaining in the North while his enemies, including a potential Tudor invasion force, could seize control of the South. As late as 15 July, Buckingham had been granted the positions of constable and steward in Salop and Hereford, which suggests that Richard was not suspicious of his loyalty. It seems more likely that the news came as a surprise, judging by the severity and swiftness of the king's response.

Richard turned to his pen before his sword. Immediately he called for the royal seal to be brought to him in Lincoln. A letter composed there on 13 October, warning the Mayor and Aldermen of Southampton of the threat and desiring them to raise troops in his support, must have been typical of a number of appeals issued on or about that date. The king informed his 'trewe subgiettes' that 'the Duc of Buckingham is traterously turned upon us contrary to the deutie of his liegeaunce and entendith thutter distruccion of us ... whose traiterus entent we with goddes grace entend briefly to resist and subdue'. The loyal armies he requested were to converge on Coventry on 22 October 'withouten faile in any wise as ye tendre our honnour and your owne wele'.[17] As the disorganised Kentish rebels were dispersed by John Howard, Duke of Norfolk, Richard sent Francis Lovell to the South Coast to repel Tudor and marched to Salisbury to confront Buckingham. Circumstances had already conspired against the duke, though, to make his attempted coup a failure even before Richard arrived. He had met with little success in raising troops and a spate of bad weather prevented him from crossing the River Severn and joining with other rebels, who were now heading west. Those men who had joined him, unpaid and hungry, were already beginning to desert. When he heard of Richard's approach, he deserted and fled into hiding with Morton at Weobley, the home of Lord Ferrers. The king then put a price on his former friend's head. Fabyan describes the proclamation he issued, 'that who so euer that might take the said duke, should haue for a reward, a thousande pounde of money, and the value of an hundred pounde in lande by yere, to hym and to his heires for euermore'. In response, Buckingham 'changed his dress, and then secretly left his people; but was at last discovered in the cottage of a poor man'. He was taken before Richard at Salisbury and beheaded in the marketplace. Meanwhile, Henry Tudor had set sail with an invasion force, unaware of Buckingham's fate. Richard marched west, arriving at Exeter on 8 November and, according to Fabyan, arrived in Plymouth 'in order to ascertain the real state of affairs'. When he had done so, 'he at once hoisted sail, and again put to sea'. By the time Anne arrived back in London, the threat had been effectively destroyed.

12

Disquiet
1484

But now all thes tryumphes are passed and set on syde
For all worldly joys they wull not long endure
They are sonne passed and away doth glyde¹

For Anne and Richard, Buckingham's rebellion had shattered the triumphant mood established at the 'second Coronation' in York. Back in the capital, increasingly aware of the threat posed by dissidents within the kingdom as well as that of the exiled Henry Tudor, they set about rewarding their loyal friends and subjects. While Tudor had been sent back into exile with his tail between his legs, Richard knew from the experiences of his brother that medieval kingship was a constant battle against those who wished to challenge the existing regime. As a Yorkist, he would always be a target for Lancastrian sympathisers but, at the end of 1483, there was little reason to suppose that Richard, as a skilled commander, administrator and politician, would not be able to deal effectively with these attacks. At thirty-one, he might anticipate reigning for two decades or more, and it was important that he now established a household to demonstrate continuity with the rule of Edward IV. Those who had previously proved themselves faithful to Richard's family were provided for over the coming months.

According to the surviving Parliamentary Rolls, that December, John Lewes was granted 12*d* daily for his good service to the previous king, while a grant for life was awarded to Joan Malpas 'for her good service to the king in his youth and to his mother the Duchess of York'. The twice-widowed Joan was likely to have been in the Yorks' household at Fotheringhay and familiar to Richard since childhood. The following February John Smyth, one of the former sergeants at arms of Edward IV, received 12*d* daily and 10 marks went to Nicholas

Harpisfield for good service to Richard's father, the Duke of York and Edward in Ireland and during the 1470–71 exile in Holland. Robert Radclyff, perhaps the father of the Richard who had been a teenager at Middleham, received 60 marks for serving the family 'in foreign parts and elsewhere' and David Keting was granted the manor of Eskir, and its watermill in County Dublin, for loyalty to the king's father Richard, Duke of York, and afterwards to Edward IV. Also, the town of Waterford in Ireland was compensated for expenses arising from the last visit there of Richard's father, the Duke of York, in the 1450s. More recent servants from Middleham, Henry and Isabel Burgh, received 'an annuity of 20 marks' for their 'good service' to the king's family, in particular to their son, Edward.[2] Many of Edward IV's household remained in their posts but, as Richard and Anne settled into their new role, they transported their existing Northern allegiances and extended family network into the country's capital.

While the Palace of Westminster remained the royal family's main official residence, Anne established herself on a semi-permanent basis further out at Greenwich. Margaret of Anjou and Elizabeth Wydeville had made it their home during the previous regimes, living in 'Bella Court', which had been built in the 1420s by Humphrey, Duke of Gloucester, and later called 'Pleasaunce' or 'Placentia'. The original palace, pulled down in the seventeenth century to make way for the neoclassical 'Queen's House', stretched 200 yards from the water's edge to the foot of the hill in Greenwich Park. In 1443, Gloucester had received a grant from Henry VI to 'embattle and build [it] with stone' around at least one courtyard and 'to enclose and make a tower and ditch within the same, and a certain tower within the park'. Edward IV had enlarged the park and filled it with deer, making certain improvements for the joust held to celebrate the marriage of his young son in 1478. Around 1480, a Grey Friars convent had been built adjoining the palace, comprising 'a chauntrie, with a little chapel of the Holy Cross'.[3] Anne was following in the tradition of queens by basing herself in Greenwich and the records of payments and arrangements for Richard's journeys there show that he was a frequent visitor.

While they preserved Greenwich as a peaceful retreat, the new king and queen kept Christmas 1483 at Westminster. The hostile Croyland called it their 'pompous celebration of the feast of the nativity' but Commines, who was not even in the country, described the 'greater splendour and authority than any King of England'. Croyland was closer to the mark. Richard was short of ready cash, forcing him to sell some items from the royal household and treasury to the merchants of London and use others to raise loans. He used the money to present the city with a gift of a gold cup encrusted with gems, while members of his court received presents totalling £1,200. Christmas day itself was predominantly a solemn occasion, with the focus on devotion rather than celebration. Anne and Richard would have attended services in the abbey and perhaps given thanks, having come through the challenges of their first six months on the throne. Festivities gradually built over the twelve days following, culminating in the gift-giving of Epiphany and the masques and pageants that followed. The kitchens would have been kept busy preparing the traditional boar's head, although, given his personal device, Richard may have opted instead for gilded peacock! It was washed down with 'lambswool', which was beer mulled with apples.[4] The only note of sorrow was that their son, Edward of Middleham, remained in Yorkshire, still suffering from the illness that had incapacitated him during August and September.

Two days after the festival of Epiphany, Richard was on the road again. He progressed briefly into Kent, which had been a stronghold of Warwick's rebels, following the close connection that trade and travel had established between Calais and Sandwich. He reached the port in mid-January, stopping over at Canterbury, where he was presented with a gift of a purse containing £33 6s 8d in gold, contributed by the mayor, councillors and 'the better sort of persons of the city', although he did not accept it. The mayoral accounts indicate how the king was catered for through payments made to a local supplier: John Burton received £4 for 'four great fattened beefs' and 66s 8d for 'twenty fattened rams'. Payments were also made for carpentry work and for the carriage of furniture and hangings to the royal lodgings.[5] Traditionally, visiting monarchs would reside in the well-appointed, central Archbishop's Palace or at St Augustine's Abbey. However, a reference in the city accounts to Blene Le Hale, outside the walls, suggests Richard stayed outside the walls, possibly at Hall Place, which from 1484 was owned by a Thomas Lovell. Alternatively Tim Tatton-Brown places him in 'large temporary buildings around a great tent called le Hale'[6] on the edge of Blean forest, elsewhere called the Pavilion on the Blean.[7] As he states, Henry VI and Edward IV were frequent visitors to Canterbury, along with their queens, so perhaps Anne was present on this occasion too.

There may also have been a religious dimension to the king's visit. Richard would have been based near St Nicholas' Hospital on the hill, overlooking the cathedral at Upper Harbledown, which overlaps with the village of Blean. Founded for the treatment of lepers by Archbishop Lanfranc, with its easily cleaned, sloping floor, the hall housed pilgrims on the route to Becket's shrine in the cathedral.[8]

From 'hobble down', shoes may have been removed to allow them to process the final mile barefoot and penitent, as visitors did at the Norfolk shrine of Walsingham. In Chaucer's late fourteenth-century work, *The Canterbury Tales*, the village was also known as 'Bobbe-up-and-down', due to the poor condition of its roads. In 1484, payments were listed for repairs to the road in advance of Richard's visit, which may well have been timed to coincide with the 400th anniversary of Lanfranc's establishment of the hospital in 1084. If the king undertook the barefoot walk to make offerings at the shrine, he would have been walking in the footsteps of another monarch. Henry II had taken this route 300 years earlier as penance for his role in the death of Thomas Becket. Did Richard make an offering at the sainted archbishop's tomb? Did he, like Henry, have a burden on his conscience that he sought to alleviate?

Where was Anne during Richard's brief progress into Kent? If she accompanied him, did she also stay outside the city and make the arduous walk downhill to the cathedral? Alternatively, she may have remained in London, possibly repairing to Greenwich Palace in his absence. Richard was back at Westminster in time for the meeting of his one and only Parliament, which convened for the first time on 22 January. Joining him there, Anne received news that the Act of *Titulus Regius* had confirmed her husband's succession to the throne and her own queenship. Croyland relates how they met at Westminster, 'near the passage which leads to the queen's apartments', and swore an oath of allegiance and 'adherence to Edward, the king's only son, as their supreme lord, in case anything should happen to his father'. Did this prompt Anne to think of another Edward, who had also been Prince of Wales, to whom men had also sworn their loyalty?

Having bases in Greenwich and Westminster helped Anne maintain a division between her public and private roles. She had already fulfilled the first function of a queen by delivering a son and heir, although at least one spare was always desirable in the eventuality of illness and accident. Since his arrival, though, Anne had not produced another child. Stillbirths and miscarriages cannot be ruled out, although the Prince of Wales featured in national prayers as Richard's 'first-born son'. No doubt, like Anne's parents, they continued to hope for another pregnancy and, according to Croyland, continued to sleep together until early in 1485. Edward's existence added to Anne's prestige, as it was more socially acceptable for her to take an active public role for the sake of her son than as the king's wife. There was little differentiation in role between a queen and an aristocratic wife besides the rise in status. As Richard's consort, her role was paradoxically ceremonial and informal. She was required to head her own establishment and appear at his side during important rituals and court occasions, yet her influence had to be informal. The recent example of Margaret of Anjou's active and 'warlike' queenship was considered the antithesis of what a benign, modest and gentle woman should be. Equally, Elizabeth Wydeville had been criticised for her family's ambition and her 'haughtiness'. Anne had to forge her own style of queenship along different lines, acting as a patron of the arts, an intermediary between supplicants and the king and subtly influencing him with her 'feminine wiles'. While this may sound, to the twenty-first-century reader, like a reductive cliché, the 'advice' of fifteenth-century manuals on female roles conform to this notion, particularly that written by a woman, Christine de Pisan. Her 1405 *Book of the City of Ladies* advocated that a 'Good Princess' speak softly, be kind, patient and humble, in the knowledge that she had 'no strength, power or authority unless it is conferred on you by someone else'. She should 'live in peace' with her husband and be humble and welcoming, putting up with bad behaviour and 'dissimulate wisely'.[9] However, Anne and Richard already had an established marriage dating back a decade. There was little need to readjust to each other, and redefine the way they interacted in private. Perhaps publicly both of them were more guarded, but they assumed the mantle of leadership as a team. It was a team that had been working successfully, even harmoniously, for years.

Anne's household followed Richard's in recruiting from among women who were her Northern relations. At over fifty, Alice FitzHugh, *née* Neville, had married into a prominent Yorkshire family based at Ravensworth Castle, which stood about 16 miles from Middleham. A formidable matriarch, Alice had outlived her brother Warwick, and her husband, and was now a vocal supporter of the new regime. She recruited a number of her children, the cousins Anne would have known in childhood, to her cause. Now, some of them joined her at the new queen's court as ladies-in-waiting and received gifts of cloth in order to make new dresses. Alice's daughter, Elizabeth Parr, had been married at the age of twelve and bore her first child at sixteen. By 1483 she was twenty-three and widowed with four small children, one of whom was the future father of Henry VIII's final queen, Catherine Parr. Two more of Alice's daughters were Agnes, or Anne, who had been married for seventeen years to Francis Lovell, and Margery, wife of Sir Marmaduke Constable, who served Edward IV on his French campaign of 1475 and helped crush the Buckingham rebellion. One of Alice's sons, George, was elevated to Dean of Lincoln in 1483.

Anne's illegitimate half-sister Margaret Huddleston was among her waiting women listed in the Coronation records, along with Elizabeth Bapthorpe, Elizabeth Mauleverer, Grace Pullan, Joyce Percy, Katherine Scrope, Alice Skelton and Anne Tempest.[10] Other women in Anne's company may have been the Duchesses of Norfolk and Suffolk, who had been prominent at her Coronation, and perhaps Frideswide Norris, *née* Lovell, Francis' sister, who had just become the mother of Henry Norris, a victim of the Anne Boleyn scandal. In 1485, Frideswide would be given a yearly salary of 100 marks and a Thomas Norris, perhaps her brother-in-law, received grants drawn from the Middleham estates, suggesting he was employed there. Possibly Agnes, Lady Scrope, wife of Richard Ratcliffe, and her half-sister Margaret, married to William Catesby, were also among the number. Shakespeare assigns her two women called Tressel and Berkeley.

Likewise, Richard promoted those he could trust to key positions. Catesby, Ratcliffe and Lovell, known to history as the 'cat', the 'rat' and the 'dog' of Shakespeare's play, were to feature prominently in the new regime. All were Richard's contemporaries, their loyalty unquestioned. William Catesby had been a Warwick retainer in the service of Hastings and then briefly on the council of Edward V before being appointed as Chancellor of the Exchequer on 30 June and, later, Speaker of the House of Commons. Ratcliffe and Lovell had progressed from being teenage henxmen at Middleham to soldiers fighting alongside Richard in Scotland in 1480. Now both were made Knights of the Garter. Lovell, who came to be known as 'the king's spaniel', hence, the 'dog', became Lord Chamberlain and Chief Butler of England, which had been 'voided by the death of Anthony, late Earl Ryvers',[11] while Ratcliffe received grants of the lands confiscated from traitors. John Howard, Duke of Norfolk, now aged around sixty, already had a long and distinguished career in the service of the House of York. He had been knighted by Edward IV on the battlefield at Towton in 1461, and had been among the party accompanying his sister Margaret to her wedding in Burgundy seven years later. Richard had awarded him his dukedom in June immediately after his succession, as well as the offices of Marshall of England and Admiral of England, Ireland and Aquitaine.[12] Another appointee was Robert Brackenbury, who had served as Richard's treasurer during his time as Duke of Gloucester. A grant of 17 July 1483 made him Master and Worker of the King's Money and Keeper of the Exchange as well as Constable of the Tower of London. The following March, he was rewarded with land and annuities for his good services against the rebels and was given custody of the lions and leopards in the Tower, receiving 12*d* daily for wages and 6d to feed the animals. Other kinsmen Richard promoted were William Berkeley, Earl of Nottingham, whose second wife was Joan Strangeways, niece of Cecily of York, and Humphrey Dacre, Lord Dacre, son of Philippa, another Neville sibling.

In spring 1484, Anne received another group of girls into her household. Edward's queen, Elizabeth Wydeville, had remained in sanctuary throughout the second half of 1483, with her surviving children, five girls. All had been disinherited by the Act *Titulus Regius*, which proclaimed them illegitimate as their parents' marriage was supposedly invalid due to a pre-contract Edward had entered into with an Eleanor Butler, *née* Talbot. Their mother had come under increasing pressure to leave her Westminster confines, but, after the loss of her two sons, Edward V and Richard, was reluctant to do so. A plot had been uncovered and quashed soon after the Coronation, by which the girls were to be spirited away to safety overseas and, as Edward's heirs, they retained a strong claim to the throne as well as popularity with the people. Given Elizabeth's backing of the failed Tudor invasion, Richard was keen to keep the bastardised princesses within his reach and thus prevent any further suspicious alliances from being made. Early in the New Year, he conceded to Elizabeth's request to swear a public oath to defend and protect her five remaining daughters, his nieces, and to become their protector, responsible for arranging suitable marriages for them all. Out of sanctuary came the five girls, Croyland's 'most sweet and beautiful children'. Named after her mother, Elizabeth of York had been her father's favourite and was the eldest at seventeen, with her long, blonde hair and the good looks she inherited from both parents. Next came Cecily, almost fourteen and reputed to be the most beautiful of them all, followed by Anne, Catherine and Bridget, who were all under the age of ten. With their mother still in custody, they entered the queen's household, based at Greenwich, where they had spent much of their childhoods already. What exactly was Anne's role in their care? As their aunt, she oversaw the arrangements for their board and provisions but, given the girls' desirability as potential figureheads of Lancastrian rebellions and alliances, she may also have been charged to be their guardian, even their keeper. Richard would have been aware that Henry Tudor swore an oath in Rennes Cathedral, on Christmas Day 1483, to marry Elizabeth of York. In private, he may have specifically asked his wife to keep a watch on the eldest princess's correspondence and visitors, as well as her comings and goings.

Anne was also involved in the provisions made for the care of her sister Isabel's two surviving children, the eight-year-old Edward,

Earl of Warwick, and his elder sister Margaret, now ten. Elizabeth Wydeville's elder son from her first marriage, Sir John Grey, had been the boy's guardian until his execution in the summer of 1483. The children now entered Anne's household at Greenwich, possibly joining the routine already arranged for Edward IV's younger daughters. Edward, though, would have required a different form of training and education if he was to fill his grandfather's shoes and was later given his own establishment at Sheriff Hutton. In March 1484, Parliament ruled that John Fortescu(e), 'the king's servant', was to receive an additional 10 marks annually during the minority of the king's nephew and, on the same day, Robert Chambre and his wife Marion had their long-term annuity of 10 marks confirmed by Richard. This would have been originally given to them by Edward or Clarence himself, as they had been in the family's employ as far back as 1477. This suggests they may have been family servants, perhaps in the household of the two children, whom, the grant's renewal implies, they were continuing to care for. In the boy's minority, provision was made for the maintenance of his lands, which were awarded to Richard's allies in safekeeping until Edward attained his majority. A Roger Holdern was granted the manor of Sutton in February 1484, 'to yield 2d daily during the minority of Edward, son of Isabel and Clarence', and Robert Russell was to benefit from the £5 annuity from Elmeley Castle in Worcestershire. The actual castle of Warwick, where the king and his family had stayed during the northern progress, was bestowed on 15 November 1484 upon John Higgeford and Humphrey Beaufo or Beowfo, to be constable and steward at salaries of 10 marks yearly.[13] Anne appears to have seen less of her own son, whose illness kept him at Middleham for much of the year. Included in the arrangements of July 1484 for the King's Household in the North were provisions for 'the children' at Sheriff Hutton. Perhaps Edward had his cousins for company in his parents' absence, or else this referred to expenses incurred by Richard's illegitimate children, John and Katherine.

A picture of the royal household emerges from the appointments Richard made over the following months. John Kendall became the king's secretary and Stephen Fryon was Master of the Signet and secretary in the Gallic tongue, while the royal physician was one William Hobbes, who was granted £40 a year on 12 December 1483. More grants were confirmed by Richard's first and only Parliament, which met in the January of 1484. In spite of Margaret Beaufort's recent treachery, her husband, Thomas Stanley, was made a king's counsellor in February 1484 and awarded a grant for £100 in his role as Constable of England. A London goldsmith, Hugh Brice, and his son James, were appointed as clerks of the king's mint, money and exchange within the Tower of London in March 1484, while Henry Wedehoke was made yeoman and Keeper of the King's Armour within the Tower of London, receiving *6d* daily for wages, and William Daubeney became Clerk of the King's Jewels. One Ralph Bygot was named as Master of the King's Ordinance, or keeper of his firearms, and John Crochard was appointed chief smith within the Tower of London at a fee of *8d* a day. A Thomas Hunte became Clerk of the Works at Westminster, Windsor, Tower of London and all the king's manors, with commission to control workmen, materials and to sell branches, bark and residue of the trees within the royal parklands. Thomas Wyntersell was made sergeant of the king's 'herthoundes' and John Piers was made Master of the King's Vine at Windsor in February 1484, while Simon Dowsing was made Keeper of the King's Garden at the Tower of London the following month. In April, John Hudde and Walter Mathyn, yeomen purveyors of the office of the poultry of the household, were granted the right to acquire fowls, lambs and other dairy products for daily provision. William Poche became Keeper of the Beds within the Tower of London, 'alias the office off the little wardrobe within the tower' at a salary of *6d* daily and *3d* provision for two grooms under him, while the Windsor Castle beds were given into the keeping of Thomas Cresey. Parliament's final grants and rulings for the provision of Edward IV's daughters were concluded towards the end of March, 1484.[14]

As spring began to spread across the country, Richard and Anne headed out of the capital on a second progress. Perhaps it was the lure of the North that summoned him, or Anne's desire to see her son, or the imperative to maintain order with his presence. Their first stop was Cambridge, where they stayed for a week and made gifts to King's and Queen's Colleges. By 20 March, they had arrived at Nottingham Castle. When antiquarian John Leland visited the place, in the sixteenth century, it was already partly in ruins but a stately bridge crossed the drawbridge, 'with pillars bearing beasts and giants'. Inside was 'a fair green court fit for any princely exercise' with stone staircases leading through the rock to the river and an underground 'vault, [with] rooms cut and made out of the very stone, in the walls whereof the story of Christ's passion and other things are engraven, by David, King of Scotland, [as they say] who was kept prisoner there'. Later records mention the extensive meadows, the dovecote and the cony gate, where rabbits were caught. There had once been a chapel dug out of the rock under the castle, as well as three others on the site, and a college of secular priests.[15] It was while they were staying there, on 20 April, that terrible news reached Richard and Anne. In their absence, their son had died at Middleham.

Surrounded by his long-term household, Anne Idley, the Burghs and his treasurer, John Dawney, Edward of Middleham had slipped away on 9 April 1484. He was probably aged between seven and ten but the cause of death is unclear. The records are full of medieval children of all classes falling victim to various illnesses, accidents and diseases and the usual attribution of tuberculosis may well apply in Edward's case. He had been too ill to go with his parents to London for their official Coronation and had needed to be carried into York on a litter for his investiture as Prince of Wales that August. Either he was suffering from a long-term debilitating illness, of which his parents were aware, or else he experienced a series of different complaints as Croyland implies, when he states that the boy was 'seized with an illness of but short duration'. Rous called it an 'unhappy death' and one twentieth-century historian suggested appendicitis. There is no doubt, though, about his report of his parents' reaction: 'You might have seen his father and mother in a state almost bordering on madness, by reason of their sudden grief.' The irony was not lost on the chronicler, who stated a popularly held belief that this loss was somehow a punishment for the fate of the Princes in the Tower, Richard's nephews. Croyland expresses a typically medieval satisfaction in the turning wheel of fortune, stating 'it was fully seen how vain are the thoughts of a man who desires to establish his interests without the aid of God', juxtaposed with a reminder that this was almost exactly a year since the death of Edward IV.

The blow for Anne and Richard must have been appalling. Even if they had known the extent of his illness, their absence during the boy's last hours intensified their pain; perhaps it had even been Edward's inability to travel that underpinned their own northern itineraries. They left Nottingham at once and arrived in Middleham on 5 May, probably in time to arrange his funeral, although this was already almost a month after his death. The battered tomb in the church at Sheriff Hutton, topped with its alabaster effigy, which has usually been claimed for Edward, does not contain his bones. The window contains Yorkist imagery but the vault is empty and the body lies elsewhere. Edward of Middleham's final resting place remains unknown to this day. His death had a significance beyond the personal; now Richard had no direct heir, the next in line being Clarence's son, the young Earl of Warwick. It made the king vulnerable, as Henry VI had been, and made the prospect of his overthrow all the more attractive to his enemies. Some went so far as to suggest this was a divine punishment for various crimes attributed to Richard, such as the deaths of Henry VI and the Princes, as Rous had recorded. This must have been in the king's mind as the couple made their way back to York at the end of May. Archbishop Rotherham repeated an ungracious tale that Richard had complained 'unto many noble men of his wife's unfruitfulness, for that she brought him forth no children'.[16] Richard may have regretted his lack of legitimate heirs but Rotherham was a strange choice of confidant, as he still had to prove himself a friend to the new regime.

Edward's death marked the turning point in Anne's life; sadly, she would never be as happy, secure or healthy again. Nor would she enjoy as close a relationship as she had had with her husband during the Middleham years. She was not old, her twenty-seventh birthday was only weeks away, but the loss of her only child must have proved a heavy burden. It was equally momentous for Richard, raising the question of divine disapproval and the reality of a disputed inheritance. From this point onwards, there appears to have been a shift in the marriage, as if Edward had been a bond which broke them with his death. Perhaps Richard did direct some of his grief and anger at the wife who had not been able to provide him with the dynasty he required. Perhaps he felt the irony of her current situation, surrounded by her profusion of nieces, when she had only been able to produce one child. It may have seemed unjust that Edward IV had almost had too many children when his one legitimate son was taken. From this point onward, Richard and Anne's marriage was torn apart by rumours and resentment, grief and illness.

For much of 1484, the threat of a Scottish invasion and the establishment of a council at York kept Richard busy. In May he was in Durham, in June naval matters occupied him at Scarborough and July was spent launching the quarterly Council for the North. Where exactly was Anne during this activity? Records seem to confirm that she was with him at Scarborough, staying in the 'square' or 'queen's tower' as he supervised a fleet for the repulsion of Henry Tudor. She may well have also been with him in York that summer but changes made to Sheriff Hutton, now the official home of Edward, Earl of Warwick, suggest she might have been there. That July, the property was designated the king's 'Household in the North' under the rule of his nephew and heir, John de la Pole. Elizabeth of York and her sisters are likely to have been present there too, included in provisions which were made for 'the children' that also covered Richard's illegitimate offspring. Sheriff Hutton, an old Neville property which had been granted to Richard after the Battle of Barnet in 1471, was close enough to York to allow the pair to see each other during the inauguration of the council. Commanding an impressive view over the Vale of York, it had four towers of reddish stone and long ranges lit on the first floor by large square windows and heated by 6-foot-wide fireplaces.

Anne and Richard were back in London that August when the bones of Henry VI were transferred from Chertsey Abbey to St George's chapel, Windsor. How did Anne feel, standing over the tomb of her father-in-law, recalling the events of over a decade ago? The re-interment had been made at Richard's request, and perhaps she appreciated this small, retrospective gesture of respect. It may be that the king decided it was time to give his fellow monarch a more suitable resting place, or maybe he was responding to the many reports of miracles carried out in Henry's name, which had already begun to develop into a minor cult. The bones were laid to rest to the south-west of the altar, incurring £5 10s and 2d in expenses. Richard had also commissioned the original tomb which was a flat alabaster slab, featuring a recumbent Henry, bearded and in armour, with a leopard and antelope at his feet and an angel bearing his shield of arms on the side. It no longer stands, having been dismantled around 1600; Henry VI is commemorated today by a slab set into the floor.[17]

Whatever reunion the pair might have had was short-lived as, by the following month, Richard had left London again, to return to Nottingham Castle. From this point, according to Paul Kendall, he referred to the place as his 'Castle of Care'; a continual reminder of the news he had received there. Now, it was a venue for the visit of a delegation of Scottish ambassadors, who proposed a three-year truce and marriage between Richard's niece, Anne de la Pole, and James III's son and heir. Richard remained there all through October before returning to London on 11 November. He was welcomed back into his capital, being met by the mayor and alderman, dressed in their brightly coloured ceremonial robes. The scarlet and violet velvet must have been vivid on the autumnal day of St Martin, traditionally the occasion when animals were slaughtered for the winter. Anne was probably already waiting for him, having spent the intervening time at Greenwich, now moving back into Westminster. Settling back into their royal apartments overlooking the Thames, a winter of discontent certainly lay ahead for Richard and Anne. And for both of them, it would be their last.

That December saw the trial of William Collingbourne, whose apparently light-hearted efforts to mock the new regime belied the serious nature of his treasonable activities. Once employed in the household of Cecily Neville, and therefore probably known to Richard in his youth, Collingbourne is best known as the author of the lampoon, 'The Catte, the Ratte and Lovell our dogge rulyth all Englande under a hogge.' These heraldic references to Richard, Catesby, Ratcliffe and Lovell (the king's spaniel whose badge featured a wolf) were demeaning when pinned on the door of St Paul's Cathedral that summer. However, it proved to be just one example of the 'various bills and writings in rhyme' that proclaimed the author's Lancastrian sympathies.[18] Collingbourne was the probable author of a longer version of the couplet and its explanatory key, which first appeared in Fabyan's chronicle in 1516 and then in the 1559 cautionary poetry collection, *Mirror for Magistrates*. This was more explicitly critical of Richard and the circumstances of his succession, although the references to his 'crooke-back' may suggest a post Tudor authorship:

> The Cat, the Rat and Lovell Our Dog
> Doe rule all England under a Hog.
> The crooke-backt Boar the way hath found
> To root our Roses from our ground.
> Both flower and bud he will confound
> Till King of Beasts the swine be crown'd.
> And then, the Dog, the Cat and Rat
> Shall in his trough feed and be fat.[19]

The author's 'key' described Catesby as 'a craftee lawyer catching all he could', while Ratcliffe was 'a cruel beast' who 'gnawed on whom he should'. Lovell, in turn, 'barked and bit whom Richard would' but such an explanation would hardly be required by an audience of 1483.[20] All three of Richard's close friends had helped in suppressing the Buckingham rebellion and received lands and grants as rewards.

After Collingbourne's arrest, it was proved that he had been in contact with Henry Tudor and other exiles, encouraging his invasion plans. It has been suggested that he was a disgruntled ex-employee who had lost his place after being implicated in Buckingham's revolt or that he wrote in revenge for the loss of lands and offices he had been promised: he had served as a commissioner for the peace in Wiltshire, in July 1483, but did not feature in the records by December of that year. On trial at the Guildhall, a commission of dukes and earls convicted him of high treason. He was then taken to Tower Hill and suffered the horrific hanging, drawing and quartering reserved for traitors. More fortunate that season was John Morton, Bishop of Ely, who received a general pardon on 11 December for his role in Buckingham's rebellion.

It was not the first time that year that Richard had been forced to deal with slander and libel. One source of annoyance was the preferment of his Northern magnates in roles that had previously been held by Southerners. Croyland was exaggerating when he commented that Richard had 'planted' them 'in every spot throughout his dominions ... to the disgrace and lasting and loudly expressed sorrow of all the people in the South', but the appointments had caused some annoyance. Although he did try to bind his critics to him with grants, alliances and titles, those with Lancastrian leanings, who had escaped punishment for the 1483 rebellion, began to resurface in hopes of a Tudor invasion. A surviving letter written by Richard on 5 April 1484 to the Mayor of Southampton shows the nature of the problem and his response. It had come to the king's attention that 'diverses sedicious and evil disposed persounes' in London and elsewhere had begun 'to sowe sede of noyse ... ayenst our persoune and ayenst many of the lordes and estates of our lands'. Their purpose was to 'averte' the minds of loyal subjects to 'theire mischevous entent and pourpos' by setting up bills and messages and 'sending furth of fals and abhominable languages and lyes'. Richard had called together a meeting of the London mayor and aldermen to 'represse al such fals and continued invencions' by apprehending all those attempting to 'stir commontions', raise 'unlawful assembles, or any strif and debate aryse betwix lord and lord'. Such malcontents were to be 'punisshed according to [their] defautes'.[21] Fabyan's chronicle is more specific regarding the rumours that surfaced around Easter. His marginal headings, 'Innocents' and 'Death of the Innocents', indicate the subjects of the accusations, which included such wild stories as smothering, poisoning and drowning. Fabyan even proposed that either Sir James Tyrell, High Sheriff of Cornwall, or an unnamed 'servant of the king' had murdered Edward IV's sons in the Tower. He also says these rumours lost Richard 'the hearts of the people'.

Richard knew how damaging seditious speech could be and seems to have spent considerable time in the final year of his reign countering various rumours and challenges to his reputation. Of course, he had his advocates too. In a private letter to William Selling, prior of Christchurch, Canterbury, in the summer of 1483, Thomas Langton wrote that Richard 'contents the people where he goes best that did prince ... I liked never the conditions of any prince so well as his; God has sent him to us for the weal of us all.'[22] The clerk of York later recalled Richard as a 'most famous prince of blessed memory' and Rous' first version of his history was full of glowing praise. Archibald Whitelaw, a Scottish ambassador visiting England in 1484, wrote,

'Never has so much spirit or virtue reigned in such a small body.'[23] By the end of that year, though, new threats were to emerge to his person and his name. Around Christmas, he received information that the planned Tudor invasion force would be launched the following summer. Before that, it was the state of his marriage that became the talk of Westminster.

13

Elizabeth of York
1484–1485

Her hands together can shee wringe,
and with teares shee wipes her eye;
'welladay, BESSYE!' can shee sing.[1]

Now the long winter nights began to draw in at the palace. As Anne looked out of the windows of the royal apartment, looking over the long, snaking line of the Thames, the sky was white and full of massing clouds. In her chamber, fires were built up in their wide hearths, cracking and blazing bright, yet the chill still managed to enter her bones. If she ventured out into the formal gardens, laid out to the north of the complex, the walkways and plants were often tinged with frost and, when she crossed the yard to pray in the abbey, her breath formed clouds in front of her eyes. As the nights grew darker, she would sit waiting in the light of the flickering candles, playing cards or dice with her ladies, reading, singing or watching while the young princesses danced to a tune played on a lute. Perhaps Richard would come and warm her bed that night. She waited for the soft knock on the door that announced his arrival, but it did not come. Where was he?

Since March 1484, Anne's household had contained the 'sweet and beautiful' Elizabeth of York. She and her four younger sisters probably travelled with them to the North that spring and had been present when the bad news arrived from Middleham. As the eldest child of Edward IV, the blonde eighteen-year-old had spent the majority of her life at Greenwich and Westminster, having been raised in the full expectation of marriage to a king or prince. It had been no secret that the rosy-cheeked little girl had been the favourite of her father, with her even temper and gentle ways. She was equally beloved of the people of London, who had turned out to cheer her whenever she made a public appearance. For a number of years she had been referred to as the Dauphine, following her betrothal to Charles, son of Louis XI, but that match had been abandoned by the time her father died. The death of her brothers should have made her the direct Yorkist heir, had *Titulus Regius* not declared her illegitimate as the result of reputed discrepancies in the marriages of her parents and grandparents. One condition of her release from sanctuary, by her mother, had been Richard's promise to suitably bestow her. She was now well past what was considered the necessary year of consent and had reached the age at which both Anne and Elizabeth Wydeville herself had contracted their first matches. As her uncle and guardian, it was Richard's responsibility to find her a husband, but, as her king, he needed to make a very careful choice. Since the Wydeville–Beaufort plot of 1483, Elizabeth's significance in Henry Tudor's invasion plan had become clearer, culminating in the oath he had sworn to marry her on Christmas Day 1483. The 'Ballad of Lady Bessye', probably written by Humphrey Brereton during the reign of Henry VII, describes her in the usual literary conventions as 'white as any milke' and 'faire on mold'. One later ambassador called her 'very handsome', while another commented on her large breasts and comely figure which promised health and fertility. The epitome of a princess, Elizabeth was beautiful, eligible and available, yet twelve months after Tudor's pledge, she remained unwed. What did her king have in mind for her?

Elizabeth Wydeville's agreement to release her daughters from sanctuary into the care of their uncle has raised speculation for centuries. The disappearance of her sons, Edward and Richard, in the Tower, in the summer of 1483, has never been satisfactorily explained and probably never will be. Some have taken Elizabeth's 'surrender' as evidence that she did not believe Richard capable of having murdered them, although this simplifies the situation she found herself in and her need to provide for her surviving daughters. The king did have a motive for procuring the deaths of the boys, although this does not imply guilt, but he could hardly have derived any benefit from removing Princess Elizabeth and her sisters. As women, unable to directly inherit, they were far more useful to him alive, as marriageable commodities. By swearing the oath, Richard bound himself 'in surety of their lives' and would suffer no hurt done to them 'by way of ravishment or defiling contrary their wills'. He would put them 'in honest places of good name and fame … to have all things requisite and necessary', to marry them suitably as his kinswomen. He did this publicly, in front of an assembly of the nobility, clergymen and leading Londoners. To break his word would have incurred serious consequences.

In fact, the wording of the oath suggests the dowager queen did believe in Richard's guilt but was faced with little choice, given her confinement at Westminster and the continual, increasing pressure he put on her to leave it. It may seem hard for a modern reader to accept that she would trust her daughters to the care of their brothers' murderer but the situation was complex and necessity dictated her actions. Her sons were beyond her reach. She could act now only for the benefit of her children still living. Her posthumous reputation has contributed to the misunderstanding of her motives and needs to be unravelled. The late sixteenth-century Holinshed accused her of being won over by Richard with 'glorious promises and flattering words', which made her 'blot out the old committed injurie and late executed tyrannie', as she was but a 'weake woman of timorous spirit'. In contrast, More presents a powerful image of her distress: 'the quene sat alone on the rushes all desolate and dismayed'. More has her call Richard 'he that goeth about to destroy me and my blood'. According to Vergil, she 'fell into a swoon and lay lifeless a good while ... she wept, she cried out loud and with lamentable shrieks made all the house ring. She struck her breast, tore and cut her hair ... prayed also her own death ... condemning herself for a madwoman ... for [sending her younger son] to be murdered by their enemy.' It seems unlikely, as the Victorian Gairdner asserted, that the 'queen dowager had been completely won over by Richard'. Elizabeth Wydeville has been accused of ambition and arrogance but there is nothing to suggest that she was unintelligent. There seems little reason to doubt the sincerity of the bereaved mother's grief or the lack of choices that now forced her into a corner. It would have been wise for the ex-queen to concede to Richard's wishes in early 1484, as she was not blessed with foresight and could not have predicted the success of Henry Tudor's invasion the following year. As far as she knew, Richard may retain the throne for decades and the fortunes and lives of herself and her daughters depended on his favour; as such, she can hardly be blamed for making a 'deal with the devil'. Her two eldest daughters were of marriageable age and could not be kept indefinitely in sanctuary. Elizabeth made her decision in 1484 as a mother. She could no longer do anything to help her sons, so she wisely did the best she could for her girls, who were now included in Anne's household. Perhaps she was counting on the influence of the new queen to keep them safe.

The loss of their son may not have brought Richard and Anne closer. In fact, it may have had the opposite effect, as their movements in the second half of 1484 are suggestive of physical and emotional distance. Her exact location during this time is unclear but his busy schedule could well have excluded his wife, even if she was staying relatively close at Sheriff Hutton. Given that she only had months left to live, Anne may have already been suffering for poor health or exhaustion, choosing to remain in one of their residences, perhaps at home in Middleham, while he was on official business. She may have consulted her physician, who would have bled her and suggested changes in her diet. Perhaps his diagnosis was one of melancholia, the intense grief caused by her loss and the sense of failure at her low fertility. However tempting it is to speculate, records of her illness do not emerge until the winter. It is possible that, during those summer months, she had not yet experienced any symptoms that caused concerns regarding her health or, at least, they were not too severe.

If Lisa Hilton is correct in her diagnosis of tuberculous endometritis, which affects the fallopian tubes, Anne's illness would have produced few external signs. She may have experienced some abdominal pain, irregular or heavy bleeding and perhaps mucus discharges, which contemporary medicine would have seen as an imbalance of the humours. The damage would have been internal, with scarring, calcification and deformation of the uterus. Very rare in the modern era, it more commonly occurs in older, post-menopausal women, often secondary to other forms of tuberculosis. It can, though, be the result of a bacterial infection or, even, of sexually transmitted disease.[2] To suggest that Anne had contracted some sort of venereal disease is a step too far, though. Records of the spread of such conditions are infrequent if they exist at all; the first recorded case of syphilis was in 1494, when it swept across Europe, claiming up to 6 million victims. Diseases of this kind were poorly understood and proved untreatable. Anne only had two sexual partners. While the extent of Prince Edward's experience is unknown, although probably very limited, Richard had certainly been sexually active before his marriage. As far as can be ascertained, he experienced good health and did not display any symptoms of infection, although his early death meant they may not have had a chance to develop. Throughout his reign, his punishing schedule and wide travel about the kingdom do not suggest he was at all unwell. If Anne was experiencing any symptoms during the summer of 1484, as a result of tuberculosis in any form, she may have seen them within the context of her general health. Those months may have passed peacefully in retreat in the countryside, awaiting her reunion with Richard.

However, Edward's death had brought her health more into focus, especially if Richard's complaints about Anne's infertility, as reported by Archbishop Rotherham, are to be believed. His criticism of her, in the aftermath of Edward's death, may have been unguarded comments made in the extremes of grief. Equally, it may have tapped into an existing source of grievance which he had previously voiced in private. Low fertility and infertility were largely considered, at the time, to be the fault of the female, and the existence of Richard's illegitimate children may have seemed, to him, to validate this. The inability to produce a surviving male heir could tear apart what would, under other circumstances, have been a happy marriage, as Catherine of Aragon was to discover with Henry VIII in the 1520s and 30s. According to Alison Weir, Richard's intention to put his wife aside and remarry in order to father an heir was already widely spoken of. Holinshed relates that Richard complained to 'diuerse noble men of the realme, of the infortunate sterilitie and barennesse of his wife, bicause she brought foorth no fruit and generation of hir bodie' and shunned her company. In Yorkshire, Anne may have been sheltered from such gossip but when the king returned to London in November, Anne may have travelled south with him. Alternatively, she may have gone on ahead of him to Greenwich, as her activities in the summer of 1483 proved that she had an independent household and had previously made the journey to the capital independently of him. Anne settled back into her Westminster apartments for the Christmas season, which provided many opportunities to surround herself with her nieces and nephews during the devotions, feasting and festivities. At some point, she became aware of rumours that were circulating the court regarding her own health. Worse still, people were also hinting at a possible liaison between her husband and Elizabeth of York. Perhaps a trusted lady-in-waiting passed on what was being whispered in the corners of the hall. Did Anne give them any credence?

The truth of Anne's relationship with Elizabeth is hard to ascertain. As the girl's aunt, only ten years her senior, Anne would have known the girl during her childhood, seeing her at court on the occasions when she visited with Richard. During the 1470s and early 80s, the position between them would have been reversed, with Elizabeth's rank as royal princess placing her higher in status than her aunt, a duchess. The girl's mother, Elizabeth Wydeville, had been very conscious of the protocol surrounding such gradations of privilege and would have raised her daughter in the full understanding of the deference due to her. This is not to suggest any arrogance or vanity on the part of either Elizabeth; it is simply how the strictly hierarchical court operated, at all levels, from the king down to the scullion. Edward's family had suffered a number of falls from their high position, plunging the princesses first into sanctuary and now supposed illegitimacy. At the court of 1484, Elizabeth was required to defer to her aunt, previously her inferior, yet she may still have held out hopes of gaining a crown for herself. Even though Henry Tudor had declared his intention to marry her and invade England, those events lay in the future and could not be predicted, no matter what 'The Ballad of Lady Bessye' says. Brereton wrote of Elizabeth's prophetic abilities in 1486, once she was married to the Tudor conqueror. As far as Elizabeth knew, Richard was to be her king for years to come. She had to carve out the best future path for herself in his reign. Anne, though, may have been another matter.

As Elizabeth's elder by a decade, the queen may well have seen herself as fulfilling the role of substitute mother, sister or guardian. The nature of their bond would depend on Elizabeth's feelings towards her uncle and her understanding of the queen's role in the events of 1483. Did the princess believe her uncle responsible for the murder of her brothers? If so, did she believe that Anne knew the truth, or had colluded with his plans? On Anne's side, her guardianship of the princess may have been affected by the need to keep her under observation as the target of Tudor's intentions. One possibility is that the two women may have been wary of each other, distrustful and distant; by another, they may have become close friends and confidants. Weir asserts that the princess 'was ranked familiarly in the queen's favour, who treated her as a sister'. As an older woman, experiencing the trials of queenship that Elizabeth had been raised to expect, she may have been something of a role model. Alternatively, it may have been difficult for the princess to forget the comparison between the new queen and her mother, who had remained in sanctuary in order to buy her daughters' freedom. Elizabeth Wydeville would still have been influencing her daughter's behaviour, directly or indirectly. The oath she had imposed on Richard that May implies that she did not trust him and believed that her sons had been killed in the Tower on his orders. Still, she recognised the need to come to terms with him for the future of her surviving children. It is impossible, now, to ascertain the feelings of aunt and niece that would provide the essential context in which the events of Christmas 1484 need to be interpreted.

The celebrations began along traditional lines. Fabyan described how the 'feast of the Nativity was kept with due solemnity at the Palace of Westminster', after which, the more lively Epiphany was held 'with remarkable splendour'. Reminiscent of his London Coronation, Richard appeared in the Great Hall wearing his crown, in his royal state of 'potency and splendour'. The doors would have been decked with ivy or holly, box and broom, which was also wrapped around

frames and suspended from the ceiling. A multitude of candles would
have been lit to ward off the gloom, games played and carols sung.
Richard may have appointed his own Lord of Misrule to entertain the
court with jokes and jests; besides this, there would be the inevitable
disguisings and plays that followed dinner and ended with dancing.
Presents were exchanged, but the fact that the king gave Elizabeth his
copy of *The Romance of Tristan* as a gift can hardly be construed as
evidence of an affair. A later poem of 1580 describes the type of fare
that would have been provided that season, which had not significantly
changed in a century and still sounds familiar today:

> Good bread and good drinke, a good fier in the hall
> brawne, pudding and souse, and good mustard withal.
> Beefe, mutton and pork, shred pies of the best,
> pig, veal, goose and capon, and turkey well drest;
> Cheese, apples and nuts, joly carols to heare,
> as then in the countrie is counter good cheare.[3]

Not everyone had much appetite for the revelry. The hostile Croyland,
writing in 1486, described himself as 'grieved to speak' that 'far too
much attention was given to dancing and gaiety' but he adds that
Elizabeth was sent, with her four sisters, 'to attend the queen at court'.
Over the twelve days of Christmas, Elizabeth apparently attracted
her uncle's attention in a way that 'caused the people to murmur and
the nobles and prelates greatly to wonder thereat'. Perhaps he had
always found her appealing but the loss of Edward turned his mind to
the need to father a new legitimate heir. The occasion that prompted
speculation was the fact that Anne and her niece wore similar clothing.
The potential threat to the queen lies more in the interpretation of
this line than the description. Their 'vain changes of apparal' were
not uncommon in a period of festivity, nor was the co-ordination of
clothing between family members on ceremonial occasions. Croyland
was not present in Westminster that season, yet he records that 'many'
said the king was 'bent ... on the anticipated death of the queen ...
or else ... divorce' in order to marry Elizabeth. 'Many' may have
believed this. How 'many'? The apparent identical appearance of the
women, 'being of similar colour and shape', has been taken to imply
the substitution of one for the other, yet this must have been suspected
within the context of other interactions between the king and his niece.
Croyland does hint at other 'things so distasteful, so numerous that
they can hardly be reckoned' which were 'pernicious and perfidious'
and were 'shameful to speak of'. The 'anticipated death' of Anne is

also sinister, giving rise to the allegations of murder that find fruition in Shakespeare's play. Frustratingly, the chronicler goes no further, leaving the modern reader wondering exactly what happened between Richard and Elizabeth at Christmas that year.

The most significant piece of evidence used to argue for Richard's relationship with Elizabeth has been a seventeenth-century copy of a letter, known as Buck's letter. Buck was an historian, born around 1560, who found a copy of *Titulus Regius* folded within the Croyland manuscript and produced his own history of Richard III's life and reign. Buck claimed to have seen Elizabeth's letter in 1619, then in the keeping of the Howard family, who were patrons of his work. Apparently written by Elizabeth of York herself in February 1485, to John Howard, Duke of Norfolk, Buck stated that the letter asked for the duke's assistance in her intended marriage to the king and expressed impatience that the queen, her aunt, was not yet dead. Assuming for a moment this letter's authenticity, it would mean that Elizabeth and Richard had come to some sort of understanding and that the whole court, including Anne, was aware that her illness was terminal. Either that, or that her death was imminent.

However, the letter is not a reliable source. For starters, it is an edited version of a lost original, published by Buck's great-nephew in the 1640s. The original version (BL MS. Cotton Tiberius E. x. f. 238v) is fire-damaged and has been reconstructed to an extent that suggests liberal degrees of 'interpretation' by Buck junior.[4] The first version's assertion that Elizabeth 'feared the queene would nev...' has become 'feared the queen would never die'. To play devil's advocate, this could even have related to concerns for Anne's health and good wishes for her recovery. The second version says Elizabeth belonged to Richard 'in heart and in thoughts, in body and in all', although the suggestive word 'body' is absent from the letter of 1619, turning a conventional phrase into a potential physical affair. However, as his niece, whom he had sworn to protect and suitably marry, Elizabeth was his to dispose of bodily. The earlier letter asks Howard to be 'a mediator for her to the K ... [space] ... ge ...', which Buck junior interpreted as a mediator for her in her marriage to the king himself. It is possible, though, that this letter must be viewed in the context of Richard's attempts to provide his niece with a marriage, as he had promised. Tudor's oath and impending invasion made that all the more urgent. He had married Elizabeth's sister, the fifteen-year-old Cecily, to Lord Scrope and may now have been planning a joint match for himself and Elizabeth. Suitably for a king and princess, his attention turned abroad. A powerful foreign alliance could add prestige to his reign and furnish him with allies in the event of Lancastrian reprisals. Richard may now have been planning a double Portuguese marriage. The proposal had been suggested by Sir Edward Brampton, by which Richard was to marry the teenage Joana of Castile, while Elizabeth would wed Manuel, Duke of Beja, later Manuel I of Portugal, who had been born in 1469. The planned union was referred to by Alvaro Lopez de Chaves, as the Portuguese hoped for English support against Castilian rebels, and may well have been the match Elizabeth was referring to early in 1485. Although this interpretation absolves Elizabeth from callously anticipating her aunt's death in order to satisfy an 'incestuous passion', it follows that Richard was already thinking of remarriage in the spring of 1485, while Anne was still alive.

Perhaps his intentions pre-dated that. Vergil states that it was news of Richard's impending match with Elizabeth that prompted Henry Tudor to act, which assumes the rumours reached him before his declaration regarding the summer. However, he may also have believed the marriage would go ahead, as he did briefly entertain the idea of defeat and returned to the possibility of taking Maude Herbert as his wife. Jean Molinet, French chronicler and translator of the *Roman de la Rose*, believed that Elizabeth had borne Richard a child in secret but this can be dismissed as the time-scale hardly allows it. Any child conceived on or around that Christmas would have arrived, if it had been full-term, in the late summer of 1485, around the time of Bosworth. Richard did send Elizabeth away to Sheriff Hutton in the spring, where a pregnancy could have been concealed, although with his desire for a legitimate heir, he would surely have married her after Anne's death, despite the disapproval of his council. The five months or so that Elizabeth spent in Yorkshire allow for such speculation; even, following romantic lines, a secret marriage or miscarriage. Yet no other source mentions a child. Molinet probably did not visit England during that period; he was the librarian of Margaret of Austria, step-granddaughter of Richard's sister, Margaret of Burgundy, and, as such, hostile to Elizabeth and Henry Tudor. It is highly unlikely that Henry Tudor would have made the Yorkist princess his queen if he had any suspicions regarding her virtue. The further five-month time-lapse between Henry's succession and marriage has also been interpreted as his deliberate delay, in order to ascertain whether or not Elizabeth was pregnant by Richard. These individuals were no strangers to controversy or gossip, though. This single report that Elizabeth had conceived a child by Richard must be dismissed as one of the worst examples of contemporary slander.

Had Richard been drawn into a relationship with his niece? Rumours at court do not translate into incontrovertible fact, no matter how many people repeat them. And they were repeated frequently in later years, usually to blacken Richard in the eyes of Elizabeth's Tudor descendants. 'The Ballad of Lady Bessye' states unequivocally the princess's distaste of her uncle as well as her belief that Richard intended his wife's death in order to satisfy his lust.

> He wolde have put away his Queene
> for to haue lyen by my bodye.

She would not be drawn into marriage with her uncle no matter what punishment she might suffer as a result: the union was clearly damnable in her eyes.

> I care not whether I hange or drowne
> so that my soule saued may bee.

The 1614 poem 'The Ghost of Richard III' demonstrates the king's awareness of the inappropriateness of the match.

> Yet to establish and secure my state
> I sought with wilfull lust and powerfull awe
> To crosse the bancs [banns] and over-rule the law[5]

An anti-Ricardian tragedy, the *Roode en Witte Roos*, by Lambert van den Bos, published in Amsterdam in 1651, may have been based on a now lost English play, rather than that of Shakespeare. Richard's wooing of Elizabeth is gentler than in the Bard's version, conducted at court, in the presence of her mother. The king appears to be a man in love, calling the young woman 'lovely creature' and 'beautiful child in which the world takes pride'. He politely asks her, 'if it please' her, to 'grant him your right hand in marriage' as a way to possess her father's throne. Elizabeth, in response, expresses 'real terror at your vile deed'. While her mother urges her to 'dissemble, dissemble', she calls Richard mad and states she cannot forget his 'evil deeds', threatening to 'pierce [his] cursed entrails'.[6]

Then there is the question of Elizabeth's private feelings. What would her motives have been for involvement with her uncle and how would her mother, Elizabeth Wydeville, have viewed this? With Buck's letter discounted, the simple answer is that we do not know for certain how Elizabeth felt. Traditionally, she has been portrayed as passive and reactive, along with the glorification of her beauty and gentle qualities, creating a degree of ambiguity about her character. Perhaps there is a good reason for it. As the mother of the Tudor monarchs, later accounts have been coloured by the dynasty's dependence on her lineage and the vilification of Richard III. Any relationship she willingly entered with Richard would have been a source of deep embarrassment to subsequent generations. Yet again, the question of hindsight is central to understanding her actions at Christmas 1484; even as late as the following summer, there were no guarantees that Henry Tudor's bid for the throne would be successful. Richard was the reigning king and, at the age of thirty-one, might anticipate at least another decade in power. Evidence to suggest that he contemplated marriage with his niece has recently been explored seriously by historians, where it has previously been dismissed as impossible. Some have concluded that Elizabeth was urged into the match by her mother, who coveted the crown for her. The princess had been raised in the expectation of queenship and the recent decades proved that fortunes could quickly turn and opportunities had to be capitalised on. With the Wydeville power on the decline, it may be that Elizabeth and her mother saw this as a last chance to seize some sort of security for themselves. The imperatives of survival and propagation could not be overlooked in a world where illness and death, accident and conflict played such a prominent role. Nor can it be ruled out that Elizabeth was released from confinement in order to seduce her uncle.

To the modern mind, there is an obvious impediment to such a relationship. Richard was, of course, Elizabeth's uncle by blood, not just through marriage. While his marriage to Anne had, in theory, required several dispensations, his affinity to Elizabeth was closer but was still not considered prohibitive according to the standards of the medieval Catholic Church. It was within the power of the Pope to grant a dispensation for alliances of this nature, so although it would not contravene religious codes, it was still rare. Richard had already understood the need to provide the correct papal documents for his marriage to Anne: some still argue they were incomplete, although their union went unchallenged at the time. Marriages between those connected in the first degree went against the grain of popular sentiment. Pairs of brothers and sisters did marry but Henry VIII's marital trials illustrate just how problematic they could prove. The rumours appear to have provoked disgust in Richard's contemporaries, with his council uniting against the idea and close advisers, Catesby and Ratcliffe, warning him of a possible public backlash. In the event, Richard appears to have listened to them, issuing strongly worded public denials that he had ever considered Elizabeth as a wife.

In January 1485, though, any affair was at its height. Whether fuelled by mutual passion, ambition or the imperative for an heir, if Richard and Elizabeth had become entangled, they were committing adultery. As Hall stated, one thing 'withstood' Richard's desires. Anne, his queen, was still alive. It cannot have been a happy time for her. In the last weeks of her life, she cannot have been unaware of the extent of the rumours, which perhaps contributed to her rapid decline soon after Epiphany. Croyland reported that her sorrow was exacerbated by Richard's cruelty: she was 'extremely sick … [and] still more and more because the king entirely shunned her bed', on the advice of his physicians. This has the ring of truth. If Anne was in the final stages of a terminal illness, that is exactly the recommendation they would have made, for her benefit and his. The chronicler added that the queen understood that she had become a burden to her husband, so 'soon became a burden to herself and wasted away', while Hall would later report that daily quarrels took place between the couple. If the success of their relationship had hinged upon the existence of Edward, his death was the catalyst for its rapid disintegration. This does suggest that the marriage had been one of expediency, on Richard's side, at least. It was Anne's tragedy if this possible ill feeling and estrangement coincided with the deterioration of her health.

Yet the case for the couple's estrangement is based in gossip. The rumours originated with Croyland and were repeated by Vergil and Hall, thus entering popular legend. To quote Richard Marius, the king was 'crucified by hearsay'. The second half of 1484 had already demonstrated that Tudor agents were actively spreading rumours ahead of the intended invasion, and the reports of his liaison with his niece must also be considered in the light of this and other, later, defamations. A 1614 poem, 'The Ghost of Richard III', states that although Anne's presence 'did deny' his match with his 'fayre niece', he had some genuine feeling for her, especially as she weakened. The two approaches are not necessarily incompatible, as Richard's position as king may have come into conflict with his private relationship with his wife. On one hand, he may have genuinely loved her and grieved at her worsening illness, while being unable to avoid the dynastic ramifications of her death. As a king under threat, survival was uppermost in his mind that Christmas; to deny that life would go on after Anne's tragic and untimely death would have been to fail in his duty. The poem goes further; the queen

> fell sodaine sicke with griefe or jealousie;
> and all my love would not preserve her breathe.

Worse still, this sensational version affirms that Anne's low fertility had been a bone of contention between them, for which she was taking some sort of remedy. The results of this, according to the author, were startling and give another interpretation of Richard's presence in, or absence from, her bed:

> I gave her medicines for sterilitie
> And she grew fruitfull in the bed of death
> Her issue crawling worms.

The derivation for this bizarre image is unknown, as is the precise use of the term 'issue'. If, as the poem implies, Anne was pregnant on her deathbed, then it follows that some stillbirth or miscarriage is intended. His medical advisers would have certainly counselled the king not to sleep with Anne if there was any suspicion of pregnancy, advice which was commonly given to couples of all walks of life. The meaning of 'fruitfull' did not necessarily imply pregnancy then, though, as its alternative uses were simply to do with creation and production in other forms. The poet may be implying, ironically, that in her illness the medicines only brought forth worms, which 'issued' from her body, thus mocking his hopes for a pregnancy. If there was an original English source for this poem, it is now lost and no other source suggests that Anne had conceived shortly before her death. Most other accounts agree that it was the lack of a child that lay at the root of the couple's problems.

From what actual evidence survives, it is not possible to conclude that Richard and Elizabeth had an affair, or that he intended to marry her, or she him. Buck's letter is too full of holes to be useful and its provenance may have been doubtful, to say the least. What can be asserted is that, along with Anne, the pair were at Westminster that Christmas, where rumours circulated about their relationship, which the king later refuted. Some people clearly believed them. Croyland paraphrased how, that spring, Richard was obliged to call a council meeting at Clerkenwell to address his 'intention of contracting a marriage with his niece Elizabeth' which had 'never once entered his mind'. The chronicler states that some present 'very well knew the contrary' and had told Richard 'to his face' that the people of the North would 'rise in rebellion against' his desire to 'gratify an incestuous passion for his said niece', summoning twelve Doctors of Divinity to support their case. Croyland roots this objection in self-preservation. It was feared, by men like Ratcliffe and Catesby, that if Elizabeth of York became queen, she would seek to 'avenge upon them' the deaths of her relatives. Also there were indications that the North would rise in rebellion to prevent the match. Just before before Easter, 'in [the] presence of the mayor and citizens of London, in the great hall of the Hospital of Saint John', the king made 'the said denial in a loud and distinct voice'. The nature of his private feelings can only be a matter for speculation.

The Elizabeth of York episode presents a further challenge when it comes to the interpretation of Richard's marriage. Looking at Anne's relationship with him as a whole, from their childhood years at Middleham, through the separation caused by Warwick's Lancastrian fling, into their marriage and glorious Coronations at Westminster and York, the events of late 1484 and early 1485 make for uncomfortable reading. They appear to represent a sudden change in character by the king, a decisive rejection of his wife of a decade. This, in turn, forces a reassessment of their motives in entering the union and their priorities at different stages of their life-cycles. Of course, much had changed since the couple spoke their vows as teenagers in the spring of 1472. Richard and Anne were undoubtedly close from the mid-1460s, when they sat together at the table for the Cawood Castle feast, and Richard was a member of Warwick's household. A match may have been Anne's father's ultimate intention, although this was superseded by that of Isabel and Clarence and became redundant when his loyalties changed. There is not enough evidence to suggest the couple formed a romantic attachment during their youth, yet this does not mean it did not happen. When they did marry, the question of love and affection may not even have arisen. For royalty and the aristocracy, issues of pedigree and inheritance were far more important than companionship, which could be found elsewhere. Through the next decade, the pair's mutual goals allowed them to fulfil the contemporary roles of Lord and Lady of the Manor, continuing their line and upholding the peace. Even after the events of 1483, when Richard's new status forced a change in their priorities, the initial months appear to have been harmonious. Until this point, it is possible to speculate that the Gloucesters had a happy, successful marriage. At least, there is little to imply otherwise.

What continues to bind a couple together for over a decade? Then, as now, love and attraction are the primary factors, overriding the fluctuations of 'better and worse'. In a less romantic sense, habit, compatibility, children and shared mores establish an exclusive connection that remains successful as long as it is satisfying to both partners. Nor does this remain static; it must evolve as those concerned change and age. Yet, in the fifteenth century, for individuals like Richard and Anne, this was not enough. The primary function of a marriage was religious and dynastic. It was intended to safeguard against various sexual 'sins' and to legitimise any children born in order to facilitate inheritance. The Gloucesters had been able to produce only one surviving heir. With Edward's death, their marital equilibrium began to unravel. Additionally, the balance of priorities had shifted massively for Richard. His initial reluctance to accept the throne in the summer of 1483 has been portrayed by Shakespeare, and accepted by many, as disingenuous, but an alternative reading might highlight a tension between Richard's ambition and the enormity of the transformation such a role would bring. As Duke of Gloucester, he had been no stranger to responsibility but, as king, his private self was, of necessity, moderated by the good of the 'common weal'. His kingdom was about to be invaded and he had no son to secure his succession. This made him vulnerable.

The thorny question remains. Did Richard love Anne? If so, why do the rumours suggest that he treated her cruelly in her last months of life? Setting aside the scurrilous stream of gossip that dogged Richard during and after his life, what happened between husband and wife during what must have been, for Anne, a 'winter of discontent'? If she loved him, the disintegration of their family unit and her health must have been the tragic cost of the crown she now wore. While fifteenth-century definitions of marriage render these responses anachronistic, a modern analysis of his behaviour of 1484–85 cannot avoid such a question. If Richard had loved her, at any point, was this overridden by political imperatives and the need to protect himself and the fragile dynasty from increasing attack? Had his affection been gradually eroded over the course of their years together? Had he married her purely for her inheritance? It would be wrong to assess Richard through a romantic filter when it comes to his marriage; kings did tire of wives they had once loved and seek to replace them with younger models in order to father sons. Elizabeth of York's own son, Henry VIII, provides enough evidence for this. There is no doubt that he was romantically in love with Catherine of Aragon as a young man, yet their failure to produce a living son undermined his emotion. The desire to qualify the Gloucesters' relationship as a love match is strong, but there is little evidence to support or disprove such a theory. It is also natural to seek positive interpretations, in the interests of balance, when rejecting the centuries of defamation that had done so much damage to assessments of Richard as a man and a king. It may have been Anne's tragedy that their previously harmonious marriage did not fit the requirements of a royal match. Richard may have loved her as a wife, but considered that she failed in her primary function as a queen. If any turning point can be identified, the loss of Edward must be it. If they had remained as duke and duchess, the boy's death would have had predominantly personal ramifications. As king and queen, it opened the kingdom to invasion and conflict. Sadly for them as individuals, the Gloucesters' marriage was undone by their lack of fecundity. If Anne was Richard's tragic queen, he was, no less, her tragic husband.

The 'what-ifs' of history can become fascinating but dangerous dead ends. However, so long as they are considered in a similar vein to the best examples of historical fiction, they can add to the understanding and interpretation of enigmatic individuals. We cannot know what direction English history would have taken if Richard had not been killed at Bosworth. We can only speculate about what sort of king he would have proved to be and whether he would have remarried, and to whom. No doubt he wanted an heir. Would he have got his way? At what cost? Forty years before the marital trials of his great-nephew Henry VIII, would Richard's quest for a son have proved as tortuous as he sought increasingly young wives in the interests of Yorkist propagation?

14

Eclipse
1485

Strange shadows from the midst of death
Are round our being strangely cast:
Thus the great city, tower'd and steepled,
Is doubly peopled,
Haunted by ghosts of the remembered past.[1]

Early in 1485, Richard was thinking about his successor. After the death of Edward, he had initially nominated Clarence's son as his heir but, considering the boy's perceived feeble-mindedness and youth, then declared in favour of another of his nephews, John de la Pole, Earl of Lincoln. John was the son of his sister Elizabeth, who had married the second Duke of Suffolk. By 1485, her eldest son was already twenty-two, a far more viable successor than the ten-year-old boy. Richard appointed him President of the Council in the North and King's Lieutenant in Ireland. He also made provision for his illegitimate son, John of Pontefract, who was assigned the captaincy of Calais on 11 March 1485. In the grant, the 'well-beloved' youth is described as having a 'disposition and natural vigour, agility of body and inclination to all good customs', which promised 'great and certain hope of future service'.[2] Given his loss of Prince Edward, it is not impossible that Richard was lining up his bastard as his spare heir. He was certain now that he would never have another child by the queen, whose condition was weakening every day.

One grey morning, Anne was dressing in her chamber when one of her ladies-in-waiting made a startling admission. The rumours regarding Richard and Elizabeth had not abated; now, in fact, they were joined by another, stating that Anne herself was already dead. Perhaps she had appeared less and less in society since the New Year, taking meals in private and resting in the company of her women. She may well have had a spell in bed, her absence giving rise to speculation. Croyland and Vergil report that she was distressed by the news and went straight to her husband, in tears, her hair loose, asking why he should 'determine her death'. Richard, in turn, reassured her, 'kissing hir [and] made awnswer loovingly comfortyng hir, bad hir be of good chere'. Holinshed stated that the slanders had originated with the king, as a ruse to scare the queen to death; 'to the intent that she taking some conceit of this strange fame ... in ... sorowfull agonie' and puts Richard's faith in the rumours to cover up his dastardly intention, if Anne 'should fortune by that or anie other waies to lease her life'. As may be expected, Shakespeare developed this idea of a whispering campaign, designed to tip an already terminally ill woman prematurely into her grave. In Act 4, Scene 2 of *Richard III*, he instructs Catesby to 'rumour it abroad, that Anne, my wife, is sick and like to die'. His motive? 'I must be married to my brother's daughter, or else my kingdom stands on brittle glass.' A scene later, the audience learns the queen had 'bid the world goodnight', not even meriting a death on stage. She returns as a ghost for a brief riposte on the eve of Bosworth, directing her prayers in Tudor's favour against the man with whom she 'never slept a quiet hour'. Anne Neville was dead and the audience believed Richard had killed her.

In 1699, the fashion for 'improving' Shakespeare saw poet laureate Colley Cibber produce his own version of *Richard III*. In a scene invented for the play, he portrays Richard and Anne at the point in which their marriage breaks down. His Anne cannot help but compare her second husband with her first, considering matrimony to be a 'blessing to the virtuous' rather than the 'scourge of our offences' it has now become. Now her life 'yields only sorrow', with Richard the 'constant disturber' of her rest, as she, 'night after night, with cares lie waking'. She asks him, 'Have I deserved this usage?' To which he replies, 'Out-liv'd my liking,' now that he 'lov'd another'. Anne then invites him to kill her, which he declines, as 'the meddling world will call it murder'. She wishes she could 'with deadly venome be anointed' but is done away with by Richard's 'physician'. The 1995 McKellen screenplay portrayed Richard encouraging the queen's developing depression and drug addiction, to the point at which she overdoses, either by her own hand or the administration of another. In the original version, Shakespeare's Anne also wishes for her own death, through the symbolic medium of Coronation:

I would to God that the inclusive verge
Of golden metal that must round my brow
Were red-hot steel to sear me to the brain.

In March 1485, Anne's actual death was to prove hardly less dramatic or mysterious. In fact, all that can be stated for certain is that she died, in the Palace of Westminster, on the 16th of that month. Lisa Hilton states that, given the rumours, Anne's 'death was all too convenient' but her illness may well have triggered the gossip, rather than been their intended result. Subsequent sources recorded that she passed away during an eclipse of the sun. The symbolism of this, as an indicator of the demise of the Yorkist dynasty, with its motif of the sun in splendour, would not have been lost on her contemporaries. Fabyan related that it was bad rumours arising from the death of the queen that caused Richard 'to fall in much hatred of his subjects', although Vergil gave a non-committal account of her end: 'The quene, whether she wer dispatchyd with sorowfulness, or poyson, dyed within few days after, and was buryed at Westmynster.'

So how exactly did Anne die? Tuberculosis (TB) and cancer have been suggested as the most likely causes, which could fit with theories regarding her low fertility. Richard's detractors favoured the poison theory and some of his contemporaries believed that enough to repeat it. In an essay of 1980, *The Death of Queen Anne Neville*, Anne F. Sutton explores how the circumstances of Anne's final illness are consistent with the diagnosis of TB. Firstly, there is the suddenness of her death. According to the Croyland Chronicle, she showed no signs of illness through 1484, but fell ill soon after Christmas, which allows for a rapid decline over a period of twelve weeks. Although there are many different kinds of tuberculosis, the most common, pulmonary TB, is an infectious bacteria spread through coughs and sneezes. It is not inherited but can easily thrive in shared living quarters, suggesting that Isabel Neville's premature death at twenty-five may not just have been a result of childbirth. The symptoms of pulmonary tuberculosis can include fever, breathlessness, night sweats, coughing up blood, weakness, weight loss and anorexia. Perhaps this may explain the physical similarity between the eighteen-year-old Elizabeth of York and Anne, a woman a decade her elder, who had borne a child. Secondly, a severe shock, such as the death of her son, could also trigger a latent infection to become a full-scale disease. Physicians of the medieval period did not understand the illness. Twelfth-century Hungarians asserted that it was caused when a dog-shaped demon 'occupied' the body and began to consume the lungs. She may have been prescribed garlic and the poisons mercury and arsenic. Perhaps these accelerated her demise. Thirdly, her symptoms would have been considered contagious and caused sufficient alarm for Richard's doctors to advise him to keep his distance. Anne's death, amid the prophetic eclipse, can never be completely resolved. Tuberculosis may fit the known facts but those facts are limited. There may have been a number of other causes. Equally, the rapid time-scale, rumours, symptoms and possible 'cures' could indicate poisoning by person or persons unknown. Did someone take advantage of the temporary darkness and smother her? Did she sink into a Lady Macbeth-style derangement, prompted by guilt, just weeks before her husband's own violent death? In the twenty-first century, it is not possible to know for sure.

Few tributes to Queen Anne remain. Her reign was one of the shortest in English history, lasting only twenty-two months. According to Fabyan, she was a woman of 'gracious fame, upon whose soul ... Jesus have mercy'. Agostino Barbarigo, future Doge of Venice, wrote to Richard III, regretting the loss of his 'beloved' consort and exhorting him, 'endowed with consummate equanimity and marvellous virtues, of your wisdom and grandeur of mind to bear the disaster calmly and resign yourself to the divine will'. According to the Italian, who had never met Anne, she lived a 'religious and catholic life, and was so adorned with goodness, prudence, and excellent morality, as to leave a name immortal'.[3] In the intervening centuries, though, it was Anne's mortal name that was often overlooked. Her life has been overshadowed by the controversies of Richard's reign and his death in battle. Today the site of her burial is disputed; perhaps Richard intended to erect a tomb in her honour but he ran out of time. In 1960, the Richard III Society established a memorial plaque on the wall of Westminster Abbey, close to where her remains are thought to lie, inscribed:

Anne Nevill[e] 1456–85, Queen of England, younger daughter of Richard, Earl of Warwick, called the Kingmaker, wife to the last Plantagenet King, Richard III. In person she was seemly, amiable and beauteous ... And according to the interpretation of her name Anne full gracious. *Requiescat in pace.*

What, exactly, was Anne's contribution to her times? While Richard III has inspired his own cult following, Anne has received far less critical attention. However, the nature of her relationship with her husband can help provide answers to some of the key questions of his accession and reign. More significantly, though, Anne must be allowed to stand alone as a late medieval woman, wife, mother and queen. She deserves to be studied as more than just a foil for the men in her life and as a far more complex individual than a mere pawn of their schemes. Her tenure as queen was so brief and poorly recorded as to make analysis of her achievements difficult. Difficult, but not impossible.

Firstly, as a wife and queen, Anne's role was to validate her husband in his position. Of course, Richard was king in his own right. As the only surviving son of Richard, Duke of York, following the declared illegitimacy of Edward IV and the invalidity of his marriage, he did not need Anne in order to claim the throne. However, the events of summer 1483 left him vulnerable to gossip, criticism and attack. His regime needed every symbol of validity to demonstrate its pre-eminence and durability, so Richard sought to embed himself at the heart of Westminster by establishing networks of ties by blood, marriage and loyalty. This began as early as his Coronation. The presence of a devoted wife, and queen of long standing, added a further level of respectability. Anne was no insignificant individual in her own right; embodied in her was the memory of Warwick's status and 'kingmaking' activities. If, by implication, she stood beside Richard, so should others who may have doubted his claim and role in the disappearance of the princes. Even today, the question of Richard's involvement elicits comments that Anne would not have remained loyal to him, had she believed in his guilt, yet this is a modern perspective. Anne had known her husband since they were children and continued to back him once he became king, whatever she may or may not have known. No doubt her own considerable ambition contributed to this, but, more importantly, they presented a powerful union.

Equally, a queen was seen as an indispensable facet of medieval monarchy, tempering her husband's warlike majesty with charity, mercy and gentleness. As the figurehead of a network of female and juvenile dependants, the queen represented an interface between a divine regime and its subjects. There had not been a double Coronation since that of Edward II and Isabel of France in February 1308. From her role as Duchess of Gloucester, Anne was already known as a sponsor of various religious establishments and the cults of saints, as well as having represented Richard at the York courts. Her political function was as an intermediary, patron of the arts and example of piety. As the embodiment of these, her visible presence at Richard's side, on occasions such as the Coronations at Westminster and York, the royal progress and Christmases at Westminster, completed what her contemporaries would have sought as the desirable model of a royal family. Thus, her function was a confirmatory one, for Richard the individual and as king.

Secondly, the role of a medieval queen had to encompass motherhood. Anne had already provided Richard with one son, the minimum requirement for the continuation of the dynasty, but the absence of any other surviving children was clearly an issue, as it made Richard's inheritance as tenuous as the young boy's life. Yet Anne's low fertility cannot be assumed. Modern medical studies have ascertained that the responsibility for a lack of fertility in couples can lie with either partner or be an unfortunate consequence of their specific pairing. Richard had fathered at least two illegitimate children but there is no way of knowing what Anne's levels of fecundity would have been if she were with a different partner. To her husband and his contemporaries, though, the lack of children in a marriage was always attributable to the woman. Through fifteenth-century eyes, Anne had failed in this aspect of her duties as a wife and queen.

The brevity of Anne's reign makes it difficult to state decisively what model of queenship she provided. During her lifetime, she witnessed the reigns of two other women, both of whom she was related to through marriage. Her mother-in-law, Margaret of Anjou, presented herself as a warrior queen, equal to the task of kingship, which she assumed during the periods of her husband's illness. The unpopularity of her favourites, coupled with the unruly nature of the armies under their command, made her into a figure of fear for many of her contemporaries. Margaret can hardly be blamed for actively defending her husband and son, and her contemporary warlike queen, Isabella of Castile, attracted epithets such as powerful, forceful and brave when she met rebels in person. One difference was that Isabel was part of a functioning couple, supported by her formidable husband, Ferdinand of Aragon; in England, Margaret was despised for blurring the lines between kingship and queenship. For most of Anne's life, her sister-in-law Elizabeth Wydeville had worn the crown and made her influence felt through the sphere of family and household. Her undeniable sexual hold over Edward led to accusations of 'pillow-talk' and resentment was caused by the advancement of her large and ambitious family. The greatest cause of dislike was her supposedly humble roots and rapid ascendancy to power, which meant her marriage had been conducted in secret. Neither modelled a type of queenship that would have appealed to Anne, as far as her character can be understood. As half of a married couple of ten years' duration, her position was unusual, as her reign was an extension of an established partnership. Unlike her contemporaries, she had not chosen Richard in expectation of a crown and did not have to undergo the process of integration and acceptance as queen. Nor did she need to define herself as a wife in the public eye, as Margaret and Elizabeth had done. As a result, she and Richard are likely to have approached their rule from a position of mutual understanding and shared ambition. Under different circumstances, Anne Neville could have proved to be a very successful queen.

Epilogue

Lord Jesus Christ, deign to free me, your servant King Richard, from every tribulation, sorrow and trouble in which I am placed ... hear me, in the name of all your goodness, for which I give thanks, and for all the gifts granted to me, because you made me from nothing and redeemed me out of your bounteous love and pity from eternal damnation to promising eternal life.[1]

On 1 August 1485, Henry Tudor set sail from Harfleur and landed at Milford Haven six days later, with an army of exiles and French mercenaries. According to Fabyan, he knelt down 'and with meke countenaunce and pure deuotion', recited a psalm 'and kissed the ground mekely, and reuerently made the signe of the crosse upon him', then 'he commaunded soche as wer about him, boldly in the name of God and S. George to set forwarde'. Nearby was Sir William Herbert, of Raglan Castle. Herbert was the son of Henry's old guardian, Earl of Pembroke, on whose estates the boy had grown up. William was six years his elder and must have known the young Tudor since their teenage years, when he had been intended as a husband for William's sister, Maude. Henry may have hoped to find support from his guardian's son. However, the previous year, Herbert had married Richard's illegitimate daughter Katherine, for which he received an annual payment that nearly doubled his income. Charles Ross has suggested that it was probably an agent of Herbert who brought news of Tudor's landing to the king.

Croyland claimed that Richard had been uncertain 'at what port [Tudor] intended to effect a landing', so 'betook himself to the North', leaving Francis Lovell in the vicinity of Southampton. The chronicler dates this to shortly before the feast of Pentecost, which fell that year on 22 May. The Court Rolls can provide some answers which disprove Croyland's time-scale. Richard was at Westminster as late as 1 August, after which he proceeded to Nottingham. The news reached him at the castle there, ten days later. At once he sent out messengers to summon his lords to rendezvous, with their armies, at Leicester, although he did not arrive there himself until 20 August. Fabyan says Richard 'gathered his power in all haste', while Croyland believed him to have been complacent, rejoicing as the 'long wished-for day had arrived, for him to triumph with ease over so contemptible a faction', resulting in 'uninterrupted tranquillity' for the kingdom. Both chroniclers wrote with the benefit of hindsight. In 1485, the king prepared himself as best he knew how, as a seasoned commander, with experience from battles such as Edgecote and Tewkesbury. In Leicester, he was reputed to have stayed at the old Blue Boar, or White Boar Inn, also known as King Richard's House, which was the city's 'principal hostelry'. Legend has it that the populace tore down the sign after the battle that August and the whole building was pulled down in 1836.[2] From Leicester, he led the royal forces west, where they camped upon Ambion Hill, near Bosworth Field, and lay down to rest for the night.

Shakespeare's depiction of Richard's terrible nightmares before the battle is well known. Describing herself as 'wretched', the ghost of Anne appears in order to curse her husband, with whom she 'never slept a quiet hour'. The spectral presence of supposed victims, speaking their allegations and curses, was a common literary device, which the Bard also used in *Julius Caesar*, written in the same year as *Richard III*, and later in *Macbeth* and *Hamlet*. Medieval Catholicism explained the existence of ghosts as souls trapped in purgatory, who could manifest in order to ensure that justice was done. The Protestant view, though, relevant for the context in which Shakespeare wrote, was that purgatory and, therefore, ghosts, did not exist; instead, these would be seen as devils, sent to taunt and alarm the living. These two interpretations, polarised along religious lines, correspond with the most dichotomic views of Richard's life and reign. According to one, he is the murderer troubled by his crimes; on the other side, he is a pious, responsible ruler on the eve of a critical battle, struggling against forces of evil.

Where exactly did the story of the nightmares originate? More's history does not cover the battle and neither the London chronicler, Fabyan, nor the *Ballad of Bosworth Field* poem mention them. The account appears first in the Croyland Chronicle, written in April 1486. According to this source, Richard declared he had 'seen dreadful visions' and imagined himself 'surrounded by a multitude of daemons'. Apparently, this made his usually 'attenuated' face 'more livid and

ghastly than usual'. Recording these events only months after the
marriage of Henry Tudor and Elizabeth of York, Croyland is keen to
state the godlessness and general disorder of the losing side, which
lacked any chaplain 'to perform divine service' or anyone to prepare
breakfast 'to refresh the flagging spirits of the king'. Similar stories are
repeated by Polydore Vergil, who had completed a draft of his history
by 1513, although it was not published for twenty years. Vergil adds
that Richard was mindful of his troops, 'refresshy[ng] his soldiers that
night from ther travale, and with many woords exhortyd them to
the fyght to coome'. His 'horryble ymages as yt wer of evell spyrytes'
replicates Croyland's in description, although he adds that they bred in
the king a fatal and 'suddane feare' so that he 'dyd not buckle himself to
the conflict with such lyvelyness of corage and countenance as before'.
Vergil also attributes this to 'a conscyence guiltie of haynous [heinous]
offences'. In 1587, Shakespeare's source, Raphael Holinshed, reputed
these details to 'fame', implying that, in the intervening century, the
story of the nightmare had become widespread. In terms reminiscent
of the fate of Marlowe's *Doctor Faustus*,³ Richard saw 'diuerse images
like terrible diuels, which pulled and haled him, not suffering him to
take anie quiet or rest', after which 'his heart being almost damped'.
According to legend, he had seen a soothsayer (fortune-teller or seer)
in Leicester, the night before the battle, who predicted 'where your
spur should strike on the ride into battle, your head shall be broken
on the return'. Apparently, his spur struck the bridge stone of the city's
Bow Bridge as he left it in the morning. Independently of the battle, he
had already planned to be buried in York, in a chantry chapel of the
cathedral, where a hundred chaplains would pray for his soul.

Perhaps there is something in the accounts of the nightmare. After
all, on paper, Henry Tudor should not really have won the Battle
of Bosworth that August day. He had no experience of combat and
had fewer troops, as well as challenging an anointed king who was a
veteran of such campaigns and had the higher ground. He also firmly
believed God was on his side, parading the cross before his troops
and hoping for a swift and decisive validation of his reign. Estimates
have placed Richard's army at around 8,000, with Henry's a little over
half that. The flower of English aristocracy lined up behind their king,
who had taken steps to ensure the loyalty of those who had previously
been his enemies, through alliances, grants and titles. The *Ballad of
Bosworth Field*, thought to have been composed by an eye-witness,
possibly based in Stanley's camp, lists those who turned out to fight
at his side: the Duke of Norfolk, 'Earls of Lincoln, Northumberland
and Westmorland, Lords Zouche, Maltravers, Welles, Grey of Codnor,

Bowes, Audley, Berkeley, Ferrers, Lovell, Fitzhugh, Scrope of Masham, Scrope of Bolton, Dacre, Ogle, Lumley, and Greystoke', as well as a multitude of knights including Henry Percy, John Grey, Robert Brackenbury, Marmaduke Constable, Richard Radcliffe and John Neville. Richard is described as having dignity and suffering 'great misfortune' and was the 'causer of his owne death', brought down by 'wicked counsel'. The account of Richard charging single-handedly at Tudor, as he stood surrounded by his troops, may have been an act of bravery or desperation. It cost him the battle. Many of his expected 15,000 troops had failed to commit themselves during the conflict, with Sir William Stanley, husband of Margaret Beaufort, reputedly launching a personal attack on the king in order to save Tudor. Richard died with the words, 'Treason, treason,' on his lips. His close associates, John Howard, Duke of Norfolk, William Catesby and Richard Ratcliffe fell at his side, while Lovell escaped to an uncertain fate.

Richard's end has attracted controversy since he fell at Bosworth on 22 August 1485. Further legends arose surrounding the desperate search for a horse and Tudor's discovery of the crown in a hawthorn bush, which Stanley then used to crown him. 'The Ghost of Richard III' gives a graphic account of Richard's end and the removal of his body:

> My braine they dasht, which flew on ev'ry side,
> As they would shew me my tracts of policie:
> My yeares with stabs, my days they multiplide
> In drops of blood, t' expresse my crueltie:
> They pierst my hart, evaporating pride,
> And mangled me like an anatomie,
> And then with horses drag'd me to my tombe.
> Thus finish't I my fate by heaven's just doome.

Fabyan describes how Richard's body, 'spoiled and naked', was carried 'unreverently ouertwharte the horse back ... untl ye friers at Leiceter', where he was 'with little reverence buried'. Holinshed adds that he had 'nothing left about him, not so much as a clout to couer his priuie members' and contrasts this with the way the king had 'gorgeouslie [the day before] with pompe and pride departed' from the same city. It is Holinshed who presents the disturbing image of the dead king 'trussed ... like a hog or calfe, his head and armes hanging on the one side of the horsse, and his legs on the other side, and all besprinkled with mire and bloud', in which condition 'he was brought to the graie friers church within the towne, and there laie like a miserable spectacle'. This was probably at the church of the Annunciation of

Our Lady, before he was buried in the church of the small monastic community at Greyfriars. In 1495, Henry Tudor, then Henry VII, paid for a marble and alabaster monument to be erected over his tomb, at a cost of £50. The church was demolished following its dissolution in 1536 and the bones were reputed to have been thrown into the nearby River Soar.

Few voices were raised in lamentation. One of the only surviving tributes came from the one place where he had perhaps been most at home, from whence he derived his family name. The Mayor of York's sergeant recorded that 'King Richard, late mercifully reigning over us, was through great treason … piteously slain and murdered, to the great heaviness of this city'. Yet, within the year, allegiances had changed. Such were the times. In 1486, Henry VII paid his first visit to the city so closely associated with Richard and Anne, where they had sat enthroned for four hours with their son, at the height of summer 1484. The mayor and aldermen rode out to meet him, dressed in their official robes of scarlet and violet, mulberry and red. At Micklebar Gate, which had been graced in 1460 by the head of Richard's father, the Duke of York, children lauded the new king. A huge red-and-white rose was displayed to symbolise the union of Henry and Elizabeth of York, and crowds sprinkled the party with rose water and sweetmeats. It seemed that while Anne had been forgotten, Richard would continue to be vilified forever. That is, until 527 years later.

*

In late August 2012, a team of archaeologists from the University of Leicester began to excavate a city-centre car park, believed to be the site of the old Grey Friars church. Unsure of exactly how the layout of the church mapped out over the modern site, they dug three long trenches and hit at once upon some bones, which they set aside for further explanation: surely they could not be so lucky as to have discovered the king on their first attempt? By 5 September, they had uncovered glazed floor tiles and fragments of stained glass, consistent with expectations of such a building. Now they knew for certain that they were actually inside the church, even within the location suggested by John Rous, for Richard's burial. This made them return to the original bones, uncovered on that first day, and begin to scrape away the soil around them. The skeleton of an adult male emerged, located in the most prestigious burial location of the church, the choir. The skull showed evidence of fatal injuries caused by a bladed weapon, as well a number of other blows. It appeared that the individual had met a violent end, probably in battle. More controversially, the bones indicated the presence of scoliosis, a condition that can result, to varying degrees, in curvature of the spine. Even *in situ*, the skeleton's spine formed a distinctive 'S' shape. The circumstantial evidence for its identity as the lost Yorkist king looked strong.

A sample of mitochondrial DNA was extracted from the teeth and compared to a sample taken from Michael Ibsen, a British Canadian who had been identified by genealogist Dr John Ashdown-Hill as a direct descendant of Richard's sister, Anne of York. While forensic pathologists worked to establish the exact cause of death, specialists in medieval weaponry were summoned to give advice on the types of instrument that might have inflicted the injuries to the skull. The bones were thoroughly cleaned and closely examined to establish the individual's age, height and state of health, before being radiocarbon dated and given a CT scan, to allow for a three-dimensional reconstruction to take place. Soil samples were also collected and analysed, as were mineralised dental plaque deposits, to help ascertain details about diet and living conditions. The world waited to hear the results.

On 4 February 2013, the archaeologists' findings were presented in a press conference, organised by the university. Having subjected the remains to 'rigorous archaeological investigation', some 'truly astonishing' conclusions had been reached. The body had lain only 680 millimetres below the surface of the car park and had almost been destroyed by nineteenth-century building works, which were probably responsible for its lack of feet. No evidence was found of a coffin, shroud or any other funeral formalities; likewise it appeared not to have been buried with any clothing, adornment or personal objects. The torso was twisted, with its head propped up and jaw open. The hands were crossed, right over left, across the pelvis, suggesting they had been tied. Detailed skeletal analysis confirmed that it was the remains of an adult male, aged from his late twenties to late thirties, consistent with Richard's age at death of thirty-two. The evidence also showed he had enjoyed a diet rich in protein during his life, particularly meat and fish, indicative of high-status living. Ten separate wounds were found on the body, two of which, to the skull, would have proved fatal and could only have been caused if Richard had lost his protective helmet during the final melee. They were made by a range of weapons, including at least one dagger and possibly a halberd, while others appeared to have been inflicted after death as further acts of humiliation. Radiocarbon dating placed his year of death somewhere between 1450 and 1540. Two lines of DNA descent were established, from Richard's sister, Anne of York, which provided the final confirmation that the bones did, in fact, belong to him.[4] That night, a Channel Four documentary, *The King in the Car Park*, revealed the reconstructed head of the king for the first time, similar to the portraits of the 1520s with his strong nose and jaw. With a half-smile playing on his lips, unexpectedly charismatic, a face stared back at the camera that had not been seen for 527 years.

According to archaeological practice, the bones will be laid to rest at the nearest location to their discovery, at Leicester Cathedral. There are no plans to reunite him in death with his wife Anne, whose exact resting place in Westminster Abbey is still uncertain.

Acknowledgements

Thanks go to the team at Amberley, Jonathan for suggesting this book and Nicola and the publicity department for their continuing support and promotion. I would also like to thank the many wonderful people I have met online whilst writing, who have offered me their expertise and enthusiasm, asked and answered questions and kindly shared their images, resources and ideas. They are too numerous to mention, all around the world, but they have made a significant contribution to this book. Thanks also to all my family, in particular to Tom for his love and support; also the Hunts, for Sue's generosity and John's local knowledge and continual supply of interesting and unusual books. Most of all, thanks to my mother for her invaluable proof-reading skills and my father for his enthusiasm. This is the result of the books they read me, the museums they took me to as a child and the love and imagination with which they encouraged me

Notes

Introduction
1. Ian McKellen official website.
2. *Ibid.*
3. *Ibid.*

1 Battles and Births, 1453–1456
1. Complaint made by Cade's rebels; Seward.
2. Ditchfield, P. H. and W. Page, 'Windsor Castle: History', *A History of the County of Berkshire: Volume 3* (1923).
3. Furnivall, F. J. (ed.) and Andrew Boorde, *Fyrst Boke of the Introduction of Knowledge* (Early English Text Society, 1870).
4. Brunschwig, Hieronymous, *Buch der Cirurgia* (1497).
5. Seward, Desmond, *A Brief History of the Wars of the Roses* (Constable & Co. Ltd, 1995).
6. Kendall, P., *Richard III* (Norton & Co., 2002).
7. Hall, Edward, *Chronicle; containing the History of England, during the reign of Henry the fourth and the succeeding monarchs, to the end of the reign of Henry VIII, in which are particularly described the manners and customs of those periods* (Collated with the editions of 1548 and 1550) (London: J. Johnson, 1809).
8. Seward.
9. *Ibid.*
10. *Ibid.*
11. SLP Henry VI July 1455.
12. *Ibid.*
13. SLP Milan 1455.
14. Licence, A., *In Bed with the Tudors* (Amberley, 2012).

2 Castle Life, 1456–1458
1. Hanawalt, Barbara, *Growing up in Medieval London* (Oxford University Press, 1993).
2. *Ibid.*
3. *Ibid.*
4. Orme, Nicholas, *Childhood in Medieval England 500–1500* (Unpublished paper).
5. Calendar of Close Rolls for Edward IV, 1483.
6. Hanawalt.
7. *A Collection of Ordinances and Regulations for the Governance of the Royal Household, made in divers reigns from King Edward III to King William and Queen Mary* (London: Society of Antiquities, 1790).
8. Nichols, John Gough (ed.), *The Chronicle of Calais* (Camden Society, 1846).
9. Phillips, Kim M., *Medieval Maidens* (Manchester University Press, 2003).
10. Orme.
11. Rickert, E. (ed.), *The Babees' Book: Medieval Manners for the Young, Done into Modern English from Dr Furnival's Texts* (Chatto & Windus, 1908).
12. Strutt, Joseph, *The Sports and Pastimes of the People of England* (Methuen & Co., 1908).
13. Rickert.

3 Warring Cousins, 1458–1460
1. Pepys 1, 64–5. *A most sorrowfull Song, setting forth the miserable end of Banister, who betraied the Duke of Buckingham, his Lord and Master.* EBBA ID 20265.
2. www.devonperspectives.co.uk.

3. Connors, Michael, *John Hawley, Merchant, Mayor and Privateer* (Richard Webb, 2008).
4. Chaucer, G., *The Canterbury Tales* (*c.* 1387).
5. SLP Henry VI May 1458.
6. *Ibid.*
7. Ingham, Patricia, *Sovereign Fantasies: Arthurian Romance and the Making of Britain* (University of Pennsylvania, 2001).
8. Weir, Alison, *Lancaster and York: The Wars of the Roses* (Vintage, 2009).
9. Gairdner, James (ed.), *Gregory's Chronicle 1461–9* (London, 1876).
10. *Ibid.*
11. Weir, *Lancaster* (2009).
12. SLP Venice July 1460.
13. Edward IV: November 1461, Parliament Rolls of Medieval England.
14. Henry VI: October 1460, Parliament Rolls of Medieval England.
15. *Ibid.*
16 *Ibid.*
17. *Ibid.*
18. Hall.

4 Boy and Girl, 1461–1465
1. Shakespeare, William, *Henry VI, Part 3*.
2. Nichols, John Gough, *Inventories of the wardrobes, plate, chapel stuff, etc. of Henry Fitzroy, Duke of Richmond and of the wardrobe stuff at Baynard's Castle of Katharine, Princess Dowager* (Camden Society, 1855).
3. http://www.english-heritage.org.uk/publications/middleham-castle-info-for-teachers/.
4. Amt, Emilie (ed.), *Women's Lives in Medieval Europe, A Sourcebook* (Routledge, 1993).
5. *A Collection of Ordinances and Regulations for the Governance of the Royal Household, made in divers reigns from King Edward III to King William and Queen Mary* (London: Society of Antiquities, 1790).
6. *Ibid.*
7. Wilkinson, Josephine, *Richard, the Young King to Be* (Amberley, 2009).
8. Weightman, Christine, *Margaret of York, Duchess of Burgundy, 1446–1503* (New York: St Martin's Press, 1989).
9. Hicks, Michael, *Warwick the Kingmaker* (Blackwell, 1998).
10. *Ibid.*
11. Calendar of Close Rolls for Edward IV, Nov 1461.
12. Rhodes, Hugh, *The Boke of Nurture*.
13. *Ibid.*

5 Romance and Chivalry, 1465–1469
1. John Rous on Anne Neville.
2. Sutton, Anne F. and Livia Visser-Fuchs, '"Richard Liveth Yet": An Old Myth', *Ricardian*, 9 (June 1992).
3. Payne Collier, J. (ed.), 'The Ghost of Richard III' (First pub. 1614; London: Shakespeare Society, 1884).
4. Laynesmith, J. L., *The Last Medieval Queens: English Queenship 1445–1503* (Oxford University Press, 2004).
5. Weightman.
6. Gravett, Christopher, *Knight: Noble Warrior of England, 1200–1600* (Osprey, 2008).
7. Clephan, R. Coltman, *The Medieval Tournament* (Dover, 1995).
8. *King René's Tournament Book* (1406; trans. E. Bennett, 1997).
9. *Ibid.*
10. *Ibid.*
11. *Ibid.*
12. Clephan.

6 Queens in Waiting, 1469–1470
1. Anonymous, 'How the Good Wife Taught her Daughter' (1430).
2. State Letters and Papers, Milan 1470.
3. *Ibid.*
4. *Ibid.*
5. *Ibid.*
6. *Ibid.*
7. Abbot, Jacob, *Margaret of Anjou* (Harper and Brothers, 1904).
8. SLP Milan Oct 1458.
9. Abbott.
10. SLP Milan 1470.
11. *Ibid.*
12. Abbot.
13. SLP Milan 1470.

7 Lancastrian Princess, 1471
1. Pepys 3.235 *A Courtly New Ballad of the Princely Wooing of the fair maid of London, by King Edward.* EBBA 21249.
2. Bruce, J. (ed.), *Historie of the Arrivall of Edward IV in England and Finall Recouerye of his Kingdomes from Henry VI* (Camden Society, 1838).
3. *Ibid.*
4. Commines.
5. Jesse, John Heneage, *Memoirs of King Richard III and Some of his Contemporaries* (London: Richard Bentley, 1862).
6. Bruce, *Arrivall.*
7. SLP Milan 1471.
8. *Ibid.*
9. Weir, Alison, *Lancaster and York: The Wars of the Roses* (Vintage, 1995).

10. SLP Venice June 1471.
11. *Ibid.*
12. Wilkinson.

8 A Strange Courtship, 1471–1472
1. Bogin, M. quoted in Shahar, Shulamith, *The Fourth Estate: A History of Women in the Middle Ages* (Methuen, 1983).
2. *A Collection of Ordinances and Regulations for the Governance of the Royal Household, made in divers reigns from King Edward III to King William and Queen Mary* (London: Society of Antiquities, 1790).
3. *Ibid.*
4. *Ibid.*
5. *Ibid.*
6. Hilton, Lisa, *Queens Consort: England's Medieval Queens* (Phoenix, 2009).
7. Hicks.
8. Hilton.
9. Cheetham, Anthony, *The Life and Times of Richard III* (Weidenfeld & Nicolson, 1972).
10. Page, W. (ed.), *A History of the County of London: Volume 1: London within the Bars, Westminster and Southwark* (1909).
11. Hicks.
12. Twemlow, J. A. (ed.), *Calendar of Papal Registers relating to Great Britain and Ireland*, August 1473.
13. *Ibid.*, March 1485.

9 Richard's Wife, 1472–1483
1. Bernardino of Siena, 'Sermon on Wives and Widows' (1472).
2. Calendar of the Patent Rolls Preserved in the Public Record Office of the Reigns of Edward IV, Edward V and Richard III, April 1477.
3. CPR Richard III June 1484.
4. Jones, M. and S. Walker (eds), 'Private Indentures for Life Service in Peace and War', *Camden Miscellany*, XXXII (Royal Historical Society, 1994).
5. Idley, Peter, *Instructions to his Son* (Greifswald, Druck von J. Abel, 1903).
6. *Ibid.*
7. *Ibid.*
8. *Ibid.*
9. *Ibid.*
10. Hammond, Peter W., 'The Illegitimate Children of Richard III', in Petre, J. (ed.), *Richard III: Crown and People, A Selection of Articles from The Ricardian Journal of the Richard III Society, March 1975 to December 1981* (Alan Sutton, 1985).

11. Kendall.
12. *Camden Miscellany*, XXXII.
13. Mitchell, Dorothy, 'York and Richard III' (Silver Boar, 1984).
14. *Ibid.*
15. Bernardino of Siena.
16. Sutton, Anne F., 'Caxton the Cult of St Winifred and Shrewsbury' in Clark, Linda (ed.), *Of Mice and Men; Image, Belief and Regulation in Late Medieval England* (Boydell Press, 2005).

10 Crisis, Summer 1483
1. Richard III, Letter to the Mayor of Southampton, 1484. 'The corporation of Southampton: Letters and loose memoranda', *The Manuscripts of the Corporations of Southampton and Kings Lynn*, Eleventh report, Appendix; part III (1887), pp. 97–134.
2. Davies, Robert, *Extracts from the Municipal Records of the City of York During the Reigns of Edward IV, Edward V and Richard III* (London: J. B. Nichols, 1843).

11 Queen, July–December 1483
1. Reputed to have been written by Henry VI when a prisoner in the Tower.
2. More.
3. Hicks.
4. *Ibid.*
5. Anne F. Sutton and P. W. Hammond (eds), *The Coronation of Richard III: The Extant Documents* (Gloucester: Alan Sutton, 1983).
6. *Ibid.*
7. CPR Richard July 1483.
8. *Ibid.*
9. *Ibid.*
10. *Ibid.*
11. *Ibid.*
12. *Ibid.*
13. Croyland.
14. *Ibid.*
15. *Ibid.*
16. Pollard.
17. 'The Corporation of Southampton' (1887).

12 Disquiet, 1484
1. K. Dockray, 'Sir Marmaduke Constable of Flamborough' in Petre, J. (ed.), *Richard III* (1985).
2. CPR Richard III 1483–5.
3. Walford, E., 'Greenwich', *Old and New London: Volume 6* (1878), pp. 164–76.
4. *Ibid.*
5. Sutton, Anne F. and R. C. Hairsine,

'Richard III at Canterbury' in Petre, J (ed.), *Richard III* (1985).

6. Tatton-Brown, T., *Canterbury: History and Guide* (Alan Sutton, 1994).

7. 'Addenda to Volume 12: Minutes of the Records and Accounts of the Chamber', *The History and Topographical Survey of the County of Kent: Volume 12* (1801), pp. 612–662.

8. Thanks to John D. Hunt for local information on this.

9. Pisan, Christine de, *The Treasure of the City of Ladies or the Book of the Three Virtues* (trans. Rosalind Brown-Grant: Penguin, 1999).

10. Hicks.

11. CPR Richard III 1483.

12. *Ibid.*

13. *Ibid.*

14. *Ibid.*

15. 'Section II: Nottingham Castle', *Thoroton's History of Nottinghamshire: Volume 2, Republished with large additions by John Throsby* (1790).

16. Hicks.

17. Mortimer, R. and T. Tatton-Brown (eds), *Westminster Abbey: The Lady Chapel of Henry VII* (Boydell Press, 2003).

18. Fabyan.

19. Hillier, K., P. Normark and P. Hammond, 'Colyngbourne's Rhyme' in Petre, J. (ed.), *Richard III* (1985), pp. 107–8.

20. *Ibid.*

21. 'The Corporation of Southampton' (1887).

22. Baldwin.

13. Buck in Kincaid, A. N. (ed.), *The History of King Richard III* (1979).

13 Elizabeth of York, 1484–1485

1. Brereton, Humphrey, 'The Ballad of Lady Bessye'.

2. uuuwell.com.

3. Peachey, Stuart, 'Festivals and Feasts of the Common Man 1550–1660' (Stuart Press, 1995).

4. Okerlund, Arlene Naylor, *Elizabeth of York* (Palgrave Macmillan, 2009).

5. Brereton.

6. van den Bos, Lambert, *The Position of the Roode en Witte Roos* (Amsterdam, 1651).

14 Eclipse, 1485

1. Thornbury, W., 'Westminster: Introduction', *Old and New London: Volume 3* (1878).

2. Cunningham, Sean, *Richard III, a Royal Enigma* (Kew: National Archives, 2003).

3. 'Venice: 1481–1485', *Calendar of State Papers Relating to English Affairs in the Archives of Venice, Volume 1: 1202–1509* (1864), pp. 141–59.

Epilogue

1. Taken from Richard III's prayer book, held in Lambeth Palace.

2. Goddard, 'Richard III's House in Leicester', *Journal of the British Archaeological Association*, 9 (1863).

3. Extant by 1594, although composed before, as Marlowe died in 1593.

4. From my notes, taken whilst watching the live conference on the BBC website.

Bibliography

Primary and Contemporary Sources

A Collection of Ordinances and Regulations for the Governance of the Royal Household, made in divers reigns from King Edward III to King William and Queen Mary (London: Society of Antiquities, 1790).

Anonymous, 'How the Good Wife Taught her Daughter' (1430).

Bernardino of Siena, 'Sermon on Wives and Widows' (1472).

Bird, W. H. B and K. H. Ledward (eds), *Calendar of State Papers, Henry VI, Edward IV, Edward V, Richard III* (1953).

Brereton, Humphrey, 'The Ballad of Lady Bessye'.

Brown, Rawdon (ed.), *Calendar of State Papers Relating to English Affairs in the State Papers of Venice, 1202–1509* (1864).

Bruce, J. (ed.), *Historie of the Arrivall of Edward IV in England and Finall Recouerye of his Kingdomes from Henry VI* (Camden Society, 1838).

Brunschwig, Hieronymous, *Buch der Cirurgia* (1497).

Chaucer, G., *The Canterbury Tales* (*c.* 1380).

Cornazzano, Antonio, *La Regina d'Ingliterra* (1466–8).

Davies, Robert, *Extracts from the Municipal Records of the City of York During the Reigns of Edward IV, Edward V and Richard III* (London: J. B. Nichols, 1843).

Ellis, Henry (ed.), *Three Books of Polydore Vergil's English History, comprising the reigns of Henry VI, Edward IV and Richard III* (Camden Society, 1844).

Ellis, Henry (ed.), *New Chronicles of England and France in two parts by Robert Fabyan, 1516* (London, 1811).

Fortescue, Sir John, *De Laudibus Legum Anglae* (First pub. 1543; ed. Amos, A., Butterworth & Son, 1825).

Furnivall, F. J. (ed.) and Andrew Boorde, *Fyrst Boke of the Introduction of Knowledge* (Early English Text Society, 1870).

Gairdner, James (ed.), *Gregory's Chronicle 1461–9* (London, 1876).

Gairdner, James (ed.), *The Paston Letters, 1422–1509* (Edinburgh: John Grant, 1910).

Hall, Edward, *Chronicle; containing the History of England, during the reign of Henry the fourth and the succeeding monarchs, to the end of the reign of Henry VIII, in which are particularly described the manners and customs of those periods* (Collated with the editions of 1548 and 1550) (London: J. Johnson, 1809).

Hinds, Allen B. (ed.), *Calendar of State Papers, Milan* (1912).

Holinshed, Raphael, *Chronicles of England, Scotland and Ireland* (London: J. Johnson, 1807).

Idley, Peter, *Instructions to his Son* (Greifswald, Druck von J. Abel, 1903).

Jones, M. and S. Walker (eds), 'Private Indentures for Life Service in Peace and War', *Camden Miscellany*, XXXII (Royal Historical Society, 1994).

King René's Tournament Book (1406; trans. E. Bennett, 1997).

Mancini, *The Occupation of the Throne by Richard III* (1483).

More, T., *The History of King Richard III* (ed. J.Rawson Lumby. Cambridge University Press, 1883).

Nichols, John Gough (ed.), *Inventories of the wardrobes, plate, chapel stuff, etc. of Henry Fitzroy, Duke of Richmond and of the wardrobe stuff at Baynard's Castle of Katharine, Princess Dowager* (Camden Society, 1855).

Nichols, John Gough (ed.), *The Chronicle of Calais* (Camden Society, 1846).

Nicolas, N. H. (ed.), *The Privy Purse Expenses of Elizabeth of York* (London: Pickering, 1830).

Pisan, Christine de, *The Treasure of the City of Ladies or the Book of the Three Virtues* (trans. Rosalind Brown-Grant: Penguin, 1999).

Rickert, E. (ed.), *The Babees' Book: Medieval Manners for the Young, Done into Modern English from Dr Furnival's Texts* (Chatto & Windus, 1908).

Riley, Henry T. (trans.), *Ingulph's Chronicle of the Abbey of Croyland* (London: H. G. Bohn, 1854).

Rous, John, *This Rol was Laburd and finished by Master John Rows of Wararrewyk* (London: Pickering, 1848).

Twemlow, J. A (ed.), *Calendar of Papal Registers Relating to Great Britain and Ireland, Volume 14: 1484–92, March 1486* (1960).

van den Bos, Lambert, *The Position of the Roode en Witte Roos* (Amsterdam, 1651).

Secondary Sources

Abbot, Jacob, *Margaret of Anjou* (Harper and Brothers, 1904).

Amt, Emilie (ed.), *Women's Lives in Medieval Europe, A Sourcebook* (Routledge, 1993).

Ashdown-Hill, John, *Eleanor, the Secret Queen; the Woman who put Richard III on the Throne* (The History Press, 2009).

Ashdown-Hill, John, *The Last Days of Richard III* (The History Press, 2011).

Baldwin, David, *Elizabeth Woodville* (new ed.: The History Press, 2004).

Baldwin, David, *Richard III* (Amberley, 2012).

Brooke, Iris, *English Costume of the Later Middle Ages* (A. & C. Black, 1935).

Burke, John, *The Castle in Medieval England* (The Anchor Press, 1978).

Cheetham, Anthony, *The Life and Times of Richard III* (Weidenfeld & Nicolson, 1972).

Clephan, R. Coltman, *The Medieval Tournament* (Dover, 1995).

Connors, Michael, *John Hawley, Merchant, Mayor and Privateer* (Richard Webb, 2008).

Coss, Peter, *The Lady in Medieval England* (Alan Sutton, 1998).

Cunningham, Sean, *Richard III, a Royal Enigma* (Kew: National Archives, 2003).

Ditchfield, P. H and W. Page, *Windsor Castle: History, A History of the County of Berkshire*, Volume 3 (1923).

Falkus, Gila, *The Life and Times of Edward IV* (Weidenfeld & Nicolson, 1981).

Goddard, 'Richard III's House in Leicester', *Journal of the British Archaeological Association*, 9 (1863).

Goldberg, P. J. P., *Women in Medieval English Society* (Alan Sutton, 1997).

Gravett, Christopher, *Knight: Noble Warrior of England, 1200–1600* (Osprey, 2008).

Gregory, Philippa, David Baldwin and Michael Jones, *The Women of the Cousins' War: The Duchess, the Queen and the King's Mother* (Simon & Schuster, 2011).

Hammond, P. W and Anne F. Sutton, *Richard III: The Road to Bosworth Field* (Constable, 1985).

Hanawalt, Barbara, *Growing up in Medieval London* (Oxford University Press, 1993).

Hancock, Peter A., *Richard III and the Murder in the Tower* (The History Press, 2011).

Harvey Lenz, Nancy, *Elizabeth of York, Tudor Queen* (New York: Macmillan, 1973).

Hasted, Edward, *Minutes of the Records and Accounts of the Chamber, The History and Topographical Survey of the County of Kent*, Volume 12 (1801), pp. 612–662.

Hicks, Michael, *Anne Neville: Queen to Richard III* (Tempus, 2007).

Hicks, Michael, *Edward V: The Prince in the Tower* (Tempus, 2003).

Hicks, Michael, *Richard III* (The History Press, 2003).

Hicks, Michael, *Warwick the Kingmaker* (Blackwell, 1998).

Hilton, Lisa, *Queens Consort: England's Medieval Queens* (Phoenix, 2009).

Ingham, Patricia, *Sovereign Fantasies: Arthurian Romance and the Making of Britain* (University of Pennsylvania, 2001).

Jenkins, E., *The Princes in the Tower* (Hamish Hamilton, 1978).

Jesse, John Heneage, *Memoirs of King Richard III and Some of his Contemporaries* (London: Richard Bentley, 1862).

Kendall, Paul Murray, *Richard III* (Norton & Co., 2002).

Lamb, V. B., *The Betrayal of Richard III: An Introduction to the Controversy* (Alan Sutton, 1959).

Lander, J. R., 'Marriage and Politics in the Fifteenth Century: the Nevilles and the Wydevilles', *Journal of Historical Research*, 36 (94) (November 1963), pp. 119–152.

Laynesmith, J. L., *The Last Medieval Queens: English Queenship 1445–1503* (Oxford University Press, 2004).

Leyser, Henrietta, *Medieval Women; A Social History of Women in England 450–1500* (Weidenfeld & Nicolson, 1995).

Licence, A., *Elizabeth of York, The Lost Tudor Queen* (Amberley, 2013).

Licence, A., *In Bed with the Tudors* (Amberley, 2012).

Maurer, Helen E., *Margaret of Anjou: Queenship and Power in Late Medieval England* (Boydell, 2003).

Mitchell, Dorothy, 'York and Richard III' (Silver Boar, 1984).

Mortimer, Ian, *The Traveller's Guide to Medieval England* (Vintage, 2009).

Mortimer, R. and T. Tatton-Brown (eds), *Westminster Abbey: The Lady Chapel of Henry VII* (Boydell Press, 2003).

Okerlund, Arlene Naylor, *Elizabeth of York* (Palgrave Macmillan, 2009).

Orme, Nicholas, *Childhood in Medieval England 500–1500* (Unpublished paper).

Payne Collier, J. (ed.), 'The Ghost of Richard III' (First pub. 1614; London: Shakespeare Society, 1884).

Peachey, Stuart, 'Festivals and Feasts of the Common Man 1550–1660' (Stuart Press, 1995).

Petre, J. (ed.), *Richard III: Crown and People, A Selection of Articles from The Ricardian Journal of the Richard III Society, March 1975 to December 1981* (Alan Sutton, 1985).

Phillips, Kim M., *Medieval Maidens* (Manchester University Press, 2003).

Pollard, A. J., *Richard III and the Princes in the Tower* (Alan Sutton 1991).

Rae, John, 'Deaths of the English Kings' (1913).

Ross, Charles, *Edward IV* (Yale University Press, 1997).

Rymer, Thomas, *Foedera* (1704–1735).

Santiuste, David, *Edward IV and the Wars of the Roses* (Pen and Sword, 2010).

Saul, Nigel, *The Three Richards: Richard I, Richard II and Richard III* (Hambledon & London, 2005).

Seward, Desmond, *A Brief History of the Wars of the Roses* (Constable & Co. Ltd, 1995).

Shahar, Shulamith, *The Fourth Estate: A History of Women in the Middle Ages* (Methuen, 1983).

Shakespeare, William, *Henry VI Part 3*.

Shakespeare, William, *Richard III*.

Snell, Melissa, 'The Medieval Child: Childbirth, Childhood and Adolescence in the Middle Ages', *Medieval History* (Dec 2000).

Strutt, Joseph, *The Sports and Pastimes of the People of England* (Methuen & Co., 1908).

Sutton, Anne F. and Livia Visser-Fuchs, '"Richard Liveth Yet": An Old Myth', *Ricardian*, 9 (June 1992).

Sutton, Anne F., 'Caxton the Cult of St Winifred and Shrewsbury' in Clark, Linda (ed.), *Of Mice and Men; Image, Belief and Regulation in Late Medieval England* (Boydell Press, 2005).

Sutton, Anne F., 'The Death of Queen Anne Neville' (1980) in Petre, J. (ed.), *Richard III, Crown and People* (Alan Sutton, 1985).

Walford, E., 'Greenwich', *Old and New London: Volume 6* (1878), pp. 164–76.

Walpole, H., *Historic Doubts on the Life and Reign of Richard III* (1768).

Weightman, Christine, *Margaret of York, Duchess of Burgundy, 1446–1503* (New York: St Martin's Press, 1989).

Weir, Alison, *Lancaster and York: The Wars of the Roses* (Vintage, 1995).

Weir, Alison, *The Princes in the Tower* (Vintage, 2008).

Wilkinson, Josephine, *Richard, the Young King to Be* (Amberley, 2009).

Index

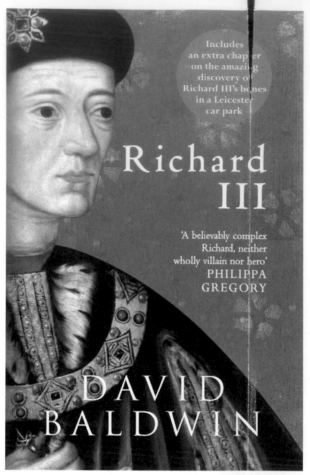